Advanced Medical Intuition

8 Underlying Causes of Illness and Unique Healing Methods

SECOND EDITION

Tina M. Zion

North Carolina

Published in the United States by WriteLife Publishing
(An imprint of Boutique of Quality Books Publishing Company, Inc.)
www.writelife.com

978-1-60808-286-5 (p)
978-1-60808-287-2 (e)

Library of Congress Control Number: 2023937920

Book and cover design by Robin Krauss, www.bookformatters.com
Cover artwork by Corey Ford, www.coreyfordgallery.com
Toroidal Field illustration by Jacqueline Rogers, www.jacquelinerogers.com

Editor: Andrea Vande Vorde

I dedicate this book to Rebecca, who kept encouraging me to write it so everyone can have the opportunity to become excellent medical intuitives. Rebecca supports me, this book, and understands the physical and the nonphysical world as a physician, a business partner, and my life partner.

Acknowledgments

Terri Leidich, my very caring, spiritually aware WriteLife Publisher, came into my life many, many years ago. We were both so delighted that the Universe brought us together. Then along came Glenn, who was willing to bounce and banter thoughts and ideas back and forth with me. Thank you, Glenn, for being you. I am grateful for the artistic realms of Corey Ford, who has been the source of many of my book covers. Julie Bromley is always there for me, creating my newsletter designs and attending to my social media. And I want to give acknowledgment to Andrea Vande Vorde, my skilled editor for this book. Thank you for patiently guiding me to be a much better writer.

I deeply treasure all of these people. I am a better, more advanced, and yes, even a more mature human because of each one of you.

Praise for Tina M. Zion
and Advanced Medical Intuition –
First Edition

"Tina Zion's *Advanced Medical Intuition* is a beacon to all who would heed the call of the Light Worker and Healer. In simple, clear, and practical terms, Zion gives readers the tools they need to rise into their natural gifts as Intuitives and Healers. A combination of instruction based on her decades of experience, as well as case studies, references, and powerful exercises, this book is a comprehensive toolkit covering a range of topics from Healer protection and self care, to working with your Spirit team to help clients achieve healing on the deepest levels. Zion dares to cover topics not found in many other books such as the truth about working with cords of attachment, entities in the Spirit realm, and the client's role in participating in their own recovery. A must read for novice or advanced practitioners who are serious about sharpening their intuitive skills and getting to the heart of healing with clients."

—Angela Kaufman, Author of
Queen Up! Reclaim Your Crown When Life Knocks You Down

"This book is riveting. Tina Zion's clear, concise, detailed approach, combines inspiration, tools, and scientific explanations. She gives us blueprints and follows with specific tools for healing and transformation for both the client and yes, for us the practitioner. As a professional medium and teacher for over 48 years, I was inspired by Tina's spiritual clarity, down to earth common sense, and practical applications. Every once in a while a book comes along that has what it takes to change lives, this is one of those books."

—Rev. Elaine D. Thomas, MS,
Director of Fellowships of the Spirit's School of
Spiritual Healing and Prophecy

"As a participant in Tina Zion's workshop, I have found her to be an extraordinary teacher of medical intuition. I admire her uncanny ability to teach medical intuition in an accessible way. In her latest book, she continues to provide a concise, easy to follow guide for learning the root causes of illness and dis-ease states and their healing. She provides techniques and tools which anyone with a sincere interest can learn and use. Guiding by example, she encourages the reader to trust in their own intuition towards the healing of others. As a physician and psychiatrist, I welcome Tina Zion's voice to our evolving knowledge of Alternative medicine."

—H. Pankowsky, MD, Author, and Speaker

"Written in a clear, easy to understand style, the book offers insight and guidance into utilizing the techniques of unique healing methods. With references to cases of real life situations, Ms. Zion lists essential points and methods in using intuitions in healing. Case studies range from simple intuitive healing to more complex methods. In all cases methods are included to engage and educate the client throughout the process. Very well written and informative book."

—Irene McIntosh
T Mitchell Bean Books

"Tina Zion's 2nd book, *Advanced Medical Intuition*, is written simply and powerfully providing optimal value to many. I didn't want to blink soaking in knowledge so imperative for intuitives. Besides her brilliance as a Medical Intuitive, she is a gifted, patient, and compassionate teacher who inspires others to have courage, confidence, and conviction to help others. Her humility in delivery and use of practical examples makes the content palpable and relevant for specific HEALING of illnesses' point of origin including negative interference across many realms and dimensions."

—Maryann Kelly, B.S., R.T.R,
Advanced Medical Intuition, Reiki, Light Grid, Energy Medicine

---

"*Advanced Medical Intuition* is an illuminating guide that provides much needed direction and clarification to the emerging field of medical intuition. Tina's explanations of the six causes of illness and unique healing methods provides practitioners—as well as non-practitioners—a clear methodology to use to assist people with their own emotional body, mental body, and physical body healing. This approach allows people to live in present time as the powerful creators intended by Source."

—Therese McGinnis
Life Coach, Intuitive, Soul Realignment Practitioner

"This book is a follow up book from *Become a Medical Intuitive* though it stands alone as a work in its own right.

Divided into two parts, the first being a review of the role and scope of a medical intuitive with reminders of self-care, preparation guidelines, and how to perceive causes of illness. Part two goes into the causes of illness and healing techniques. There is a very useful appendix with a summary of the Primary Energetic Healing Techniques.

Though I am not a practicing Healer, I thoroughly enjoyed this text. It was well laid out and very interesting and informative with real life examples in the form of case studies which helped to cement the validity of this work.

I would recommend this book to anyone with an interest in Health Spirituality and healing."

—Diana Woodhead
BSc Health Studies
MSc Advanced Nursing Practice

Other Books by Tina M. Zion

The Reiki Teacher's Manual (1st edition, 2008)
Become a Medical Intuitive (1st edition, 2014)
Become a Medical Intuitive (2nd edition, 2018)
Advanced Medical Intuition (1st edition, 2018)
Reiki and Your Intuition (2019)
The Reiki Teacher's Manual (2nd edition, 2020)
Be Your Own Medical Intuitive (2021)

Contents

Part Two

The Invocation

Created by Betsy Bergstrom

I give thanks to those that I am about to invite!

I ask that this room, this home or building, and the grounds become a sacred space.

I invite the Divine to be present.

I invite Great Spirit, Mother, Father, God to be present.

I invite Great Mystery to be present.

I invite the Compassionate and loving Ancestors to be present, and I give thanks to them because without them we couldn't be here.

I invite the Great Teachers and Masters to be present, especially those that we have connections to and affiliations with.

I invite the Angels, the great beings of light, especially the Archangels, the guardian angels, and the angels of healing.

I invite the Power Animals, the Totems, and I give thanks to them for loaning their power, their qualities and for relationship.

I invite the Healing Spirits of all the realms and give thanks for the healing that I know is going to happen.

I invite the Elements—Earth, Water, Fire, Air, and Sacred Space—and I ask for a balancing of the Elements.

I invite the Compassionate Spirits and Devas.

I invite the Earth, the Sun, and the Moon.

I give thanks to the Stars and the Compassionate Star People.

I invite the Directions and the Guardians of the Directions.

I invite the Four Great Winds.

I give thanks to the Great Spirits of the Land, and I ask to be in
harmony with you and to prosper here.

I give thanks to the Spirits of this place for allowing this work
to happen here.

And as always, I give thanks in advance for the blessings that
I know will happen here.

Thank you!

Introducing
Advanced Medical Intuition,

2ND EDITION

Over the years, it has shocked me how many students tell me they did not know a medical intuitive can accomplish healings too! I want you to succeed as an excellent, accurate medical intuitive healer. I want you to be powerfully safe as you do this level of work. I want to teach you not only to be an extraordinarily accurate intuitive, but also a wise healer who achieves dramatic results. This book is all about stretching beyond old and limiting rules, opening your awareness to controversial concepts, and manifesting profound healings within your medical intuitive sessions.

When I wrote my first edition of *Advanced Medical Intuition* in 2018, I had no idea that I was teaching controversial topics, concepts, and experiences. Now, even more, I want to highlight these different, unusual, and yes, controversial concepts of the nonphysical realms of life. I have expanded the six categories causing illness to a total of eight categories. I have updated the healing steps and concepts, and have rewritten many of the commands to help you deliver more powerful signals to the Universe.

Each of us learn differently, so I present this information in a variety of ways for you to truly absorb the material and *excel* as a medical-intuitive. For your success, I offer the following educational features:

- Eight categories describing the causes of illness, how to find these causes, and techniques to heal them.

- Ten keys to become an accurate medical intuitive, and how to guide clients through profound, positive healing.

- Detailed steps to empower your protection.

- Eighteen pathways to communicate with the nonphysical realms.

- Case studies transcribed from my recorded medical intuitive sessions, presented in narrative form.

- Comments and demonstrations of healing techniques within these transcriptions.

- Step-by-step explanations describing purpose and healing goals.

- A list of Essential Points at the end of each chapter for your convenience.

- Different approaches to engage and empower your clients.

- Guidance on structuring a one-hour medical intuitive session.

- A complete summary of the healing techniques in the Appendix as a quick guide for your success.

PART ONE

The Excellent Medical Intuitive Healer

"There is never a crowd on the leading edge of thought."

—Abraham, channeled by Esther Hicks

Chapter 1

Controversial Topics and Key Concepts

"Those who say it cannot be done should not disturb those who are doing it."

—Unknown

Interacting in a knowledgeable way with the nonphysical realms seems like an "everyday normal" to me. So, for quite a while, I did not realize that many topics I speak about in my books and my courses are controversial to so many people all around the globe. I have had people jump up and run out of the room, become angry and confront me, rock in their chairs, or quietly weep while the larger number of students in the room are delighted that someone is finally discussing the forbidden.

For this second edition of *Advanced Medical Intuition,* I decided to begin with the controversial topics so you will quickly learn more about yourself and how you might emotionally react, or perhaps feel a sense of relief. Many students declare aloud in class, "Finally, someone is discussing the nonphysical realms in the ways that I have already been sensing!"

Here is a brief summary of the controversial topics within this book:

1. **We living humans are powerful.**
   I work with my power and teach others how powerful they are, and every day I am surprised by the abilities I have, and those that my clients display. The more we know how powerful we are, and the more we utilize the power of

direct, precise thought energy, the faster and more distinct the Universe responds to us.

2. Stop putting a bubble around you for protection.

This is not protecting you at all. When we put an energetic form around us, that form becomes denser each time we create it. We usually only create the form around us when we are afraid or worried about something. But negative emotions such as fear and worry will vibrate at such a thick, slow, heavy build up and replace the protective energy.

3. We must command the Universe.

People are often appalled when I discuss the concept of commanding. I first heard about commanding the spirit world or the Universe decades ago in the St. Germaine teachings. I, too, was shocked and refused to even consider it. Who am I to boss around angels, guides, and God? Decades later, my own Divine and Sacred guides directed me to command and to be commanding. That got my attention.

4. Meditation is not necessary to be intuitive or spiritual.

I bring this up as a controversial topic because nearly every day I hear my mentoring clients struggle to meditate, or to schedule the time for it in their busy schedules.

In short, I ask that you bring meditation into your day rather than blocking out a time in your day for it. I ask that you meditate for only a few minutes, or moments, at a time, and all throughout your day no matter where you are. Instead of grumbling while standing in the line at the grocery or waiting for the car to be repaired, I close my eyes and go into a moment of meditation.

5. The higher self is simply a larger portion of our individual soul, not a more advanced one.

Our individual soul is larger than what can fit into a human body. Our higher self is not any more advanced than the portion residing within our physical body. The soul is all one energy. In this case, I sense that the higher self has received that title because the remaining portion tends to be above the physical body and is interconnected to the matrix of the whole. This is one of the latest "downloads" of information that I received from my Divine and Sacreds.

6. Do not cut energetic cords.

First, not all cords are negative, and second, cutting cords is not a healing. It is just making two pieces of something. True healing signifies the release of something negative. If a cord between two people is cut by some well-meaning energy worker, nothing has been removed, or released, or healed.

7. Deceased people do not float up to heaven and turn into angels.

Dying does not mean sudden enlightenment. Most people readily release the Earth plane and go directly into the Light to continue in an alive but bodyless form. Many people do not. These people need healings on many different levels after leaving the physical body. Deceased people will respond to living people communicating with them, but more importantly, deceased people quickly respond to a medical intuitive facilitating a profound healing with them.

8. Positive and negative nonhuman entities are real.

Nonhuman entities are not just the imagination of ancient folklore. Negative entities interfere with both the living and the deceased. An excellent medical intuitive knows that negative entities must be considered clients too. They need healing just as much as living humans. Most negative entities appear hideously ugly.

Remember this forever: You are the empowered, knowledgeable medical-intuitive healer. Ugly does not mean they are more powerful than you. It just means they are ugly.

The Medical Intuitive Travels Throughout Many Dimensions

The medical intuitive travels through many dimensions of existence. Our work includes not just the living, but also the dying and those who have already made their transition. The medical intuitive travels through levels of energy, from light to dark and back to the light again. We move through time and space at will because there are no restrictions and no limitations. Those borders exist only in the limited mind.

Alberto Villoldo, in *A Shaman's Miraculous Tools for Healing*, beautifully describes the energetic healer in this way:

> "I remember the lines from the Bible, 'Many are called, but few are chosen.' I welcome all souls into this sacred work if they wish, but the chosen are those who respond to the call. They are a self-selected group and are the chosen only because they have said yes. They are seekers who walk with pure intent and open hearts, willing to experience the joy and suffering of humanity."[1]

The medical intuitive's work not only focuses on the physical body but also the mind, the emotions, and the eternal soul. The intuitive's sensors enter into a person's current story, their body, their energy field, and their eternal story. We begin to see how their current life and their past lives are affecting their well-being. We perceive someone's secrets, emotions, fears, and struggles. We find their beliefs, emotions, hidden pain, joy, and agony, but also their possible future. We discover the ugly, the weird, the deeply private, and the sacred. The medical intuitive must be compassionate, confidential, and without judgment. Above all, before you enter into your client's sacred moments, you must ask for permission either intuitively or in person. This is a journey that you must take side by side.

The most powerful healing happens at the energetic level. Most societies rely on healing at the mental or physical level, and are

---

1 Alberto Villoldo, *A Shaman's Miraculous Tools for Healing* (Newburyport, MA: Hampton Roads Publishing 2015), 37.

not aware of the energetic level. This is why traditional medicine and mental health counseling are the primary mechanisms for healthcare throughout the world. It is only a small percentage of energetic practitioners, quantum scientists, metaphysicians, and psychics who are aware of this vibrational level of life. The energetic realm is ultimately the most effective healing method because the possibilities are infinite. Energy healing has no limitations or parameters. All the lab tests, MRIs, and x-rays will never find the true, original cause of someone's illness or suffering.

The medical intuitive discovers the person's eternal essence. He or she may be drawn to one's current childhood, a past life, a vitamin deficiency, a forgotten trauma, or many other surprising possibilities. The practitioner is pulled by a thread of energy within the eternal essence of the individual they are working with. The energetic threads of our eternal life can either give energy to us or pull energy away from us. Energy can drain the vitality from a certain organ of a person, or it can rush into that same organ and provide profound healing. The push or pull can be either positive or negative for our health. There is much more going on in the unseen world than is ever going on in the physical world.

The Medical Intuitive Becomes a Healer

This book is the result of many students speaking up at the end of my weekend workshop, "Become a Medical Intuitive: Seeing with X-Ray Eyes." Students would say some variation of the following:

"We have all really popped open and are picking up all kinds of accurate information about each other, but now what? How do we use the information to bring healing and relief to our own clients?"

This is the most phenomenal question of all.

Once again, I set out on a mission to study myself in the same way that I did when I wrote *Become a Medical Intuitive*. After each client left my office, or we hung up the phone, or closed our Skype connection, I examined the interaction between my client and me. I also focused on what I did after receiving the initial intuitive information. I quickly realized the profound healing techniques that were happening. First and foremost, I discovered that the client and I did something together with Spirit leading the way. Together, we created a sacred moment. We humans were never meant to be alone in our healing process.

The observations of myself and the clients' responses led to the creation of an advanced training day. That training day led me to write this book. My first time teaching the training day took place with a group of sincere and dedicated people in Bucharest, Romania. During our Sunday afternoon workshop, they asked me, through our translator, to share more with them. They wanted to know how to heal their clients with the intuitive information they were now receiving. So I sat down in my hotel room that night and developed an outline on a 3 x 5" piece of paper. I shared that information with them the next day. That little piece of paper with my tiny outline gave birth to this book. I will forever be grateful to the people of Romania.

As I developed the advanced portion of my workshop, I realized I had absolutely no idea how healing situations occurred in my sessions. People continued to contact me to say that they no longer suffered from the situation, or the negative thoughts, or the illness that once plagued them. They had no idea what had happened in their session, but they felt completely different and better than they had in years. My clients would often leave my room and go out to the front desk to make their next appointment. They would tell my office manager that they could not describe what had happened during their time with me, but they felt dramatically better. Here is a very small portion of an actual session:

Case Study:
Medical Intuitive Healing

Practice Experience:

Imagine you are the medical intuitive speaking the words in this transcript. Read it aloud or, if possible, with a study buddy, one taking part as the medical intuitive and one as the client. Practice this session as if you are actually giving these steps to someone who needs your guidance.

Tina Zion (TZ): I am beginning to see very, very low energy in your throat. You are not expressing your life, who you are. By "expressing," I mean to create, sing a song, or journal, and you're not doing it. It's not just about speaking. It is about expressing. Going to meet with people you love, and to share with them. Grieving and sadness tend to go to our lungs, and you have very, very low energy there, and in your chest. In fact, there's an emptiness. You are so empty that I'm seeing through the bones of your rib cage, and there is actually empty space where your lungs should be.

Client: Mhmm.

TZ: I would be really surprised if you don't already have breathing struggles or symptoms. You need to change some things in your life or you will have some lung problems in the future.

Client: Mhmm, mhmm.

TZ: Now let me just stop right there. I haven't looked at your heart yet, but let me just stop and see if there is anything you want to say about the things I have mentioned. Just see if there's anything you need to express about it.

Client: I guess I kind of do. I want to say . . . I guess I'm surprised that you are so thorough. I guess I'm surprised by the things you are seeing that I already know.

TZ: When you commented about my being so thorough, I thought, "Boy, we have only just begun." *(We were only five minutes into the session.)* My hope is that our time together also begins a healing or adds to the healing that you are already doing.

Client: Exactly!

Then later on in this session:

Client: What's causing the pain in my shoulder, neck, and back?

TZ: Your neck was the first thing I commented on in this session. Your energy is so low from your back, and it goes straight through into your lungs. It's a very, very depleted place, but I would like to look more deeply if you'll allow me. I'll look up and down your spine and see what I'm noticing there. I see up at the top of your spine where it connects with your skull that you have a sore or hot spot there. You also have a hot spot between cervical 3 and 4. This hot spot is very tight, tense. It looks as if the padding in between the vertebrae is thinner right there. Let me see what else. May I continue?

Client: Yes, of course.

TZ: Then down around your cervical 7 vertebrae, where it turns into your thoracic vertebrae, I am seeing a very tight, tense area. I know you've already told me that you have pain across your shoulders and back, but what I'm actually saying is that you have three places in your spine that are causing you pain. Do you ever go to chiropractors? Do you believe in chiropractors?

Client: I have tried that.

TZ: What do they say? Have they mentioned the same vertebrae?

Client: I am almost certain one of them did. The three and four.

TZ: Yes, those are very prominent.

Client: They have not been able to unlock it, I guess I would say.

TZ: Well, what an interesting word that you used for it! Our neck, in that mind-body connection, allows us to turn and look in different directions. Our neck gives us, hopefully, flexibility. Over the years you're losing some of your flexibility, and it's interesting that you used the word "locked," because you're becoming more locked down in life. You can only look in one direction rather than remembering how flexible you could be to turn and look in another direction in life.

Client: Mhmm.

TZ: So, our necks are all about that. They are all about either struggling to realize that we can turn and take a different step, or we struggle to remember how flexible we could be in life. In your situation you feel like life is heavy and feels like you're in cement, and you forget you can take a different step.

Here's what's coming up now. It feels as if you think you have to take a giant step, and that step has become too giant, too large, and too big. I'm going to ask you now to tell me what is the tiniest, tiniest doable step that you can take to just begin to have some flexibility in your own life. You are lugging around a tremendous amount of responsibility, and I'm here to tell you it is not all your responsibility. You think it is, but you're lugging it around, carrying it around on your shoulders like a big boulder. That is what I'm seeing sitting on the top of your shoulders, and it's not all yours to carry. You're not responsible for everything, but I'm pretty sure you think you are.

Client: Yeah, that's pretty spot on.

TZ: I feel like this might have been a struggle for you to even take time to have this session with me.

Client: Spot on! *(giggles)*

Intuitives pick up what is prominent in a person's energy field. What is prominent at the moment is not permanent. The outcome can be altered during a healing, for example. The client's energy field brightened as the session progressed. I kept her informed as those changes happened. Medical intuition, as well as other alternative healthcare modalities, is truly a complementary option. It does not stand alone, just like Western traditional medicine does not stand alone. It usually includes multiple physicians and other specialists to assist in the patient's care. The alternative community does not need to stand alone either. It can function in coordination with traditional medicine. More and more physicians, nurses, respiratory therapists, and physical therapists come to my workshops. They let me know they are picking up intuitive information that is not based on the patient's chart, lab tests, or MRI. They recognize a "knowing" that just sweeps through them as they approach their next patient. They tell me they want to explore and build upon this experience. Many nurses tell me their doctors are beginning to listen to their intuitive hits too. The movement of integrative medicine is beginning to happen.

The medical intuitive not only receives information about a person's physical body, but also the emotional body, thought body, and their eternal energy body. He or she is able to pick up the most personal and even intimate information within an individual's body, their current life, their past lives, and their future possibilities. Please understand that there is nothing more intimate than another person's existence unfolding before your eyes.

While it is usually part of the session, the medical intuitive does not focus on the more common things of life. In other words, the medical intuitive will not focus on the next boyfriend and when that boyfriend will show up. The practitioner will not focus on buying and selling your home, or what car would be the best for the client to have. While the medical intuitive may have the ability to sense opportunities in the future, their work focuses on living, learning, and the healing of the soul. People yearn to understand why they keep getting sick and what they can do about it. Many people have no idea that they can take charge of their lives, their body, their mind, and their health.

The Medical Intuitive Communicates Throughout Many Dimensions

We humans are energy beings who have a grand experience of pulling, pushing, dragging, and lugging around a lot of cellular matter called the physical human body. As with everything, some people are much better at this than others.

The physical body is determined to draw our attention to it in all kinds of ways. We quickly forget around the age of six that we are truly an eternal soul within an eternal megacosm. We megacosmic-energy beings do our best to convince ourselves that we are filled with limitations and unable to be the creators of our own lives. We are, in fact, filled with abilities and power we rarely notice or experience. The human energy field and the physical body constantly vibrate with information. The excellent medical intuitive recognizes that their abilities are always expanding. Two of those powerful abilities are astral projection and remote viewing. Many are not aware of these two expansive abilities, but they are vital key steps to access detailed information about a client.

Astral projection is the ability to deliberately stretch our energy field outward like a laser beam or flashlight, to the client we are assisting. That person can be in a chair three feet away or on the other side of the globe. Distance does not matter with energy. We stretch our energy field outward toward the client, creating a laser-like beam of focused energy.

The medical intuitive utilizes another natural ability called remote viewing. **Remote viewing** is the ability to receive information from a distance. When we are remote viewing, we are receiving intuitive information through the tip of our astral-projected laser beam. The tip of our laser beam has hypersensitive sensors which receive the information. In short, you are astral projecting outward to the client, then pausing to receive intuitive information by remote viewing.

Here is an example of how I have used astral projection and remote viewing. When my mother was dying in the hospital, I sat in my car in the hospital parking lot and stretched my energy field outward to her hospital bed. I perceived shimmery, transparent beings surrounding her . . . many of them. They stood shoulder to shoulder, forming a complete circle around her like a strong privacy fence holding back the outside world. Their unblinking eyes silently watched her until I interrupted this sacred space. In unison they eerily turned toward me. I felt a gentle push against my chest, sending me a strong impression not to interfere. I looked over their shoulders to see my mother motionless on the hospital bed, dying. I pulled my energy out of the room, out of the hospital, and back into my own body, which sat in my cold car in the hospital parking lot. The day before, the pulmonologist told me that I must give the doctors permission to unplug my mother from the ventilator.

I told him that I could not do that yet. "You must give me more time," I said. What I really meant was, "You must give me time to meditate and ask my mother and the beings surrounding her if she is ready to transition." The image that I had just seen gave me the answer. I walked into the intensive care unit and said, "No, you can't unplug her yet."

The next day the same doctor was livid, red-faced, and yelling at me. He said that I was drawing out the situation longer than necessary. "She cannot survive!"

I could not tell this man of modern medicine that I was waiting for my mother's spiritual process to finish. I was not waiting for her body and mind to mend. I was waiting for a sign from the guardians that encircled her. I didn't understand what I had witnessed from the parking lot, but I did know that I was not to interrupt in any way.

The next morning, I sat in the car and psychically asked my mother again if she was ready to transition. It surprised me to see that, as the spirit people surrounded her, her spirit self sat in bed, playing with a ball of light as if it were a softball, throwing it above her and catching it again and again. She seemed so very childlike in her play. The spirit people did not notice me this time. They watched my mother as if intrigued by her play with the patience of eternity. I pulled my energy away from the surreal scene.

Two days later, I sat in my car in the hospital parking lot for the third time. Once again, I drifted from my physical body and floated my spirit toward my mother. I expected to see my mother and her spirit guardians continuing to do whatever it was they'd been doing for days. This time nothing happened. I was surprised. All was quiet, so I stood waiting in the dark. The scene in my mind's eye opened up. Sky first, and then trees wrapping around a large lake, silhouetting a faraway horizon. The water, still and glasslike, was not water at all but a thick, silvery liquid like mercury.

My mother floated on her back in the thick, shiny liquid. All I could see above the mercurial water were her toes, belly, and face.

Deep within my mind I called out to her: "What should I do about unplugging the life support?"

The sound of my voice vibrated inside my head and echoed out across the thick water-like substance. Only my own echo answered me. In slow motion her left arm rose up out of the silver liquid, and then her right. Slowly, she paddled away from where I stood on the bank. I watched until she floated and paddled so far across the lake that I could no longer see her. I knew it was time.

I called my brother and sister and told them what happened during this last meditation. They knew it was time as well. We gathered that day, all sixteen of us—children, grandchildren, spouses, and two great-grandchildren. We all stood in silence as the nurse pulled the ventilation tube from my mother's mouth. My son sat on the window sill, holding his sister's newborn child, softly singing to her. His song floated across the room, soothing us, as Mother crossed over.

Medical Intuition Requires Noticing but Not Hard Work

All this is accomplished without any work. Do not work at this. Energy always follows your thoughts. Think all the above and it will happen.

Esther Hicks, channeling Abraham, describes it in this way: "We are all vibrational beings. You're like a receptive mechanism in which you set your tuner to a station and hear what is playing. The object of your focus is where you set your tuner, and when you maintain focus on that object for as few as seventeen seconds, you activate that vibration within you. Once you activate a vibration within you, the Law of Attraction responds to that vibration, and you're off and running."

Over and over again, I hear my students struggle the most with one particular issue. They describe to me, in huge detail, how hard they work to be more intuitive. So, over and over again, I state to them and now to you: Intuition does not respond to working hard. Hard work completely gets in the way.

When I listen more closely to students who are "working hard to be intuitive," I notice a theme. They are seeking a fragment of something that might be described as intuition. Do not actively work to search for signals from the Universe. An excellent intuitive is a complete receiver—not a seeker—of information. Simply notice the world around you. There is no effort in noticing the subtle. We simultaneously communicate back and forth with our Divine and Sacred guides, and with the energy field and physical body of the client. Notice what effortlessly pulls your attention to it, or repeatedly comes into your awareness. The more you recognize yourself as an energy being, the more your limits will subside in your thoughts and beliefs.

18 Pathways to Send and Receive Signals of Communication

Without the barrier of hard work in the way, you can now allow your mind to effortlessly send and receive communication with your world and Spirit. Here are some common pathways that we can use to do this.

1. **Your Name**—A name is more than a name. It is a frequency of information. The name that we are given at birth sends a signal to the Universe throughout our lifetime. When a woman changes her surname to her husband's at marriage, she doesn't just change her name but her entire person's energetic signature. The key is to notice the feel of the change. Does it feel right and positive, or does it feel like something else? Sometimes people change their name to deliberately send a different signal. Now notice the feel of your own name.

2. **Your Environment**—You are an integral part of your environment. It is not just the space around you, but a manifestation of your energy signals. One client sent out a thought that if her Divine and Sacred guides were with her,

then show her pink vehicles. Pink cars, vans, and trucks suddenly popped into her world.

For example, has a book ever leaped from a shelf and landed at your feet for you to discover it was the perfect book for you at that moment? Notice an object that repeatedly draws your attention. A friend realized he was constantly seeing antennae everywhere. He asked Spirit to tell him the meaning of antennae, and a situation at work immediately popped into his mind. He realized he was not effectively listening to a coworker. Spirit sent him a symbol to improve his communication with the coworker.

3. **Clouds in the Sky**—People send me photos of clouds that look exactly like angels, or an eagle, or other significant images. I was in an airplane just above the clouds when I looked ahead to see the exact form of Santa Claus sitting in a massive chair. He had a great smile on his face. He was so massive that it took the plane a long time to pass by, so I had a long time to perceive every detail of this signal of information. Santa was a signal of information that was indeed a gift to me at that time in my life.

4. **Dreams**—So many adventures happen within our dreams that it would take an entire book to explore the ideas I am now aware of. We astral project around the globe and far beyond our Universe. We communicate with our deceased loved ones who try so hard to reach out to us. We process our day and our life. Guides constantly direct us. These are just a few examples of the activities that happen when we dream.

I teach internationally in my awake state, but I also teach internationally in my dreams as well. I will wake in the morning knowing that I was teaching in a certain location or in a specific country. Within two days, I will receive emails from people in those same countries. They ask for mentoring sessions with me, or request that I travel to teach in their area. What a powerful confirmation that we truly travel throughout time and space in our dream state.

I received an email from a woman telling me that I was in her dream last night. She said that I stood at a podium in an ornate golden building, lecturing to a class. She arrived late and hesitated to enter but finally did so. She said that I immediately stopped talking to the class, looked directly at her, and declared, "Do not ever be late again!" This woman had no idea that I am a stickler for being on time. Again, more confirmation of the realities going on in our dream state!

5. **Internet and TV**—A woman in Wales emailed me one day. She said she was on her son's computer randomly clicking on things, when suddenly my photo popped up on the screen with the words "medical intuition." I laughed as I read on. She said she was not searching those words at all, but there I was smiling at her on her son's computer. She reached out to me, took my classes, and is now a highly esteemed medical intuitive in the UK.

6. **Déjà Vu**—It is real and not your imagination. Again, we are not trapped or confined beneath our skin. We are energy beings experiencing a world of energy. Most of us tend to openly discuss our awareness of past lives but with little understanding that we have the ability to travel away from our location. We can project forward in time to moments, locations, events, and other dimensions. Time is not linear, and it is not under our control, though we attempt it with clocks and calendars. We are energy beings flowing throughout realms of energy.

7. **Deceased People**—We are all mediums. Yes, you are too. We all have the ability to send and receive telepathic communication with the deceased because they are just as alive as we are. So many of the dead still have something important to say and want the living to hear it.

Are you aware of a deceased person coming into your dreams? Deceased people tend to come to us through our dreams when they have not been able to communicate with us when we are awake. The primary struggle is that living people keep talking to the dead, but no one stops to listen. Talk to them aloud or in your mind. Ask a question first, then pause. Pausing allows you to receive their eager responses. People in spirit will usually communicate in two pathways. Either thoughts will pop into your mind, or images will pop into your mind's eye. You must become a listener and not just a talker to receive their responses.

8. **Synchronicity**—According to Gerry Ellen, the definition of "synchronicity" is "the simultaneous occurrence of events that appear significantly related but have no discernable causal connection."[2] There are no accidents and there are no coincidences. The Universe is organized, complicated, and powerfully responsive to our thoughts and our emotions. When we think and feel, we send out signals that communicate to the world, and the Universe responds to us by sending us signals in return. Universe Synchronicity is a meaningful, perfectly timed union of information.

I struggled for a few days to find the best example of synchronicity to include in this book. Then a precious event suddenly unfolded before my eyes. I was driving down a busy road while powering my toroidal field. I finished running each separate color of the rainbow, and then moved on to fill myself with the violet flame to cleanse and purify my body and my field. While I was wondering if I was using the most powerful shade of violet, I saw a panel truck up ahead. It was painted the same brilliant shade of violet with which I was cleansing my field.

First of all, who paints a big work truck violet? But

---

2 Gerry Ellen, "Understanding Synchronicity as a Tool for Conscious Living," *MeetMindful*, accessed September 1, 2022, https://www.meetmindful.com/understanding-synchronicity/.

more importantly, I mentally asked a question and received a direct and immediate answer from the Universe that made me laugh and laugh. This was not a coincidence. This was the answer to my question—a perfect example of synchronicity, and it came at the same time I was floundering about the best example to use. It was a precious moment of communication from the Universe.

9. **Nature**—I was walking alone in a large wood nearby. It had been beautifully still for an hour or so. I knew the trees, the elementals, and my guides were listening to my thoughts and ideas. I stopped on the path and asked the Universe a clear question within my mind. Instantly, a strong wind rushed through with words riding along with it. Stillness returned immediately and remained for the entire walk. Nature responds to our thoughts, emotions, and questions. You will always receive an answer. It is only a matter of noticing in a different way.

10. **Birds**—Birds of all types are the messengers for Spirit. My friend called me in a panicked voice. She had just pulled in to her long driveway to see twenty vultures sitting along the entire length of her roof. Her first response was fear. She immediately thought it meant certain death was about to befall her. After listening to her words, I asked her a couple of questions:

First, "Do vultures actually kill people, or anything else?"

"No, they eat what is already dead," she responded.

I agreed and added, "Vultures are the 'cleaners,' removing something that has already come to an end."

"That makes so much sense!" my friend declared. She went on to share her story of a long, painful relationship that had just ended, and she felt such a relief regarding it.

Then I said to her, "Twenty vultures are also a personal symbol of information for you. What does the number twenty signify for you?"

She told me she had struggled for twenty years due to a certain relationship and now she ended it.

I replied, "You see, the number of birds on your roof symbolized the number of years, but it also shows me that a huge and thorough effort is going on to clean and remove the negative that has just ended for you."

"Yes, absolutely!" my friend said.

When you receive a symbol in the form of birds, there often may be a certain number of those particular birds showing themselves to you. Some birds are symbols of certain life traits. Owls, for example, are full of information for us. Their primary traits are seeing clearly in dark times. The Universe uses nature to communicate with us. You have the ability to see the hidden wisdom even in the birds around you.

11. **Animals**—People often say to me, "How on earth can I know the exact information I'm supposed to get when I see a certain animal?"

Here is my answer to that: We humans first need to look at the way the animal survives in the world. Are they aggressive or passive? Do they tend to hide and be loners, or do they run in a pack? How do they receive their nourishment? What actions do they take when you see them nearby?

For example, only a month before I wrote this section, a movement out the window caught my eye. There was a massive coyote in my yard! He was alone. He leaped in the air, stiffening his front legs to stomp on a mouse. Coyotes have a characteristic of running alone but also meeting in large groups. When they are in a group, they greet each other and yelp loudly. People tend to be afraid of them and think they will attack their horses or cattle when, in fact, coyotes prefer mice and rabbits.

If you suddenly saw a coyote out your back window, what signal of information did the Universe just give to you?

They are loners, but they also make meaningful connections with others. They love to share information among their peers loudly and happily. They are powerful and sometimes scary, but they are not aggressive at all. At that moment in my life, that coyote gave me an amazing number of details regarding an issue I was dealing with.

From now on, notice the animals that suddenly appear around you. Notice their personalities, how they live, what sustains them, and what they are known for. The message to you is within the animal's natural characteristics.

12. **Accidents**—There are no accidents when there is an accident. My dear friend had a series of medical issues that prevented her from seeing her clients for nearly two months. She frequently commented that her physical problems were a surprise to her.

"I didn't see this coming," she would say.

On her first day back to work, she pulled out in front of a car and got into a terrible accident. Her car was totaled, and she was injured with a concussion.

Our daily thoughts and subsequent emotions are constantly sending powerful signals of information outward into the cosmos. The signals may be positive and light, or dark and dense, or anything in between. The cosmos is structured to respond to us by matching our signals. Accidents tend to happen when there is great upheaval in our emotions. When our emotions rumble and churn, the world around us rumbles and churns in response.

13. **Numbers**—Numbers are everywhere. Each number and combination of numbers vibrate with meaning. They show themselves to us by repeating a particular number over and over until we notice the signal. You might see it in different locations such as license plates, billboards, and your receipt at a restaurant.

An example of one of the most common numbers that appears is 1-1-1-1. This number sequence commonly symbolizes the gates of heaven, or the passage to higher awareness, or a doorway to the next step in your life. One day, my uncle commented that for months he had woken up every night at 2:22 a.m. I was startled, then shared with him that I also had been waking up at 2:22 a.m. for months.

Now notice the numbers that keep repeating in your everyday world. Each individual number, and combination of numbers, has meaning. What numbers tend to appear in your daily life?

14. **Repetitive Life Patterns**—Everyone has repeating patterns in their lives, some positive and some negative. Look back over your life and notice a pattern or theme that reoccurs in your life. For example, do you keep finding yourself needing money? In an abusive relationship? Are you trying to head a certain direction in your life, but nothing works out?

A negative pattern will repeat for millennia until we develop a deeper awareness of our soul's mission. A negative pattern itself is not just a signal; it is an offer for another chance to:

  1. Learn and understand something vital about your development.

  2. Heal unresolved and traumatic past lives.

  3. Heal and release a current life event or trauma.

The more we ignore the repeated appearance of a pattern, the more it will appear and the more severe the negativity will become because the Universe is trying to get your attention. Each repetition is another chance to learn, to heal, and to make more positive decisions.

15. **Meditation**—A student told me recently that she was deep in meditation when suddenly an image of a book I wrote popped into her mind's eye. She had never heard of me or my books, but still the correct image of the book clearly appeared in her vision.

Remember earlier in this book, one of my controversial

topics is meditation. Meditation is important in our lives not just because it makes us more spiritual, but because it makes us better listeners and receivers of intuition. It also sends us into a different, lighter energy frequency. It is like fine-tuning to the radio channel of the Universe.

Meditation is a prayerful time, and yet we are not praying. We are training ourselves to stop chattering, wishing, yearning, or begging the Universe for something. Take a few moments to listen for, and receive, intuition. This is the process of the most accurate intuitive.

16. **Photos**—The moments spirit communicates with us is often a great surprise. The Universe adores children. So my grandkids and I, together, call out for orbs to appear to us. Then I hand them cheap cameras. Off they go, out the door and into the night, clicking away with their cameras. I, on the other hand, stroll out the door with my expensive camera, and I click at the nighttime air around us. I get nothing, but the children's photos are full of orbs and fairies! Spirit communicates with us through old pathways, and now Spirit is utilizing cameras, the internet, and social media to open awareness that the nonphysical realms do exist. When you look at a smiling face with an orb in the center of your photo, this is hard to deny.

17. **Music**—The Universe loves music, and our guides use it to communicate with us. People often complain that a song has been stuck in their head all day, and they cannot get it to stop. If that happens to you, even occasionally, I ask that you examine it in quite a different way. Notice the exact song in a deeper way. First, notice it is usually only a piece of the song that is "stuck" in your mind, and not the entire song. The piece that is "stuck" is really only a short portion of the lyrics. What exactly is the section that repeats over and over? What are the exact words in that section? Here lies the message meant just for you. When you receive the message, the song gently subsides.

18. **Living People**—Living people around us are often unaware they are messengers for us. A stranger will sometimes direct a comment to you in a casual way, and that comment is filled with the most enlightening, profound wisdom that you have been waiting for. That comment pokes a hole through a block that you could not get through on your own. And then that stranger just walks away, having no idea they just changed the direction of your life forever.

The very day I wrote this section, someone gave me a profound moment in my life. I was sitting at the airport gate, and suddenly the woman next to me asked me where I was going.

"My dearest friend was canoeing in the boundary waters at the Minnesota and Canadian border," I said. "She had a horrible fall and is very injured. Three wilderness rescue men got her out of there and flew her to an emergency center in a tiny seaplane. I am heading there to bring her home." Then with a big smile, I chuckled, trying to make it more lighthearted than it really was.

Just then an airline worker approached this woman and said she could not take all her bags onto the plane. He said she could only take two bags.

She struggled a long time to organize her bags in many different ways, but was unsuccessful.

I finally said, "I have room to put the Pretty Pretty Princess game and the small blanket into my carry-on bag." I giggled. "I promise you, I will not run away with the Pretty Pretty Princess game." I laughed again as she handed me the objects, which fit perfectly in my case.

Then this woman looked at me quite seriously. "See, now you are saving me too."

Her words went right to my heart. I was just asking Spirit if my books and courses were truly helping people. I was given the answer at that very moment from a stranger in an airport.

A long time ago, my attorney told me I would never

make anything of myself. I was twenty-five years old, and he was an authority figure to me, so I believed him. I stood in the hallway, waiting for the elevator. When the door opened, an old man stood in the corner. I tried to hide my tears as I stepped in. He began to make the clearest, most beautiful sounds like the singing of a canary. I felt the waves of sound float into my chest, then into my heart. The birdsong floated into me, and I floated with the song. The elevator door opened. I stepped out and turned to thank him. No one was there.

My sixteen-year-old granddaughter shared an experience she had in a small restaurant where she worked. This is what she said:

> "One of my customers told me that I have the Holy Spirit in me. I think that is pretty cool. She is an older lady with black hair and has a ton of crosses on her clothes and jewelry. She actually came in almost exactly one year ago, and was dancing in the lobby to one of my favorite songs, smiling at me the whole time. I told two other people I work with that she is one of my guardian angels who has come to visit me.

> "Last year when she came in, I literally could not stop crying because her presence was so comforting, and she really doesn't seem human. She just seems like a figure made of white light."

No matter what age they are, listen to the children.

The Universe is a living being that is continually communicating with each one of us. I have given you eighteen of the many avenues in which the living Universe participates with you during your earthly life. It is simply a matter of noticing, and simply a matter of realizing that everything and every event has meaning. Within the meaning, the rich nugget of personal information is just for you.

Essential Points

- The medical intuitive's work not only focuses on the physical body but also the mind, the emotions, and the eternal soul.
- Medical Intuitives primarily pick up what is prominent in a person's energy field.
- The Universe sends signals to you through symbols in the world around you.
- Do not work hard to search for signals from the Universe.

Chapter 2

Levels of Protection

Here is a brief summary of the foundation for the medical intuitive's own self-care and daily cleansing, separated into four levels. It is imperative that you stay in the vibration of Divine Light—vital, healthy, full of confidence, and fiercely invincible.

Level 1: Run Your Energetic Toroidal Field

Science has discovered that energy follows human thought. Let that reality settle into your awareness. That discovery is the foundation for the work done by energy practitioners and medical intuitives. Each thought is a powerful, living thing with substance. Research has found that we humans can move pinballs from thousands of miles away with our focused thoughts. Intent describes the human ability to focus the energy behind our thoughts, and creating intention sends a particular type of energy outward into the Universe. So use the power of your thoughts. Get in charge of them and do not let them be in charge of you. You have the ability to create an intent more powerful than you could ever dream. Use that ability to create well-being for yourself first, and then for the many others who are waiting for you.

Science has recognized that the human energy field moves in a formation called the **human toroidal field**. When I came across this toroidal field on the internet I almost jumped out of my chair with surprise. I saw a diagram showing a fountain of energy flowing through a human, which you will find on page 38. That formation is exactly the way I perceive energy flow with people who are feeling exceptionally well physically, mentally, and emotionally.

I could not believe scientists discovered that human energy moves in the same way that I have intuitively witnessed it for years. I love it when science catches up with the nonphysical realm of life.

This fountain of energy will work with us, and for us, in planned and purposeful ways. As I have mentioned in my other books, I am not one to ask people to protect themselves with thoughts of bubbles, crystal-egg shapes, or even beautiful walls. When someone creates a wall of protection, even if it is a crystalline wall, it is often generated from fear, suspicion, jealousy, or similar emotions. Fear and other emotions at that level are energetically dense and jagged. This dense, jagged energy tends to interfere with the natural flow of human energy.

In short, the wall of protection becomes a thickened barrier that keeps the negativity out but also interferes with our ability to receive the positive in life. Instead, consider building your personal energy field from inside outward. Deliberately enrich your own energy body first and allow that richness to shine out to all the world and beyond. Here are the ways you can create an ascension and an expansion of your field.

Scan and Assess Your Energy Field

Send your "thought awareness"—like sending your ears, eyes, and fingertips—all around inside of your physical body. Notice whatever you notice. There is no way to do it wrong. Simply notice and learn more about your soul energy without judgment.

When you have quickly scanned all around and within yourself, send your thought awareness beyond your skin and out into your energy field. Send your sensors in every direction around you, and do not forget to scan your backside and under your feet. Notice where it feels strong, bright, and energized. Also notice any sense of weakened, thin, or lower energy and the location in or around your body. Remember that it will always feel as if you are just imagining it. Trust whatever leaps into your awareness. You might find that your field is rich with energy, or full in some areas yet weak in others. Any type of weakened conditions indicates the need for immediate action to bolster the natural protection that your field provides for you.

Understand the General Flow of the Human Toroidal Field

Many people tend to make the toroidal field much more complicated than it really is. Deliberately directing your own personal energy field is instant. You merely think focused and clear thought about each image and the energy is generated by your thoughts, but energy also follows thoughts. Do not let your mind wander. Here are the images on which you should clearly focus your thoughts:

- The general flow of energy is upward and inward to fill every physical cell of your body until you are so full you feel like a glowing lightbulb.

- When you are full, you become a fountain. Allow your energy to shoot up into the cosmos just like a fountain in a pond.

- The cosmos notices your new brightness and responds by matching and interconnecting its energy with your new, brighter, and more positive vibration.

- Then the cosmos sends all this combined energy back downward into your field, your physical body, and into the earth.

- All this repeats over and over again in a flowing movement: Rising up, filling up, shooting up, then coming down into your field and physical body, down into the earth, and then back up through the soles of your feet. You are like a fountain in the center of a pond.

- Think it, and the energy must follow your thoughts.

Direct and Empower Your Toroidal Field

My guides have altered the order of directing your toroidal field. Directing the toroidal field in the following way is one of the primary reasons I decided to release the second edition of this book. My guides ask that you fill yourself with the following energy. The first two focus on healing, cleansing, and then purifying while the last two bring in power and protection because the negative cannot stand its elevated high frequency.

- **Each individual color of the rainbow.** Each color has its own focus of healing. So, directing each color individually provides a more powerful healing response within your body.

- **The violet flame.** This holds a purifying, cleansing energy.

- **Brilliant diamond-like sparkles.**

- **Shimmering, glorious, golden energy.**

Here are the steps to direct and empower your toroidal field using the energy listed above:

- Imagine inhaling through the soles of your feet.

- Focus your thoughts and inhale each color of the rainbow one at a time. Fill yourself with each color one by one in this order: Red, Orange, Yellow, Green, Blue, Purple, White.

- Every time you inhale, fill yourself more and more with each shimmering, glistening color.

- Focus filling every cell of your body on sending each color up your spinal cord, every cell, every organ, every muscle of your physical body.

- Notice the fullness of rainbow energy within you.

- In your mind, direct the violet flame to rush through each cell of who you are, purifying all along the way.

- Think, imagine, and sense that brilliant white sparkles are inside every single cell of your physical body.

- Direct shimmering, electrified, precious gold energy to shoot up from the soles of your feet.

- When you are completely full of rainbows, violet, white

sparkles, and gold, then allow that fullness to shine like a lightbulb. Shine in all directions, and especially empower your entire backside. (*Note:* Do not deliberately send your energy outward. Focus on being so full of brilliant light that you naturally shine like a lightbulb.)

- Notice you are so full that your brilliant light rises upward and out the crown of your head, shooting up into your higher self and into the heavens. The heavens notice and respond positively to your new positive energy field.

- Allow your energy, and the energy of the heavens, to flow back down like a fountain through you and back into the earth.

- Every time you inhale, continue this natural flow as it comes back up through your body and spine. Allow your body to feel the sensations of this flow. As you think about the flow circulating, your body will feel the sensations of it. The energy will often give you warm vitality and the sense of taking a perfect, heavenly shower.

Your goal is to practice until you can generate your flowing fountain in just a few seconds. Remember, your entire body becomes a pumping mechanism, exactly like a fountain in a park. Practice and play with it.

Again, this is about expanding the energy of who you are and not about creating a barrier around you. When we place a barrier around us, it is usually out of fear. The element of fear creates a density that is more like a barricade. A shield or barrier will eventually become denser and impede your natural state as a pulsing, energetic being. We do not want to be encapsulated and barricaded from our pulsing, energetic Universe. As energetic practitioners, we are meant to achieve a higher state of intense, refined spark of Source and not create an energy barricade around us.

Do not work hard at this. Be playful. Practice these steps for

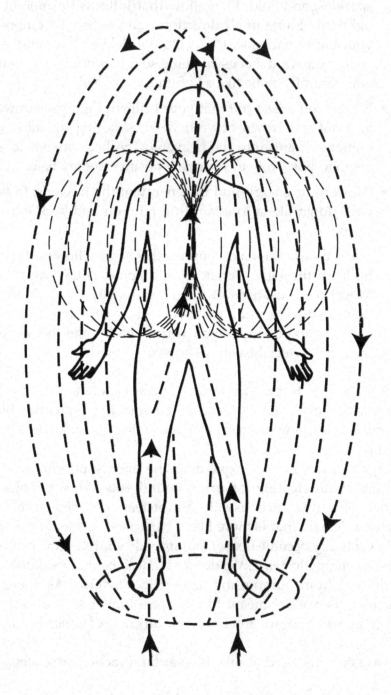

The Toroidal Field *(illustration by Jacqueline Rogers)*

only a few minutes at a time throughout your day. It will strengthen you, physically and energetically. It will replenish your auric field and create the most intense protection for you without creating a single wall or barrier between you and the world around you. You are becoming a powerful, positive link between Earth and Heaven.

Level 2: Protection that Works with the Negative

Now we will take your protection to the next level so you can excel as a healthy healer and be safe while addressing any situation that interferes with your clients or your personal life. I will magnify your protective abilities while working with any negativity. Do not wait to practice the toroidal field when you are experiencing fear. It is imperative that you practice building your field while experiencing feelings of confidence and strength. Practice when you know you are powerful, unshakable, an invincible Light of Source, doing the work with a sincere and intense frequency of Love.

We can be harmed by an emotional event or crisis. We can be harmed by another person, or our own negative emotions can contribute to weakening our field. We humans are not just harmed physically or emotionally. Our aura can have an injury as severe as a gash or even a gaping hole. This also leaves us undefended on an energetic level. If you had a hole in your home's wall, all types of things would naturally flow into it such as the rain, wind, small critters, birds, and insects. It is the same with our energy body. If there is a weakened spot or an opening, it is the nature of the Universe for anything and everything to flow into it.

Most people can conceive of their energy reaching out in front of their body because that is the direction in which we perceive life. Your personal field vibrates in *all* directions around you. It is behind you, on each side of you, above you, and below you. It should appear or feel like waves of pulsating electricity, glowing, radiant, and healthy. Assess your energy body daily for jagged edges, paleness, cloudiness, leaks (which often appear as bubbles), weakened or thin areas, holes, tears, or gashes. Finding any one of these conditions in your aura indicates the need for immediate action to bolster the natural protection that your field usually provides for you. Repeat the steps for the toroidal field when something negative happens in your life, or when someone says negative things to you. We humans are physical and nonphysical at the same time. As a medical intuitive, it is time to think of yourself not only as a physical being but also an energy being. Constantly assess, build, and repair your vitality by deliberately streaming your toroidal field in the specific steps identified earlier.

That being said, there is more you absolutely need to do. The following steps will enhance your abilities to handle any degree of negativity. Face each day with the following:

- **Attitude:** You must have a fierce attitude with anything that seems negative in any way. This comes directly from a great dowser named Raymon Grace. I have heard him say repeatedly that you must have an attitude if you do healing work. I have given this concept of "attitude" a great deal of thought. My own definition of "attitude" relates to bold thoughts, feelings of strength and assertiveness, a certain commanding demeanor and way of holding oneself, and a formidable and convincing viewpoint of self. That is exactly what you need to achieve and radiate throughout your toroidal field at all times. This attitude and these feelings emit a frequency that even the worst level of negativity cannot approach.

- **Your Protection Guides:** Call in the most Sacred, Divine protection guides and, together, create a holy protective perimeter—a sacred ground around you, your work, and your clients. You can also ask for body protectors, Sacred Specialists from the Light of Source to specifically protect your body. You and these particular guides are creating a sacred, safe protection for you as a healer, and the space you work within.

- **Your Specialists:** Here on Earth, there is a Divine and Sacred specialist for just about everything. Similarly, there are specialists in the spiritual realm. When you come across any level of negativity in your work with others, call in specific Divine and Sacred Specialty Guides who work with the exact type of negativity that you have discovered. Call out intuitively, in your mind. An example might be: "I request the perfect, Divine specialty guide from the highest order of the Compassionate Source. Immediately take this negativity to the perfect place for its transition into the Light."

- **Practice:** Deliberately running your toroidal energetic field daily is as essential for your energy hygiene as much as taking a shower and putting on deodorant is for your physical hygiene. Do not wait until you are deep within your client's energy field before you remember that you have not cleansed and protected your own soul's energy.

- **Command:** As an energetic healer, do not hesitate to command something from your specialty guides, or from the Universe. It is your right, as a Light-conscious worker, to send out your requests for yourself and your clients in a compelling manner. The following are examples of noble commands that are protective in profound ways. The key for affirmations and commands is to concentrate on the words and let your emotions feel their power. If the following three commands feel right to you as an individual, state them in a commanding manner when you wake and just before you go to sleep:

"I, *(full name)*, completely and permanently revoke and repel *all* negative people and *all* dark-force energy from me and my clients in all ways and on all levels! I, *(full name)*, am indomitable, invincible, and unassailable to all negativity on all levels. Only the divine, compassionate, loving Light of Source fills my body, my mind, my higher self, my spirit, and my eternal soul."

"I, *(full name)*, invoke the greatest guardians of the divine, compassionate loving Light of Source, to constantly guard my physical body and my energetic field to create a completely safe, sacred space around me, my clients, and our healing work."

Note: For the final command, substitute "God" for any divine name that feels correct to you, such as "Buddha," "Christ," "Krishna," or "Allah."

"Only God's compassionate Love and Light and the purest sacred Consciousness completely fill **every cell in my body** now."

"Only God's compassionate Love and Light and the purest sacred Consciousness completely fill my **mind** now."

"Only God's compassionate Love and Light and the purest sacred Consciousness completely fill my **emotions** now."

"Only God's compassionate Love and Light and the purest sacred Consciousness completely fill my **energy field** now."

"Only God's compassionate Love and Light and the purest sacred Consciousness completely fill my **higher self** now."

"Only God's compassionate Love and Light and the purest sacred Consciousness completely fill my **spirit** now."

"Only God's compassionate Love and Light and the purest sacred Consciousness completely fill my **eternal soul** now."

Take the time right now to review the descriptive words regarding attitude: Bold. Strength. Assertive. Commanding. Formidable. Convincing.

Make them yours. Make those words about you as a medical intuitive. Then practice declaring the commands stated above. Notice how different you feel. Call in the highest level of protective guides and your specialists. Do not settle on being adequate. Build yourself into the finest, top-rated medical intuitive possible. To get there, you need to attend to yourself first.

Level 3: See with Your Mind's Eye

You have accessed the clearest channel. Now it is time to notice where and how you receive intuitive information. Where is your mind's eye? Where does it project itself for you? I will tell you that mine is in the back of my eyelids. It is as if a movie is projected from my brain outward and shows itself on the screen of my eyelids.

I was amazed when students in my workshops began to describe their mind's eye showing up in many other locations. Some say it is in the center of their head. Some describe it as hanging out in the air anywhere from four inches to a foot or more from their forehead. Some say they perceive it above the crown of their head. Fascinating! The mind's eye projects itself in different locations with different people. Where is yours?

The center of our forehead, commonly known as our "third eye," is the intake center for intuitive information. Intuitive information enters into the energy center and flows to the pineal gland that sits between the two hemispheres of the brain. The pineal gland carries that name because it looks like a tiny pine cone. Ancient societies have honored the pine cone for eons. I believe the pineal gland is the brain's processor of intuitive information. Science has now discovered that the same cells in the pineal gland are also found in the retina of the human eye. There are no coincidences.

Even though we are talking about seeing intuitive information, the process of seeing with your mind's eye is not just visual. It is also about perceiving intuitively. Clairvoyance has become significant. If you think you must see everything, then you are missing all the other ways intuitive information is coming to you.

Don't forget that you will also sense information about your client in your own body. You will receive it through sound, smell, taste, and sight, or the "knowing" that waves through you. Most people who struggle to enhance their intuition ignore telepathic thought that leaps into their mind out of nowhere. Here is an excerpt from a session that explains how to open and allow your third eye to work for you, and with you.

Case Study:
The Third Eye

Practice Experience:

Imagine you are the medical intuitive speaking the words in this transcript. Read it aloud or, if possible, with a study buddy, one taking part as the medical intuitive and one as the client. Practice this session as if you are actually giving these steps to someone who needs your guidance.

TZ: They *(my Divine and Sacred guides)* want me to mention your third eye in your forehead. When people are trying to be intuitive, they tend to push out through their third eye. I want you to just imagine that you are inhaling through your third eye right now. Just as you inhale through your nose or mouth, also notice inhaling through your third eye. For you, it might be a certain color, or colors, or it might just be a physical sensation of inhaling. Imagine it and the energy will follow. *(Pause.)* Then imagine inhaling to the very center point of your head. You will just know, or sense, where that is. *(Long pause.)* Ask to receive a piece of wisdom right now that they want you to know. It will pop into your awareness instantly. *(Long pause.)*

(Pause to allow the client time to practice a new experience. Watch their energy field as they practice.)

Client: Wisdom. When I was doing that, I could see a woman. It wasn't me or a past life. I don't know who it was, but a woman with long dark hair. She is watching me as I was doing that. She is facing me. And then, when it came time for the wisdom, she stood up and came closer. She said along the lines of, "You are home," or "This is your home."

TZ: Oh, wow. Now, when you are wondering about something that comes to you intuitively, put it in the form of a question. So, take a minute and put it in a very definite, clear, short question and maybe ask her who or what she is. Put it in the form of a question that you want to know about her, and pause to receive the answer. *(Long pause.)*

Client: She knew me in a past life when I had great abilities. She is just here to help me.

TZ: So, as a guide or helper?

Client: No, not as a guide. More around techniques.

TZ: Oh, techniques. That's cool. Ask her this: Does she mean techniques to empower, or build your own intuitive nature, or something else?

Client: Yeah, it seems to be around abilities and intuitiveness.

TZ: Excellent.

Client: So, it is specifically around helping me, you know, hone in on my abilities and that kind of thing.

When we try so hard to be intuitive, we are actually pushing out from our third eye. By pushing out and trying hard, we end up making the third eye an output center, which is opposite of its true nature. The third eye is an input center. When we work hard to be intuitive, we push outward, trying to grab or pluck information out of the air. The easiest way to heal this chakra is to gently imagine inhaling from it. Soon you will realize that it has permanently returned to its primary function as an intake center, and it will remain that way for you.

Level 4: Get in Charge of Your Laser Beam

The accurate medical intuitive can hone their thought energy into a decisive laser beam, and direct that beam outward and into the energy field of the client. They then direct the laser beam even more precisely, going past the skin and into the person's physical body. Your laser beam will be pulled to the area of your client's body that draws its attention. Your specialists will be there to guide you as well. When you make that contact with your client's energy field and physical body, you may perceive a photo-like image of the person, or you may perceive a vague human form. Simply stop, watch, and wait. The wait is usually only for a few seconds. I wait because intuition is a gentle, passive movement. Receiving is the flow of information coming through your intuitive sensors and into your awareness. It is not about trying, or pushing, or working hard. It is about gentle acceptance and the gentle process of receiving.

Your laser beam is real. Your thoughts just created it, and the laser-beam energy just followed your precise and powerful thoughts. When I beam out toward my client, I tend to send it toward the person's name and the sound of their voice. The tip of the laser beam has sensors that are like hypersensitive eyes, ears, nose, and fingertips. They notice everything.

Thought is our powerful creative force. Energy naturally follows thought. Remember, we humans have no idea how powerful thoughts really are. Look at your life right now. Your thinking mind influences what you have and what you do not have. The Universe follows the lead of your thought energy. However, most of the time, people describe their thinking as scattered, negative, unable to remember detail, or weak and unintelligent. All those thoughts do, indeed, create a weaker energy signature.

No matter where I go or where I teach around the world, people consistently tell me that they cannot stop thinking the way they do. They describe the following:

"I cannot stop negativity because I grew up in a negative family."

"I cannot change things because I have been a certain way since childhood."

"I cannot do medical intuition because I am not good enough."

Underneath those words, I hear: "I am not in charge of myself." If you are not in charge of you, then who is? Somebody, or something, is determining what your thoughts are and what they do. You might as well be in charge of you!

The following thought creates a stronger energy signature:

"I am learning all the time. I think and remember clearly. I am a good-hearted person who lives an aware life."

Can you feel the difference as you read these words?

Creating intent is, first and foremost, instructing and training your thoughts, and then pointing your thoughts in the direction you want them to go. You might want to send thought energy to something three feet away, or on the other side of the world. Distance does not affect energy.

Intuitives, medical intuitives, mediums, all modalities of energy healers, as well as people focusing on self-healing, must constantly check in with their physical being, but also their energy being. Constantly assess, build, and repair your energy, and as a result, your soul will heal too. Your constant self-care must become part of your self-care like taking a shower and brushing your teeth. You will sometimes find that on some days you must take multiple energetic showers.

Essential Points

- Science has recognized that the human energy field moves in a formation called the human toroidal field.

- We humans are physical and nonphysical at the same time.

- Approach your commands to the Universe with a bold, assertive, and confident attitude.

- Energy follows your thoughts.

Chapter 3

10 Keys for the Excellent, Accurate Medical Intuitive

"When I let go of what I am, I become what I might be."

—Lao Tzu

As I prepare a new course or write my next book, I deeply study myself to notice if I have received new information from my guides or the Universe. I also study the mentoring clients who I am working with. I look for details that stand out like neon signs blinking in the dark. The following ten keys are the neon signs pointing the way to be an excellent, accurate medical intuitive.

Key 1: Work Only with Divine and Sacred Guides

Most intuitives and mediums have little idea of which level the guides they are working with fall under. If you and I sit together and call out to the Universe for a guide to help us, we are not defining who we are willing to work with. We are commanding in a vague way and not defining the special qualities, the level of skills, or the enriched awareness of guides we are willing to work with.

I now demand that I work only with guides that are at the Divine and Sacred level. I refuse to work with any guides that are less. If they are not at that level, I thank them and send them away. The negative side of life has the highest, the best, and the greatest, but never the Divine and Sacred. The Divine and Sacred are two distinct words that vibrate with instant and rapid frequencies.

When a new guide arrives, I give them a serious interview as if they are applying for an important career position. The true Divine and Sacreds never hesitate to participate in their interview. Their answers are fast, clear, and to the point. Those who show up for you and are not at this advanced level, will not answer your questions, or they will try to distract you by talking about something else, hoping you do not notice they did not answer you. Here are the steps to invite in a Divine and Sacred specialty guide:

Step 1: Command

Use the following command to call out to a Divine and Sacred specialty guide:

"I invite in now, only the most Divine and Sacred guide who specializes in working with me, *(your full name)*, for the purpose of *(clearly define the specialty that you want or need)*.

Step 2: Interview

Interview the guide so you are confident about who you are working with. Ask them these three questions. If they are truly Divine and Sacred, you will receive an instant "Yes."

- Are you truly Divine and Sacred?
- How did you achieve that status?
- What exactly is your specialty area?

Dismiss them if . . .

- They are silent and do not answer your question.
- They begin talking about something else to distract you.
- They clearly say, "No."

Step 3: Develop a Working Relationship

Communicate back and forth to develop a clear working relationship. Ask precise questions such as:

- What is my first step to working excellently with you?
- What is the first step you will take to work excellently with me?
- I just received this piece of information from you. Did I receive that correctly?

Note: The invitation is only an invitation. From this point forward, you must now clearly command each action you want or need the Divine and Sacred to take.

Many people think our guides spring into action when you invite them to work with you. This is not the case. An invitation is only an invitation. If you are truly working with the Divine and Sacreds, they will *never* take a step without your command. That is one of the primary differences between a low-level being and the more blessed. The lower-level spirits are known for interfering with humans by pushing into our energy field, body, or life.

The Divine and Sacred will *never* interfere with human choice. We humans are making choices every second of our day. The Universe is a highly intelligent, highly organized, very complex supersystem based on thoughts, and especially choices, that human beings make every moment of our current life. This is why clear directives and clear requests are essential when working with the Divine and the Sacred.

Key 2: Disconnect Your Energy from the Client
After Every Session

As the years go by, we intuitives cannot maintain our own energy and health if we allow an intense connection to continue after the client walks out the door, or we end a phone session. Their emotions will continue to affect you as your life moves forward. Try to imagine carrying that level of intense connection with hundreds and hundreds of clients that you have assisted over the years. Many of those people will continue to live in agony, and that agony will sit heavily on your back. This is exactly one of the ways that thought forms develop and how they continue to grow thicker and heavier over time.

For years, I have noticed that professional mediums, psychics, and bodyworkers are frequently ill and often hospitalized. Something is not right with this picture. I brought this up with other professional psychics and mediums that I knew. We came to a mind-blowing understanding. We came to this realization by discussing how we began our sessions with clients. For example, I use the description of laser light beaming toward my client, then moving in past the skin and into the physical body. For other professionals, it feels more like enveloping the person with their own energy as if they are throwing a net over the client. Others described different methods, but basically we all discussed how we make an intense level of energetic connections when working with clients. We begin our sessions creating energetic connections, then we bring the session to a close and move on to our next appointment.

With alarm, we noticed that no one—and I mean *no one*—ever pulled their energy back from the client at the end of each session. We intuitives were leaving energetic threads with each client. These threads allowed an energetic exchange back and forth between the intuitive and every client they had ever worked with. This exchange could continue for the rest of everyone's lives, and probably even beyond. As a result, intuitives were not living clean and clear within our own energy field. The thoughts, emotions, and traumatic events of many other people's lives continued to dramatically influence our bodies, minds, spirits, and souls. How can we work toward our own health under such conditions?

As a result of this breakthrough, I wanted to be careful how I began this book. I purposefully opened with *The Invocation* by Betsy Bergstrom. This invocation is one method of being careful about who we invite into our work. People are generally sloppy with their words and with their energetic hygiene. If you simply ask the Universe for help, you may not necessarily receive the best, most qualified help available. If you do not deliberately and thoughtfully request the specific assistance you are really hoping for, you may receive any spirit who happens to be floating by.

Each word, phrase, and sentence we declare is of vital importance. What we think, say aloud, or intuitively request will return back to us exactly with the same frequency that we send out. Use this invocation or create your own, but be careful. At the beginning of your day or your session, specifically request assistance utilizing high, fine, compassionate, and loving terminology like that of Betsy's *Invocation*.

Not only must we begin sessions with care, but it is especially vital for our well-being to consciously and carefully disconnect from our clients. We must create good, clean closure at the end of our sessions or at the end of our work day. We must also disengage from every person we have ever worked with in the past.

I discovered, with the help of other professionals and my beloved spirit specialists, valuable details and specific steps to accomplish this goal. Here are three specific steps to create good, clean closure with your client:

1. At the beginning of each session, ask that a sacred space be placed around you and your client for the most perfect work and healing to happen. Do not create the space yourself. Ask your specialty guide to create the perfect, sacred, and safe space for the work to happen. You may feel it, or you may see it. Intuitively invite each client to join you in that sacred space.

2. At the close of each session, or at least at the end of each day, invite in and direct a Divine and Sacred specialty guide to create the most powerful cleansing filter for you now. Notice the look and the feel of the filter in front of you. With deliberate consciousness, pull back your energetic laser beam from the client through the filter. You may feel

the filter, or you may actually see it working. You can assist yourself by inhaling and imagining that each inhalation pulls your energy back to you through that filter.

3. A possible command to use at the same time might be:

I now bring me, and only me, back to myself, clean and clear, through a perfect filter provided for me by my divine cleansing specialist.

Sometimes I see a thick substance clinging to the filter. I am so comforted and pleased to know that I am not bringing someone else's emotional density into my life.

During one session with me, a well-known professional psychic who was struggling with cancer made the following comment:

"I *love* the part where you point out the difference between the temporary energetic psychic connections we use in our work, and the more permanent connections that build up over time in our general relationships! I had never considered that before, but it certainly seems right, and I can feel the difference within myself. This is my newest information, and the biggest tip of all!"

The above three steps are the most important piece of information in this entire book. Every time you end a session with a client, friend, or family member, use these closing steps without fail. They will save your life.

Key 3: Take Control of Your Fears

If you say right now that you have no fears, you might be in trouble already. You may be completely unaware of your fears. Nothing gets in the way of intuitive skills more than fear. Any degree of fear or worry lurking within our conscious or unconscious mind will always stifle our innate abilities. In particular, subtle and unconscious fears squeeze the life out of our potential abilities and the flow of intuition. It is imperative that you examine your fears and make a conscious effort to release the control they have over you. The more awareness you have about your own internal struggles, and the more you allow them to come to the surface of your consciousness, the more powerful you will be.

There are all types and levels of fear. I became acutely aware of the many facets of fear when my workshop students frequently brought them up in class. Many of the fears are classical. Below is a list of the most common:

- Change.
- The opinions of family and friends.
- Being judged or criticized.
- Making mistakes.
- The unknown.

Then I began to hear some fears that I had not thought of. Students have said:

- What if I love the spirit world so much that I don't want to leave it?
- What if I miss a terrible illness for a client?
- What if I can no longer function in the physical world?
- What do I do if I begin to see spirits?
- Will the spirit world take me over?
- What if I'm wrong?
- What if I'm right?
- What if I'm just making it all up?
- I'm afraid I don't deserve to have this ability.
- I'm afraid medical intuition is too important for me to do.
- I'm afraid I'm not worthy to do this work.

Which of these fears and worries do you have? Do you have one that I did not mention above? The hidden fears are the most dangerous because they lurk beneath the surface of your life choices. Please bring your own fears to light and allow yourself to notice them. Notice how the energy of fear has a squeezing sensation. Where in your body do you feel the squeeze and the constriction? Get to know where it is located within your body and your energy field. Will you allow yourself to "feel the fear and do it anyway"? The medical intuitive path is calling you, or you would not be drawn to this book. Please allow yourself to excel so you can assist others with your awareness.

You are not the only one in the room who has fears. Your clients are afraid too. I was presenting my workshop in New York State, and one man spoke out about this subject:

"I have been a medium for many years, and people come to me to hear and connect with their loved ones. When they leave, they are so happy. It has never occurred to me that they might be afraid, but I can really understand that now."

The class agreed that clients coming to them for medical intuition are afraid of what the intuitive would find in their body. They are also afraid the intuitive might find their hidden secrets, their traumatic life experiences, and their true emotions. They are thinking:

"What if you find cancer?"

"I hope you don't find out about my childhood sexual abuse."

"What if this intuitive sees that I cheated on my spouse?"

Who knows what else they might be afraid of? Find your own fears, get in charge of your life, body, and energy field, and move past them. Be the confident, professional intuitive without any judgment or critical opinions. Create an atmosphere of openness and understanding no matter what discoveries come to light for your client.

Key 4: Always Ask for Permission

A medical-intuitive session is one of the most intimate experiences a person can have in their life. Because of that intimate connection, I ask my clients for permission before we begin a session, and then I continue to verbally ask permission throughout the session.

For example, in the middle of the session, the client might tell me they are worried about their persistent headaches. I will say, "May I have permission to look more deeply into your head?" Even though the client has already given me permission at the onset of the session, I continue to ask for permission throughout the session.

Requesting permission is the first step in teaching your client that they truly are in charge of their body and their energy field. It sends a powerful signal to the person that you, as the medical intuitive, are not in control of them. Throughout the session, I continue to inform each person they are in charge of their thoughts, their lives, and their energy field. Being in charge of themselves is probably the most valuable healing process that takes place. I emphasize this no matter what the client's goal is for the session.

Probably 75 percent of my clients ask me to check in with a loved one during our time together. That loved one may be living or deceased. I tell my client that I am respectful of everyone, alive or deceased, and do not push into other people's lives without permission. I then tell them that I will be glad to ask their loved one for permission, but if I receive a no from them, I have to honor that.

One student brought up that she could not tell intuitively if she was getting a "yes" or "no" from anyone. Here is a simple way to recognize permission: Say in your mind right now the word "yes," then pause and notice any sensations that "yes" feels like within you. Then say "no" inside of your mind and feel the sensations that the word "no" gives you. Each has a completely different feel. For example, a "yes" for you may have an uplifting feeling and a "no" may have a downward sensation. Another way to receive a "yes" happens when you intuitively ask for permission, and you immediately begin to perceive something about the client. If you immediately get information, you are automatically getting permission.

Permission is so important before doing intuitive work. Here is where "the rubber meets the road," so to speak. If we work energetically with someone without receiving permission, we are crossing a line that should never be crossed. Here is where our powerful abilities become dominant, and therefore darker. Who are we to decide what is best for someone else? Energetically altering someone's body, their life, or their decisions and choices is an instant abuse of our power. It is the first step into the dark.

Key 5: Don't Let Self-Created Rules Get In Your Way

A huge portion of my medical-intuitive workshop is the chipping away at the layers of mental barricades that students have built up for themselves. Most barricades seem to be based on self-inflicted rules. A rule is merely preconceived thoughts of what something is or should be. Many rules are given to us by family. We make a rule true by allowing it to have power over us. A thought that one thinks over and over becomes a belief. A belief can become a rule.

I first noticed one of my own rules getting in the way as I was giving Reiki to a client. I had it in my head that I could not receive intuitive information about my clients unless I had my hands on them while giving Reiki. I was completely convinced that this rule was accurate. When I realized that my intuitive rules were quite limiting, I began to push myself past the boundary of restrictive rules. I began by creating thoughts that were beyond that boundary. Next, I began to ask for volunteers. I told people that I wanted to practice intuitive readings without placing my hands on them. Everyone I asked readily agreed. I pushed through that first limiting rule.

Next I realized I could not do intuitive sessions unless my client was sitting with me in the same room. Once again, this was a self-created rule. So I asked some individuals that I had not seen lately if they would be my practice phone clients, and I offered them an intuitive session on the phone. I picked five people, and every single one of them happily agreed to allow me to practice on them. So we set up an appointment just like I would for a regular client, and I called them at the appointed time. They knew it was practice, and so I simply practiced! Each person was delighted with the information I offered them, and I pushed past that restrictive rule.

The most prominent self-created rule people have is that they must be clairvoyant. They must be able to see spirits, to see guides, to visualize everything. This is simply not true. This false belief and limiting rule comes from decades of intuitives saying, "I see this," or "I see that." To "see" is a shortened version—a lazy form—of the word "perceive."

Do not make clairvoyance the most important factor, and do not make it your only goal. If you do, you will disregard the variety of different channels through which you can receive information. You will perceive intuitive information through many channels. Release your boxed-in structure and go with the flow of the client. As I said in my first book, *Become a Medical Intuitive*, there are many pathways for intuition to enter your awareness.

Another rule that limits our intuitive abilities is the thought: *I am probably not good enough to be a medical intuitive.* The emotion within this thought is very dramatic. Negative emotions at this level give a thought more substance, more density, and thus more power to limit yourself.

People often tell me that their intuitive abilities have stopped:

"My guides have left me, and I'm not getting clear information anymore!"

"Suddenly I don't feel or see my guides!"

People are alarmed and feel abandoned. It is impossible for the nonphysical world to leave us. The only thing that gets in the way of our natural abilities is ourselves. Spiritual assistance does not leave us. We cannot even leave Spirit because we are Spirit. We live in oceans of Spirit. It is in us. It runs through us. We breathe Spirit and sit in Spirit; we walk in Spirit and constantly interact with Spirit.

We can forget our place and position as a Spirit being. We can ignore and reject Spirit. One minute, an intuitive practitioner can give an incredibly accurate reading for a client, and the next minute discredit or fail to recognize the massive amount of information they receive.

For example, one of my mentoring students struggled to understand that she was, indeed, receiving valuable intuitive information. She could only identify that she was fluctuating between physically seeing and abstractly sensing emotions and changes in her own physical body during a session.

She said, "Sometimes I am clear in what I visualize, yet for the next person I am not clear."

She had created a rule that she had to clairvoyantly see, and completely ignored that she was receiving intuitive information through other pathways. She created a vague, subtle rule that intuition had to be a certain way, and when that did not happen, she decided nothing was happening.

Are you as creative as she was in discrediting your abilities? Take a minute or two right now to glimpse into your subtle methods of keeping yourself in failure.

Now get in charge of yourself and stop it! You can be the successful and accurate medical intuitive that you are meant to be!

Our blatant self-made rules are quite easy to discover. Now look for those quiet, subtler rules that are hidden underneath your struggle to take the next action. Allow them to come to the surface. It is the subtle rules that trip us the most. If you still struggle, stop and notice your inner negative dialogue. If you continue to hold on to these self-limiting rules, my books and workshops cannot make you release them. It is up to you to expand beyond your own false beliefs. Your old rules are no longer assisting you. Take a moment now to write down your rules about intuition, and then leave them behind. This awareness will make all the difference and will open up the intuitive world for you.

Key 6: Do Not Absorb the Suffering of Others

Empaths are both profoundly sensitive and intuitive. They are primarily powerful clairsentients. Empaths are excellent at intuitively picking up the emotions and reactions of others. People who identify themselves as empaths receive strong signals of intuitive information regarding negative emotions from other people such as anger, coldness, indifference, trauma, sorrow, defeat, agony, hysteria, vehemence, terror, or loss.

Empaths tend to pick up the negative emotions much more readily than the positive emotions because negative emotions vibrate with a frequency that is slow, thick, dense, and heavy. Those same dense characteristics make it much easier to notice negative emotions, but it also makes it so much easier to negatively affect an empath.

As you read this, you must be deeply truthful with yourself for your own well-being, health, and clarity as an intuitive healer: The empath is like a dry sponge, soaking up the same exact experiences as the troubled people not only physically near them but beyond their environment when they watch the news on the internet or television. They astral project their own energy field outward toward the suffering people or animals, and absorb their energy and life with the energy of each trauma. In this sense, the empath actually becomes someone else. They lose a large part of their identity and life experiences, and merge into the negative emotional experiences of others. Then they internally try to convince themselves that this makes them a more sensitive person, and that everyone else has become hardened to the world around them. When an empath unconsciously takes these steps, they immediately add to the energy of trauma, and make more trauma as a result. This is the opposite of becoming a powerful healer for others.

Here are some simple guidelines to get in charge of the suffering you experience and instead become a healer of it:

- Acknowledge that you are an empath. If you the read above information and realize this accurately describes you, you are an empath.

- Understand that identifying with the traumatic emotions of others does not mean you are more sensitive than the general population. It means you are a struggling empath.

- Believe right now that you can get in charge of your energy field to become a clearer intuitive.

- Examine yourself so you may become more aware of what leads you to suffer with all others who are suffering.

- Take charge of your thoughts. When you alter your thoughts, you alter your energy field, and therefore your life.

- Every time you notice the dramatic struggles around you, don't merge into the darkness of suffering. Instead, become the most brilliant light. Power up with your toroidal field. Direct yourself to be the highest wattage lightbulb, shining outward, to show the others the way out of their darkness.

Dr. Norm Shealy and I were speakers for Dana Williams's Energetics of the Soul Summit. A total of twenty people were interviewed and recorded for this summit. Later on, I listened to Dr. Shealy's interview. During his interview, he states, "Every thought is a prayer."

I got chills as he gently said those words.

Dr. Shealy went on to discuss his own self-care. "I am inevitably interested in protecting my true life's energy from chaos . . . It's not worth wasting my life energy on." He continued, "The Transcendent Will of the Soul is extremely important. The Transcendent Will is paying attention to our personal soul's connection."

Take care of yourself, first and foremost. Stop feeling everyone's suffering. There, I said it out loud. Feeling and merging into the suffering of others only adds more suffering to your life. You cannot lead anyone into health if you keep merging into their suffering, life story, shame, or guilt. You will not be a healer or accurate intuitive if you carry their emotions on your back. By holding your client's story only in your mind or your heart, you can be completely engaged with them and not take on their story.

Key 7: Clarity Heals Your Clients

As a medical intuitive, you must keep your personal energy field free and clear. Do this for yourself and for your clients who will need your clarity. When we send an energetic laser beam out to each client, we must pull our energy back to our own bodies, completely releasing each person we work with. It is also not our place nor our right to remain attached to everyone we have assisted. Your client will not always understand how to control their energetic field, so it is up to us, as medical intuitives, to cleanse and maintain an unpolluted essence that is not tainted by our client's tension, sorrows, and struggles.

It is vital to our health that we do not work alone. It is natural to work with other spirits who have advanced in their own transformational lives. If I worked all alone without the assistance, guidance, and support of Spirit, my effectiveness as a healer would be greatly limited. Spirit will take your healing skills beyond your own individual resources. They will surprise you in infinite unconventional ways as they guide you in unique healing methods. Get out of their way and be ready for anything and everything, because the cosmos is unlimited. There are no healing procedures that fit every single person.

Being a committed healer or intuitive does not mean that you go home at night and continue to think about your clients and their life stories. Healing is not about giving your essence away or merging into their struggles. You must hold strong to the qualities you have built within your own dynamic energy field. You must shine your compassionate brightness into their darkness. It is the intensity of your illumination that leads them to find their own way toward health. Your profound brightness and peace is where your intuition and your inner healer resides. There will be more of you to give if you give to yourself first.

I need to add here that even the clearest intuitive will seldom receive clear intuition for people or animals whom they are emotional about. We are rarely clear about ourselves as well. First of all, it is extremely difficult to be objective. Second, even positive emotions will obscure the neutral vibration that intuition requires. I receive more questions about this than anything else. Emotions will disguise and muddy intuitive information. It is important for you to understand why you may not able to read the medical situation correctly.

For example, my sister, who has been in a wheelchair for twenty-five years, called me one evening, quite tearful, and asked me to look into her foot because she thought it was broken. I looked into her foot and thought I saw multiple tiny breaks that looked like spiderwebs. I could not bring myself to think she was injured again, and I instantly became very emotional, telling her that I did not think her bones were broken. I said if she could not stand on it in the morning, she needed to go to the hospital for an x-ray. The next morning, she went to the hospital, and the x-ray showed three small breaks in the shape of spiderwebs in her foot. Even though I saw tiny fractures, I could not be clear for her. My emotions over her struggles got in the way of my accuracy. Perceiving your family's or friends' struggles will prove difficult for most people.

Emotions have an exaggerated electrical charge, which will either be positive or negative. The clearest intuitive information will feel or seem neutral. If an intuitive is completely clear, they sense the suffering but do not make it their own experience. They work from the heart with unconditional love—not personal love— and from the mental level at the sixth chakra.

You will bond with your client when true unconditional love pours through you. In other words, it is not empathetic love that brings precise intuitive information. The refined electrical frequency of unconditional love will allow you to perceive the purest level of information.

David V. Tansley, DC, describes in his book *Chakras: Rays and Radionics* that 95 percent of diseases originate in the astral and etheric levels of a human's energetic body. This certainly applies to the healer as well as the client. Dr. Tansley states:

"Firstly we must understand that any practitioner who is focused in his or her astral body and works through the solar plexus chakra is heading for trouble . . . It is essential to dissociate the astral and etheric auras from the field of work and to be focused in the head chakras and on the mental plane at the higher levels. Empathy and identification with a patient's disease indicates a stage of astral focus and will inevitably lead to trouble, which will make itself felt in fatigue and an acutely oversensitive nervous system."[3]

In other words, aligning with the client's illness or suffering will force you into the emotional spectrum, which clouds over your ability to perceive accurately. The result for you and your client will be suffering without healing.

Constant vigilance is required to maintain your clear, finely tuned energetic field. When we are harmed in life, or emotionally impacted by an event or another person, we are not just harmed physically or emotionally. Our aura may also be harmed. It can weaken, or tear, or even develop a gaping hole. This leaves us vulnerable and undefended on an energetic level. Remember, an opening or weakness in our aura leaves us vulnerable and undefended on an energetic level, and will allow anything to enter. It is the nature of the Universe for anything and everything to flow into it. A strong or negative emotion contributes to weakening the aura, and that same level of energy will be drawn to that opening.

You can heal your aura by running your toroidal field. Strengthen, reinforce, and bolster your electromagnetic field with rainbow light flowing throughout your physical body and extending brightly around you. Let it sizzle with golden electrical power. Secure your aura around you and throughout you, generating a healthy boldness and invincibility. Most people tend to only notice their energy field in front of their body. That is a very small portion of the entire being that you are. Your personal field vibrates in all directions around you. It is behind you, beside you, above you, and below you. Take a moment now and scan your energy field, searching in all directions for weakened areas. This exercise is also a profound way to learn about and get to know yourself.

---

3 David V. Tansley, *Chakras: Rays and Radionics* (London: C.W. Daniel Publishing, 1984).

Here are some tips for maintaining vigilance regarding your clarity as an intuitive:

- Identify yourself as the healer standing strong and personally unaffected by the sorrows or negativity of your clients.

- Deliberately run your toroidal field. Identify with unconditional love and mental wisdom from the center of your heart and mind. Do not create a barrier around you. Your protection is the brilliant glow from the Light of Source within you and shining outward all around you.

- Do not do this work by yourself. Every day, invite specialty guides as your body guards to constantly protect you.

- Read and feel *The Invocation* by Betsy Bergstrom, or feel free to create your own invocation.

- Have no fear. Think and then manifest feelings of power, knowledge, and invincibility.

- Take a daily energetic cleansing shower provided to you by a spiritual guide who specializes in cleansing and healing.

Key 8: Intuitive Information Pops Like Popcorn

At the beginning of every session, stop your clients from giving you any information about themselves. Your clients will be impressed. They will truly know you are not "fishing" for information. Your client will be even more impressed when your initial assessment directly relates to their physical or emotional struggles. The information you initially share is completely based on your abilities and their personal energy field. Your credibility and reputation as a medical intuitive will soar because your clients will know, beyond a doubt, you did not probe for information.

The medical intuitive must learn to discern the difference between their own body aches, thoughts, and emotions, and the intuitive information about their clients. Before I make any contact with a client, I do an instantaneous self-check to identify my own aches and pains, and the emotions I feel. Do I have pressure in my head? What mood am I feeling? Am I up and energized or do I feel a little blue? When you notice your physical, mental, and emotional state before you make your initial contact with clients, you will know anything else is a signal about the client and not about you.

After that initial self-evaluation, focus on whatever pops into your awareness. The clearest intuitive information will be instant and sudden, like a kernel of corn exploding into a piece of popcorn. I have come to trust the information that pops for a simple reason: My analytical-thinking mind did not have time to alter the information. Sensations that your body suddenly feels are signals from the client.

If your mood quickly changes at the beginning of the session, you are sensing the vibration of their mood. If you were not feeling down prior to a session, and your mood changes during, you are receiving a signal about your client and not about you. You might find yourself gradually feeling more agitated during a session. Again, you are receiving an energy signal from your client. This sudden mood change is not about you. Use the "pop" of information as a guidepost.

Be careful. Do not unconsciously make the session about yourself. If you are worried that you may be wrong, you are really making the session about you. If you have any thoughts about yourself, positive or negative, you just took precious time away from your client by shifting the focus to yourself. Get in charge of you, your thoughts, and your energy. A medical-intuitive reading is not about you in any way. Get "you" out of the way and put your laser-beam focus completely on your client.

Key 9: Work with Your Guides

When I find myself struggling during a session, it is usually because I forgot to call out for Spirit's help. Notice what type of assistance you need as you do your intuitive work. Plan your words carefully before you call out to the cosmos. If we just call out for help, we would get just any spirit who "thinks" they can be your helper. You could get some person in spirit who just died in a car wreck, or someone who does not yet realize they have died. You could get someone who died two hundred years ago and has remained on the earth plane, unaware of their ability to transition into the Light. You might inadvertently invite in one of your relatives who has passed on, or someone in spirit who died under a bridge after shooting heroin. I also recommend that you not accept a deceased relative or friend to be a guide for your medical-intuitive work. There are specialty guides we can request, who have a more advanced "view" of the Universe than we humans, deceased or alive, can ever have on our own.

When you call out to the Universe, do it with the clearest awareness and the most descriptive, high-energy words such as "Divine," "Sacred," "compassionate," "Light and Love," "beloved," "blessed," "cherished," "dearly loved," "saintly," "pure," "kindest," "most treasured," "kindhearted," "benevolent," and the "most holy," who are dedicated to cleansing and healing humans. No matter what positive words I use, I always want Divine and Sacred Specialty Guides who are excellent with communication and discernment of the medical and emotional struggles that affect humans. I want the highest order of compassion, sincerity, and integrity. These choice words will draw in the most profound guides to assist you.

Create a relationship with your Divine and Sacred specialist simply by communicating with them. When you ask a question or make a comment, make sure you pause to clearly receive their responses. If you are the only one doing the talking in this relationship, you will miss important information that the guides telepathically send back to you. Determine how the two of you will work together. Inform your specialist, or your team of specialists, what you expect from them, how you want to work together, and what your needs are. Find out how they expect to work with you. The more regularly you communicate with your specialty guides ahead of time, the more you will recognize the strength and trust of your relationship together. You and your guides become a team, focused on the client, for his or her complete benefit. When a team works together, their focus is not on the individual members, but the goal the team can achieve when working together. So listen, sense, and feel the wisdom coming from them to you, on behalf of your clients.

We are not meant to work alone. Even though I have fifty years of intuitive experience and thirty years as a registered nurse trained in medicine, psychiatric care, and mental health, I do not have the knowledge to receive vital information for my clients without the assistance and intelligence of the greater Universe.

In *A Shaman's Miraculous Tools for Healing*, author Alberto Villoldo speaks about this in his poetic words:

> "It was only when my eyes were opened to the formless world that I discovered realms of angels, power animals, and luminous beings that surround us, and that we can befriend. One of their tasks is to help us respond to the call of destiny, which may come thundering through the psyche unexpectedly, like a summer storm."[4]

In other words, we must first be open to the formless or nonphysical realms. Then we must allow that knowledge to come to us. Last, we need to notice that the nonphysical worlds are not dense but extremely subtle. When we accomplish these three steps, wise information is suddenly everywhere around us, "like a summer storm."

Sometimes neither you nor your client will know the meaning of your intuitive information. When this happens, simply tell your client to give you a moment to check with your guides. The client will not question this at all. Ask a simple, direct, and specific question within your mind. After asking the question, pause to receive the answer. Be aware that the answer may come as thoughts, waves of knowing, smells, sounds, physical sensations,

---

4 Alberto Villoldo, *A Shaman's Miraculous Tools for Healing*, (Newburyport, MA: Hampton Roads Publishing, 2015) 189.

or images. A vague question will give you a vague response. A short, simple, clear-cut question will give you a clear response.

For example, stop wondering what a symbol means. Simply state a specific question in your mind, such as, "Give me the meaning of the butterfly I see across my client's chest," or "What does my client need to know about the gray cloud wrapping around his right shoulder in order to heal?" Stop wondering and ask your guides.

Here are the simple steps to ask your guides about a piece of intuitive information they gave you of which you don't know the meaning:

1. Create a very specific question and direct the question to your specialty guides.

2. Pause and wait for a moment.

3. Absolutely accept the first thought, image, knowledge, or sensation that pops into your awareness.

Here is another unusual example of trusting your guides no matter what. Many pregnant women will ask you to try to determine the gender of their baby. When this particular mother-to-be asked me that question, I faltered. I felt the information go back and forth. That had never happened before.

So I said, "I am going back and forth, and it does not feel clear to me like it has been for other mothers. The baby does feel more female to me. You will not have any trouble with this baby, but she does seem to be slightly frail and will need more attention."

The mother came back to me months later saying that her child was a male and he had many problems with allergies, which had weakened his system. I was distraught. Up until this point I had been 100 percent accurate in predicting the gender of babies. Five years later, that same mother called and told me:

"One night I was reading a book to Tony, now five years old, and there was a picture of a little blonde girl in the book. Tony said, 'That looks like me when I was a little girl.' I said, 'Oh really, when was that?' Tony said, 'Before there were lights.'"

The mother said he was not being silly and was quite matter-of-fact about it. Three years after that, she contacted me once again:

"Tony just blurted out that he wants to be a girl and really is a girl."

Tony's mother asked him if he needed to dress like a girl or change in other ways. Tony was thoughtful for a moment, and then, in a matter-of-fact way, said no, meaning he did not need to change in any way.

His mother said to me, "Do you remember when I was first pregnant and you sensed it was a girl?"

I smiled and told her that I certainly remembered, because it had destroyed my 100 percent accuracy rate. Being the great person that she is, she just laughed. The moral of this story is to trust, trust, and trust some more that your guides are there for you and your clients. Trust them no matter what. There is always some level of truth in what they give you.

Key 10: Do Not Tell Your Clients to Forgive

Forgiveness is both a tricky and a wonderous concept all at the same time. But it's important to understand that forgiveness is not a healing technique. Forgiveness is the end result of a true deep and permanent healing.

I was deep into the process of my medical-intuitive workshop. Everyone, including myself, was excited to be there. The group was amazed at the level of awareness they had achieved in such a short time. And then I said, "Whatever you do in the healing process with your client, do not tell them they need to forgive."

Oh my goodness, the reaction that swept through the group! One woman placed her hands over her mouth. Her reaction was so dramatic that I stopped and directed my next comment to her.

"You are really reacting to what I just said, aren't you?"

"Yes," she declared. "I tell everyone they need to forgive!"

With a smile on my face, I gently responded, "Then stop it."

The entire class, including the woman, laughed and the tension broke.

When we tell our clients they need to forgive their wrongdoer, the client reacts and instantly clamps down on their immense, pent-up emotions, and may even react with anger. They react with shock because you are the authority figure telling them to forgive, and they are not yet at that point. It is too big of a leap from where they are.

Your client might be the one who initiates the topic of forgiveness. They will tell you they must forgive their wrongdoer. I ask them to stop trying to forgive. At first the client is surprised, and then a profound release sweeps through them. The tension fades from their face and their energy field.

When that happens, redirect the client to take a different step. Ask them to tell you what the next tiny, tiny step might be, something they are convinced they can actually accomplish. Explore those tiny steps that create doable goals. That dialogue leads the person toward a different course that gives them new hope.

When healing work happens on an energetic level, you will no longer need to tell them to forgive. One day in your future, that person will appear to you in a session, or an email, to share that the healing process with you has led them to forgiveness and peace. They have naturally achieved the refined frequency of forgiveness because of your gentle support and wisdom along the way.

While I studied both myself and my mentoring clients, these ten concepts stood out more and more. My attention was drawn to them as if they were fundamental truths or standard principles in an important document. Functioning with these guidelines will allow you to stand out as a medical intuitive and an energy healer. These ten key points will keep you or your client safe and healthy. They are neon signs that point you in the right direction toward becoming an excellent, accurate medical intuitive.

Essential Points

- Be sure to only work with guides on the Divine and Sacred level.

- At the end of every session, be sure to pull all your energy from the client and back to yourself.

- Don't let your fears get in the way of your intuitive ability.

- Asking the client for permission sends a powerful signal that they are in charge.

- Learn what your rules are, then push past them.

- Do not merge into the gloom of everyone's suffering. Be the healer!

- Shine your brightness into your client's darkness.

- The clearest intuitive information will be instant or sudden.

- The Divine and Sacred guides do not leave us. We ignore them or are unaware of them.

- Forgiveness is not a healing method. It is the result of profound healing.

Chapter 4

Energy is Real and Must be Handled with Care

"The whole business of man is 'not to turn his back upon the Light.' This Light may be a poor thing, but our business is to make the best of it, try to feed and brighten it, to make it shine into dark corners."

—August Strindberg

Everything is energy. Yes, everything. The chair you are sitting on as you read these words, the car you drive, the house or apartment you live in, the land your home sits on, your body, your emotions, and your thoughts—all this is living, vibrating energy. The more you shift your awareness to that particular level of instinctual knowing, the more you will be in charge of your body, your health, your life, and your world. Look around you right now, and imagine that every material item around you is pulsing with dynamic energy.

Each session you have with a client is personal and intimate. The medical intuitive enters into a person's eternal story, perceiving thoughts and emotions—old and new—as well as one's physical body and internal organs. The intuitive perceives one's current life and one's historical life because all are living things. These living vibrations enter into our cells and radiate outward from our mind, entering into the collective of the Universe for eternity. Because of this depth of information we gather, we must be sensitive, compassionate, and extremely confidential as we direct all our awareness to the client. This is a precious and sacred time for both of you.

We are responsible for our entire eternal life. This includes our past lives, our current life, and our future possibilities. When we allow a healing to take place, for ourselves and for others, we actually springboard our energy field into a different frequency. That altered frequency flows forward into the future, back into the past, and outward in all directions. It also flows throughout our relationships and signals the Universe that there has been a transformation in our awareness. Each transformation brings us closer to true compassion without criticism or judgment. Each transformation leads us toward different opportunities and probabilities for our future.

Energy Cannot Be Killed

Science discovered a long time ago that energy cannot be stopped, discontinued, or killed. It can, however, be altered or transformed into a different type of substance. Metaphysicians, religious leaders, energy workers, and intuitives often do not offer this knowledge as they do their healing work with others. Many healing practitioners still resort to practices like exorcism, stabbing, chasing, cutting, or trapping negative energy, throwing it away, shaking it off their hands, or shouting at it. Some practitioners even draw negative energy into their own body in an attempt to heal it.

Going into battle with energy will not achieve anything lasting because the energy did not change or transform. If anything, it simply moved on. When that is the case, true healing did not take place. In fact, considering energy does not die, what are the results and consequences of the practices mentioned above? If we are running, chasing, or yelling at something, then that something will probably shift, or flee to something—or someone—else. Energy is known to attract similar energy to itself. When energy merges like this, it can only create more disharmony and negativity somewhere else.

If that makes sense to you, then you might ask yourself, "What other options do we have?"

We do have other options. We have loving, nonjudgmental

interaction with negativity. We can relate to negativity as if it is alive because it is alive. Everything in our world, and in the Universe, is alive and cannot die. It can only transform. Healing accelerates transformation and transmutes human struggles, agony, and illness into health, well-being, and peace.

What Does "Healing" Really Mean?

For many years, I struggled to define the word "to heal." My guides finally got through to me and stated this: "A healing is release of a burden." I looked throughout many sources to find synonyms for the word "burden" and found a surprising number of them. Here are only a few of them:

A load, weight, responsibility, obligation, problem, worry, trouble, pain, affliction, difficulty, misfortune, strain, encumbrance, duty, deadweight, overload, pledge, oath, vow, pact, covenant, debt, strain.

Then I researched the meaning of the word "heal." Here are those synonyms:

To cure, restore, fix, mend, rehab, fortify, rejuvenate, revitalize, repair, alleviate, relieve, remedy, gain, mend, improve, recover, soothe, ease.

Notice the only word that suggests bringing something to a complete end is the word "cure." But we humans are not going through a process here on Earth to be like a "cured, finished product" at the end of a factory's assembly line. We humans are eternal, and like the rest of the Universe, we advance, learn, and experience. We are given opportunity after opportunity to work our way to a divine level of awareness. There is no end to the assembly line.

Nearly every day, a student tells me they are failing as a healer because they have not completely healed themselves first. We medical intuitives do not need to be, nor ever will be, a finished, cured, or healed product before we can be healers for others. We are healing ourselves at the same moments we are the healers for others.

The Key to Creating a Permanent Healing

During many methods of healing, a medical intuitive removes negativity from the client, whether it is negative energy or a negative spiritual being. Whenever you remove, release, or take away anything from the human body or energetic field, you *must* immediately fill the empty space with a more powerful positive energy.

The Universe does not like a void, an opening, or an emptiness. When negativity is removed, there is a tendency to draw similar negative energy back into that area. If you allow this to happen, you will not permanently complete the healing.

Make sure to command your Divine and Sacreds to fill every single space and place with three or four positive energy frequencies. A few examples of powerful positive energy might be love, joy, cellular vitality, compassion, or confidence.

Always remember to personalize the positive-word vibrations with words that are especially meaningful to each individual client. For example, if the client mentions they lost all their confidence during a traumatic event, one positive power word phrase might be: "Fill every single space and place with powerful confidence now."

Stop Cutting Energetic Cords!

As I travel all over the world teaching medical intuition, I beg people to stop cutting energetic cords. Some of the readers might be alarmed about this. You might even be sitting in your favorite chair right now, thinking, *I have been cutting cords for years! Why stop now?*

We are, as humans, dynamic electromagnetic entities full of thoughts, emotions, and passion. We are not stuck beneath our skin, but we exude thought forms of all types beyond our bodies and our skin. Emotions empower each thought form, whether it is positive, negative, or anything in between. Energetic cords are real. Many readers have already heard of the silver cord that keeps our soul body linked to our physical body, providing vitality and stability to both forms. You might have occasionally perceived some silver cords that appear dull, dim, frayed, twisted, or even knotted. As a result, your client will often be racked with guilt; detached from self, family, and life in general; or potentially suicidal.

But there are other types of cords as well, cords that are not for connecting us with our soul or higher self. Cording happens in relationships of all types. The medical intuitive can perceive a great amount of information from these energetic cords. For example, I have noticed that cords are different lengths and thickness. Some are thick and powerful, while others are like threads pulled thin. Some cords have different intensities and pulsations. Cords are created under varying circumstances, sometimes unconsciously, other times thoughtfully calculated for a certain purpose. All cords have a dominant flow of energy, either moving toward the client or away from them.

When a great amount of positive or negative emotion is involved, it creates a cord. As a medical intuitive, you will tend to perceive cords based on tremendous emotions, either positive or negative. Cords can link us with our loved ones like our biological family, friends who have become like family, our life partner, or some other variation of positive connection. When two people cherish each other, the cord that connects their hearts is shimmery, weightless, and flexible. The medical intuitive will perceive this type of cord as balanced and fluid with positive sensations about the people involved.

However, emotions such as betrayal, anger, guilt, or trauma may deliberately or subconsciously create negative cords. Some cords control another person while other cords attach to a person out of a severe sense of neediness. For example, a sexual perpetrator or sexually interested stalker will link a cord into the targeted person's first and second chakra. Those energy centers vibrate more on an emotional plane. A person interested in controlling someone will connect into the person's head to get in control of their thoughts. A needy person is unable to generate their own power or worthiness. They feel an overwhelming sense of deprivation about being alone. This person will often cord into a strong person's back or shoulders, consuming that person's vitality. A person with unresolved issues about an event will cord into the other person involved. Someone with a broken heart may attach to the other at the heart's center.

Victims of any type of negative cord energy will constantly feel exhausted, and their physicians cannot find any reason for this level of lethargy. They may describe feeling as if they carry a huge burden on their back. People who cannot realize their own personal power will find an individual who has the qualities they believe they lack in themselves. That cord will connect into the solar plexus of their victim, attempting to capture these qualities, but also to appear much more powerful than they truly are.

Negative cords are thick, dense, or dark, rope-like forms. You will usually perceive the cord as if its energy is moving in one specific direction or another. The direction of the energy flow is determined by the person who holds the strongest negative emotions, or "unfinished business," with the other person.

However, you do not want to cut these cords. Imagine holding tight to one end of a garden hose, and I am holding just as tight to the other end. If someone cuts the hose in the middle, we are each left holding part of the hose in our hands. Thus, some of the negative energy still resides within both of our energy fields. Instead of cutting the cord, each person needs to release their end. As a medical intuitive and teacher, my goal is to assist my clients to completely release the entire cord, and any roots that may exist within them. You must remove all the energy from the cord to fully cleanse it.

Case Study:
Removing Energetic Cords

This is a session with a thirty-two-year-old female client, whom I will call Sara. We addressed the relationship with her needy ex-husband and the physical location of his energetic cording to her. We conducted a healing, but it was not complete. It made all the difference when I asked the client to participate.

Practice Experience:

Imagine you are the medical intuitive speaking the words in this transcript. Read it aloud or, if possible, with a study buddy, one taking part as the medical intuitive and one as the client. Practice this session as if you are actually giving these steps to someone who needs your guidance.

TZ: I see you are a very thoughtful person. There is a lot of energy in your head and around your neck. I want you to notice whoever, or whatever, pops into your awareness as I say these things to you. Whatever pops in is always the clearest truth for you. Your mind is thinking, thinking, thinking. It's dark where there is low energy across your throat and around your neck. I have to tell you that the dark around your neck became a cloak, and it spread out behind you like Superman or Superwoman.

Client: Yes.

TZ: Something about you being a superwoman. There is still a struggle about you expressing who you really are. You know Superman runs around helping everybody and saving the day. Rather than the cape tied to your shoulders, I am seeing it around your neck. Our necks and throats are about you needing to express more of you.

Client: I understood the description, and I think it is right in terms of my life. I think I have a thyroid condition.

TZ: The true Superman's cape went out from his shoulders, so he is shouldering responsibility. Yours is tied around your neck right where your thyroid is. Give me a minute here and let me see what pops up about this . . . I am getting tied in knots.

Client: Yes!

TZ: Tied in knots. There is a person in your life who you feel is holding you back a little bit and keeping the knot tied. Who pops up in your awareness?

Client: I think it is probably my ex-husband, although it's possibly my present boyfriend. I feel a lot of pain and I feel tied in knots. Do you have a sense if either of those is right?

(Watch the fluctuations in your client's energy. It gives you precise information.)

TZ: Yes. When you talk, I am literally sitting here with my eyes closed, watching your energy field. When you mentioned your boyfriend, the knot did nothing. He is more neutral and you are neutral about him as far as struggles. When you mentioned your ex-husband, it brightened up, so I would say it is more about your ex. Give me a second . . . Give me his first name if you are comfortable in doing that. Is that okay?

Client: Yeah. His name is Sam.

(Ask your client to wait while you receive intuitive information.)

TZ: I always tell everybody that I do not go pushing into everybody's life, so I need to ask Sam for permission. Just give me a second here. He might say no, but give me a second. (Pause.) Well, sometimes I have to say some hard stuff out loud. Tell me if this make any sense to you. He still feels sexual toward you. Now, I will tell you what I actually saw. He appeared behind you, biting your neck and shoulders. So, he is showing me that there is still a sexual connection or interest, at least on his part. Now, it is interesting to me that he is biting your neck and that's where you have struggles.

Client: Yeah! You mean like a vampire sucking blood?

TZ: Yes.

Client: He is a great guy, and I don't have anything against him, but somehow I got into taking care of him rather than myself.

TZ: Exactly. The old term "vampire" actually comes from people who literally drain energy from others. I find it interesting that he showed up behind you and not shoulder to shoulder with you. Literally hanging on your back.

Client: Yeah. Do you see any way to cut that cord? Is there any way of energetically releasing or separating myself from him?

TZ: Yes, excellent! I would say it is in your neck and your throat. If I had a rope and you had one end and I had the other and we cut it in it somewhere in between, that leaves you with a chunk and I still have a chunk. Some release would take place, but we still have some of the negative in our hands.

Client: I see that.

TZ: Give me a second . . . They want me to ask you to notice where in your physical body he is corded into. What do you notice? It will just feel like your imagination.

Client: I used to feel like it was in the solar plexus because I would feel some pulling. Now I'm feeling that between my heart and my throat. I am feeling right now tightness in my throat and a little nausea, like I want to throw up.

TZ: This will always feel like your imagination or like you're just making it up, but Sara, this is very, very real. I told you how he appeared and what he is doing, and you said it makes total sense to you. This is very real. He is still draining you, or at least drawing from you.

Client: Yes.

TZ: Don't try to make anything happen. Just see what happens in your awareness. Wait, I am getting some direction here . . . I want you to take the end that is connected in with you, whatever that cord looks like to you, and I want you to pull it out of you. I want you to invite in the highest, most beloved healing guides to help you. I am doing that too. I hope you believe, and that this is not too far out for you. Do it with their assistance and pull, pull, pull, pull. They are showing me that you should make sure you get all the roots of the cord. It is rooted in with lots of little filaments or tendrils, or something. Just imagine pulling it completely, every single bit of it, out of you and hand it back to him. I will be quiet until you speak. Take your time. *(Long pause.)*

Client: Okay.

TZ: What did you notice as you did that? There is no right or wrong about what happened.

Client: I did feel the tension releasing from around my neck, and it was interesting that the way the cord was kind of red, kind of bloody, you know? And while I completely believe in this, it is hard to believe that I can just remove it that quickly. So, I wonder if it makes sense to just repeat it every time I feel that tension.

TZ: That is interesting. It will only take as long as you think it will. So, you just sent energy into it, that it is going to take longer than just this minute.

Client: Oh, okay.

TZ: My guides are asking, "What did you do when you handed it back to him?" Did you get a sense of that?

Client: I rolled it up neatly and I said, "This is yours. I love you, but take this."

TZ: And what did he do with it?

Client: He took it. He didn't walk away; he just took it happily and held it as if he had to. I didn't spend much time thinking about what he thought about it, I guess.

TZ: Good, that is fine. I want you to look around to see if there is anything left of the cord. I think there is still some more of the cord in your brain, your third eye, and in your forehead.

Client: Oh, okay . . . I pulled out of my body, but I didn't pull from the top down at all.

TZ: Well, check that out and see what you notice. And don't do it all yourself. I hear that you are trying to do this all by yourself. Make sure you allow the higher guidance, the healers, to do this for you and with you.

Client: Okay . . . I definitely felt like I was being aided. You know that whole superwoman thing?

TZ: Yes, what about it?

Client: I really tried to ask for help. I have had to do so much by myself. I raised children pretty much by myself and tend to think I have to do everything by myself. I think I could be open to feeling guided, but I don't always feel it. That would be a big plus for me. So, in this case, I definitely felt we were working together and I pulled all these tiny little tendrils out of my nose and my third eye. Then it came to this little string and it was really a stacked-up cord, which I gave to him and said, "Thank you, but this is yours." He put it in his mouth. Somehow it just went into him through his mouth.

TZ: Well, I'll tell you why that happened. This is very cool, and it is a new experience for me. My guides are showing me that all you took out of yourself needs to be implanted into him so he has both ends of this cord. You stuck both ends in his mouth.

Client: He actually stuck it in his mouth and we did it together.

TZ: I am seeing it's as if it loops back into him. It is fascinating to me. I have not had this experience before, so that's really something. So now, if you would, ask your healing guides who have come forth to fill every single space and place where all of that used to be. Fill it with golden light, and fill it with complete healing. If you would, allow that to happen and I will be quiet again.

Client: I feel it in and around my brain, my nasal passage, my third eye, my throat, and down into my heart and solar plexus.

TZ: All of a sudden, I feel a lightness in your lungs. You did not mention your lungs, but I feel like you are breathing easier or more lightly. Your lungs are lighting up and filling up with clear energy. If you didn't notice it, that's okay, but I believe that is also happening.

Client: I feel it now that you say that, but I didn't notice it before. I do feel it there.

TZ: Grieving and sadness over the years tends to land in our lungs. As I look at you, it feels like this release and healing is taking place in many areas of your energy field. May I look more deeply into your chest area?

Client: Yes.

TZ: They are showing me that you are going to feel a difference. It was as if you were trying to breathe through a straw and now you will be breathing in the full capacity of your lungs. You are getting a homework assignment here. I am seeing a golden energy. Once in a while, during the day, feel like you are inhaling a golden energy. Practice that for a minute, just inhaling the golden energy. Allow it to flow into your neck and throat. Allow this golden energy to fill your thyroid. They are also saying that this work has made room in your life for new opportunities, new connections, and new experiences in your life. There wasn't any room in you before. Check to see if you feel that you have made more room in your life to receive.

Client: *(Sara looks at her phone.)* You know what I think is interesting? My boyfriend called when we had just finished removing my ex-husband.

TZ: Wow! A lot of people who I work with would not put two and two together. They would not see that as a symbol from Spirit. You get it, don't you?

Client: Yeah, oh yeah. I mean, that's the reason I am calling you. A lot of old grief was around my ex-husband, but it is all coming up after ten years! This is really powerful for me.

TZ: Well, Sara, my guides were showing me that they were sticking the other end of those tendrils from the cord back into him so that he does not attach onto someone else in a negative way. Wow, this is really cool.

Client: It is cool. It is really cool.

TZ: Sara, I have been doing this work for years, but when I work with someone like you, there is that "wow" factor.

Client: Yeah, and to feel this difference. I have been broken down a little bit too. I have been on the spiritual path for so long, but I am such a thinker. This whole period of grieving and trauma and anxiety has really made me go into my body and energy system in a way that I have avoided before. But this is perfect.

TZ: Well, they are telling me there is one more step. If it feels right to you, would you also take back your power from him and place it back into your solar plexus?

Client: I am uncomfortable, still tight.

(The client might hesitate to finalize an important healing step. Give them some confidence to finish the process.)

TZ: Yes, yes. Take it back from him because it is yours. It does not matter if he agrees or not. Take back from him all that is truly you. All that he took and also all that you gave to him. Take it all back and again, make sure you get it all. Ask for help and put it back into you.

Client: Okay. *(Long pause.)* I saw me and Spirit pulling from his solar plexus. The cord was blue, and it pulled all the way up from his shoulder and neck area, then up from his groin area and out. We put it into my solar plexus. I felt pretty tight in my solar plexus, but I think we got the last tendrils out.

(Direct the client's awareness to the descriptive words they say.)

TZ: Take the first thing that pops when I ask you this. Check and let the tightness tell you something. Take whatever pops into your awareness.

Client: I think it said, "sadness."

TZ: And what about the sadness? Just check it out.

Client: You know, it feels like its old and hanging around and not needed.

TZ: Ask for some help about this if you would, and do not be a superwoman.

Client: I got an image of me and guides scooping out sadness. It was a clear fat or gel substance and putting it into a bowl. A guide was holding a large bowl of it and carried it out to the sun to dissipate it. My hole is still kind of gaping. I don't know what to do.

(The more the client accomplishes on their own with their superior guides, the more powerful the client feels.)

TZ: Then ask. When we don't know something, specifically ask the greatest healing guide, "What are we to do next?"

Client: They are telling me to use golden energy again.

TZ: Well, I will tell you on my end, I am seeing the golden energy and it keeps coming, but there are now rays of spring green too. So, it is gold with spring-green vibrations. Spring green is always renewal, healing, regeneration. Okay, so check that out. Is it continuing? Just allow it to continue if that is happening.

Client: Yeah, and then they closed the hole and hugged my abdomen.

TZ: I am seeing a restructuring, a building of the fiber, and it is going from your solar plexus and rising upward, very bright and clear and going into your thyroid. Then rising up into your third eye, then up through your crown chakra. Get a sense of energy rising and restructuring into your thyroid and filling that up. Then it rises to your third eye, your brain, and filling you up through your crown and out. Oh . . . okay. It keeps rising literally up into the heavens, restructuring and reconnecting you.

Client: Yeah, it feels really nice.

TZ: I'll bet it does.

Each client is unique, and the procedure with one client may be entirely different from the client you worked with last week. Pulling the cords out rather than cutting it into two pieces will make a huge difference for your clients. One must be careful to determine whether the cord needs to be removed from both people, or if it would be best to pull the cord out of only one person. A key point: Inform the client they are to remove the cord either from their own body or the body of the other person involved. Allow your client to proceed in their own personal way. Removing the cord without your assistance will empower your client. It is critical in the healing process to recognize the destructive, energetic-binding cords that are crippling your clients.

Energetic Alerts: What NOT to Do

This section is a quick overview of what I have learned *not* to do as a result of some terrible real-life stories that I have seen or heard over the years.

1. Never draw, pull, or suck the illness from someone's body into yourself. This is an ancient shaman's technique, and I am pretty sure it did not work well for them either. We mere humans are not meant to do that. That is why we have a higher order of guidance to assist us. A so-called healer in my home city proudly told me she was drawing the illnesses out of her clients and into her own body. She then stated that she transformed the illness into something else while it was still within her own body. I pleaded with her not to do it

in that manner. She assured me it was fine. A few months later, she could barely walk with a cane. A few more months later, she was bedridden and could not walk at all. She never asked me for help or intuitively gave me permission to assist her.

2. No matter the depth of grief you are experiencing, remember my words here: Never drape yourself over the top of a person who is actively in the dying transition. In short, it will allow the dying person to accidentally transfer their soul's essence into the person lying over them. There is a story about this later in this book.

3. Do not "get to know" the negative energies that affect your clients. You will find later in this book that you will need to generate a dialogue to encourage their transformation, but that should be the extent of your interaction with them.

4. Do not work alone. Spirit specialists want to work with us. They are learning and transforming along with us. You do not need to do this work alone.

5. Never go into fear for any reason. Fear is a dense form of energy, and it will restrict and collapse your positive strength and invincibility.

Energy is not just a concept. Energy is the basis of all things in our known physical world. Energy is also the basis of all things in the nonphysical world as well. We humans are profoundly powerful because each thought we think is a specific energy signal. Those signals surge through our bodies and out into the environment, and then out to the Universe.

Essential Points

- Energetic cords are created when a great amount of positive or negative emotion is involved.

- Remove an energetic cord by having the client and the other person involved release their ends. Fill the empty space with powerful positive energy.

- We are healing ourselves at the same moment we are the healers for others.
- The client is empowered when they remove the cord without your assistance.

Chapter 5

How to Discover the Precise Cause of Illness

"We have all to specialize, more or less—but whoever boxes himself in, tries to find the whole truth inside his box, knows nothing of other approaches to knowledge or is merely contemptuous of them, is working with only one hand and hopping on one foot, when he doesn't need to."

—N. Meade Layne

Traditional Western medicine focuses completely on the physical world by assessing the physical body, the physical symptoms, diagnostic tests, and then a treatment at the physical level. As a nurse, I honor Western medicine, but at the same time we must equally honor the alive nonphysical energy that vibrates within each person's physical body. Assessing each person at the energetic level opens the box in which we exist, and leads the healer in many surprising directions.

My primary workshop focuses on opening up intuitive awareness, getting over our struggles and rules, and enhancing the laser-beam abilities that enable us to pick up specific physical, emotional, and mental struggles. Toward the end of the third day, people ask me what to do with the abundance of information they are now picking up:

"How do we begin to heal our clients with this information?"

"Will just giving the information be enough to bring healing to them?"

"Where does the healing enter into a medical-intuitive session?"

I struggled to find descriptive words or explanations, let alone the steps toward learning how to do this. Once again I had to examine myself, to learn how I was facilitating such positive changes for people.

After grappling with my students' questions for two years, I examined myself after each session. I first realized the following:

I had no preconceived plan, or any idea how healing was about to happen, for each individual.

I always asked Spirit specialists to take me to the **point of origin**, or precise cause, of this person's illness or struggle. I then asked them to direct me in the perfect ways to guide the client toward reaching a permanent healing on all levels. Spirit never failed me. I always received healing information to utilize.

It is important to trust whatever you receive. Spirit often directed me to say certain phrases that led the client toward their healing, or to guide the client to a certain awareness or time in their personal history. While I always offered verbal and energetic support, I never told the client how to experience the process. As I became more aware of what I was actually doing during a session, I shared this process in my workshop. Then I realized I needed to add more hours to the workshop in order to explain all the information and have the students practice the process.

Going Deeper Than the Physical

Many healthcare practitioners tell me they feel they are only scratching the surface of the healing process. This may be because the therapies that work on the physical level of illness are not healing at the core of an illness or disease. I have noticed that a more profound healing takes place when it is addressed on the energetic level of life.

Healing at the physical level alone is constrained by the dense nature of the physical realm. An everlasting healing has more opportunity to take place on an energetic level because energy has no boundaries. For the most incredible healing to take place for physical, mental, or emotional illness, we must go to the point of origin. If we do not discover that exact instant when the illness originated, our healing efforts will tend to be more superficial.

It would be like telling a person who just fractured their leg, "Put a dressing on it and go on a vacation for two weeks." We need to discover that the genuine cause of the broken leg was a massive fear of success. This person's fear was completely triggered by a wonderful job offer that included a promotion with a large pay increase. The cause of his injury, in this case, was an overwhelming terror of change and success. It is only when this deep-seated level of information is discovered and addressed that the most accurate and permanent healing may take place. In this example, the medical intuitive would need to discover that it was the client's fear of success that actually triggered the broken leg, thus interfering with his chance for this promotion.

Do NOT Depend on Your Human Mind Alone

Do not assume, through your intellect, that you know the cause of an illness or struggle. This means you are working only with your intellect. The excellent, accurate medical intuitive relies on the pop of intuitive information coming from their Divine and Sacred team of guides.

Consider this example. My client had just given a violin lesson to a child in the parents' home. She stated that this home was like nothing she had ever experienced before. The parents were kind and attentive. Communication between the child and the parents seemed comfortable and happy. When she finished the lesson she said goodbye and walked out their front door, onto the front porch, and immediately plunged off the top step, shattering every bone in her dominant left arm. Remember that this woman is a violin teacher who needs both arms to function well.

Many sincere and genuine healers would immediately assume that she probably became dizzy and fainted. Another practitioner might question the client in an attempt to find out what she thought happened on that top step. In both cases, the practitioner is attempting to discover cause by using their logical thinking mind, or that of the client. When practitioners use only their thinking mind to determine cause, healing techniques often fall into a more superficial level.

As a counselor, I used to try to fix people with my thinking mind. Over many years, and with thousands of clients, I discovered that depending on our human mind alone makes us less likely to access the original cause of an illness, struggle, or accident. If we do not open the doorway and retrieve the original cause of the client's suffering, we cannot facilitate a permanent healing event. The more we get out of our own way, the more precise our intuitive insights will be. In other words, the less we depend on our logical thinking minds and the more we depend on the wisdom of the Universe, the more accurate and profound the healing will be.

So, I needed to find the cause of the violin instructor's so-called accident not with my thinking mind but by using my intuition. I asked Spirit, in a commanding way, to give me the exact point of origin that caused her fractured right arm. I clairvoyantly perceived my client as a child in her current life, living in agony with an alcoholic father and a terrified mother. Her primary memory was loud fighting and beatings, and she had thought everyone lived this way until she sat in this loving family's home. Spirit said it was as if the earth shook beneath her, knocked her off her feet, and rocked her world. Now I knew the cause of this painful event. I knew where we needed to go for the most sincere and genuine healing experience.

Discovering the point of origin of any illness or injury is so simple that you will insist there must be more to it than this. Turn it over to your guides. Call out to your specialists in a commanding manner, asking for the exact point that a certain malady began. Do not just call out for help, but be specific with your request. Our words create energy, so we must be careful how we phrase what we want, and for whom we want it. Here are some examples of statements that will prompt the specialty guides to provide the most accurate information on behalf of your client.

The following phrases can be very effective:

- "Give me the exact point of origin that started *(illness/struggle)* for *(client's full name)."*

- "Show me the precise moment that started the *(illness/struggle)* for *(client's full name)."*

- "Direct me right now to the instant that *(illness/struggle)* began for *(client's full name)."*

- "Give me the original cause when *(illness/struggle)* began for *(client's full name)."*

- "Show me the exact point of origin that is causing *(illness/struggle)* for *(client's full name)."*

Remember, when you ask Spirit to give you the precise moment of your client's illness, pause to receive the information, and don't question what pops into your awareness. The point of origin you intuitively receive may take you on a wild ride or lead you to the most mundane story. You must prepare yourself to be pulled into a surprising or even shocking experience. You may witness a torture scene from a past life, or an alien interference in the person's current life. You must also be prepared for the commonplace and the humdrum. You may get something simple, like the reason for the client's hair falling out is because they are missing a certain mineral in their diet.

We humans are very powerful. We can be an open conduit or pipeline for Source to work through us to help others. We are essentially more of a spiritual energy than we are a physical body. Going to the exact point of origin of an illness or struggle and healing it at the energetic level is key for powerful healers.

Those of us who yearn to work as a medical intuitive must

consistently strive for the highest level of accuracy and integrity. You are already capable of this and much more as you assist individuals who come to you for help.

Essential Points

- An everlasting healing has more opportunity to take place on an energetic level, not merely a physical level.

- Do not assume, through your intellect, that you know the cause of a struggle.

- Don't rely on your thinking mind. Instead, ask Spirit to give you the point of origin of an illness, or the exact instant a certain problem began.

PART TWO

8 Primary Causes of Illness

"The belief that we are frail, biochemical machines controlled by genes is giving way to an understanding that we are powerful creators of our lives and the world in which we live."

—Bruce Lipton, PhD[5]

My primary goal for my previous book, *Become a Medical Intuitive*, was to assist people to open or refine their natural intuitive abilities. That refinement leads the practitioner to literally perceive information regarding the health of the physical body. This second edition of *Advanced Medical Intuition* utilizes those sharpened intuitive abilities to uncover the original cause of illness and the specific methods to create a personal healing. As I studied myself and my medical-intuitive sessions with clients, I first categorized the causes of disease, afflictions, and physical and emotional disabilities into six categories. Since 2018, I now recognize that there are actually two new categories that I have added in this second edition: the environment and our ancestors.

The ten chapters in Part Two focus on eight categories that cause illnesses or life struggles to give you, the reader, a clearer way to learn the different healing methods for each category. I have divided the category about nonphysical entities into three chapters because of the complexity of the nonphysical realm and

---

[5] Bruce H. Lipton, *The Biology of Belief: Unleashing the Power of Consciousness, Matter & Miracles* (Carlsbad, CA: Hay House, 2016) xv.

its abilities to cause illness and life struggles. Please realize that I am still describing one category that causes illness or struggles.

With that in mind, here are the eight categories that cause illness or life struggles:

- Physical Bodily Needs
- Thoughts and Emotions
- Relationships
- Nonphysical Entities: Levels 1–2
- Nonphysical Entities: Levels 3–4
- Nonphysical Entities: Levels 5–6
- The Environment
- Ancestors
- Past Lives
- Current-Life Trauma

Some causes of illness may occasionally overlap, and so will the healing techniques. However, look closely at these healing techniques, because some have subtle differences in their steps toward healing. In the appendix at the end of this book, you will find a consolidated summary that provides you with a quick reference guide of healing techniques to use as you work with individuals. This summary will allow you to quickly connect certain illnesses with their equivalent healing technique.

It is an honor when someone asks you to go with them on their healing journey. But the two of you do not need to do this alone. There is guidance all along the path if you allow it. From my last book, you found and fostered a relationship with your medical-intuitive guides, who excel in detailed information about the human body, mind, emotion, spirit, and the eternal soul. Be aware you may detect a different individual, or a group of guides, who specializes only in the healing process. Some of you might experience your medical-intuitive guides play a double role as healers and also as diagnosticians.

Chapter 6

Physical Bodily Needs Causing Illness or Life Struggles

"If you don't like something, change it. If you can't change it, change your attitude."

—Maya Angelou

This chapter delves into how our bodily needs, the choices we make about our bodies, and the traumas our bodies endure can lead to a physical illness. For some of these causes, there does not seem to be a mysterious reason hiding in some deep, hidden place in the client's subconscious. The illness does not come from childhood or past lives or negative thought forms. In fact, the remedy is often simply a physical need of our physical body not being met.

Over the years, I have noticed that the people who feel bubbly and healthy, and can think clearly, have vibrant energy fields that move in the specific pathways of the toroidal field. The flow is always streaming upward from the earth into their physical body through the feet, rising up through the spine, and bursting from the top of the head up into the heavens. The flow then rains downward throughout the external portion of the human's field, back into the earth to repeat the cycle over and over again. The current is like a huge, sparkling water fountain twinkling in the sun. People who are doing quite well mentally, physically, and emotionally appear to consciously or unconsciously run their energy in this precise pattern.

This current seems to signify that we humans are indeed

a conduit uniting heaven and Earth. Each of us is an essential segment linking the cosmos with our planet. The toroidal field is also a fundamental key for manifesting life in the physical world by drawing from the dynamic, abundant Universe. We humans are a corridor between the nonphysical and the physical world. We have a choice to participate in an open, healthy stream of energy, or we can resist and create blockages in the conduit that is our physical bodies.

Sometimes It's Simply a Change in Lifestyle

Sometimes it is simply change that calls out to us, and we simply need to take a different action in our life in order to feel fulfilled. However, there is nothing simple about changing something in life, nor is it simple to take an action that we haven't taken before. However, sometimes that is exactly what healing requires.

As the medical intuitive, you may receive an image of your client moving out of a house. When you mention that, your client might say, "Well, I'm thirty-five years old now, and I've been thinking it's time to move out of my parents' house and get my own." I have frequently been given an image of legs walking quickly down a path, and when I state this to a client they will admit they are a "couch potato," and their medical doctor has been telling them that their sedentary life is causing their illness.

As the intuitive practitioner, you may get thoughts regarding your client that a healing for their depression requires a career change that speaks to their heart and soul. You might receive information that the person longs to meditate under their favorite tree but never gets around to it. Do not diminish the importance of guiding a client to make a change, large or small, in their life. A change in lifestyle can be startling, and yet prove to be as profound a healing technique as any other offered in this manual.

Case Study:
Pain and Diminished Thinking

Here is an excerpt of an actual session with a seventy-year-old woman who suffered with back pain. She was also aware that her thinking was cloudy and unable to think clearly. Remember, I did not know her symptoms until I assessed her energy and her physical body. I walked her through the steps to influence her energy field and deliberately direct it to flow in the toroidal field pattern.

Practice Experience:

Imagine you are the medical intuitive speaking the words in this transcript. Read it aloud or, if possible, with a study buddy, one taking part as the medical intuitive and one as the client. Practice this session as if you are actually giving these steps to someone who needs your guidance.

(The location of energy gives you more specific information.)

TZ: Okay, I just saw this energy coming up from your heart, and it came up like this, and then it encircled your whole head, almost like you are looking through a Christmas wreath. I would say that your head and heart are in union more than ever before. The energy came in a strong path that I see rising up from your heart around there. The wreath is around your head and not within it, which tells me you are not incorporating it yet into your mind. I think that's because it's a new positive development, so it's not down inside your head yet because you haven't incorporated it yet.

Client: Ah . . . it's outside of my head?

TZ: Yes, it's in the beginning of the evolvement. It would be different if it was inside of your head and your face.

Client: Of course, I get it.

(Ask for permission throughout the session with clients.)

TZ: Okay, your spine all of a sudden popped up. Is it okay to go on?

Client: Yes.

TZ: Your spine has popped up and it is a beautiful reddish pink, but there is also a dark cut through it. It goes straight through from the vertebra thoracic 4 to the organ of your heart.

Client: Exactly where I have my pain!

TZ: Okay, yes. It is straight through you and into T4.

Client: Yes, because the heart is right there, and I have pain there too often.

(Teach about energy and explain the homework assignment.)

TZ: Do you know about the toroidal field that scientists are exploring? I heard (from my guides) you need to start consciously running your toroidal field and that it will be very, very helpful. Imagine and pretend you are drawing up energy through your feet, raise it up through your body, and fountain it out through your crown. Then allow it to sparkle down around you and back into the earth, and then draw it up again and again into your body until you create a pumping-like mechanism. You need to deliberately run your energy in this way often. Inside of this big toroidal field, people also have another, smaller toroidal movement through the organ of the heart. It moves in that same fountaining flow. So, there is a toroidal field through the whole body and then the heart has its own. The heart flow interlocks and interconnects with the full-body one. So, can you see it visually?

Client: I'm seeing it now.

TZ: As I watch your energy field, it is more organized now than a little bit ago. Before, it looked unorganized to me. Now it is very organized like a fountain. It's as if your whole body is a fountain.

Client: Oh, oh! Gotcha!

TZ: I have actually been seeing a dark line cutting through your spine right there. *(Pointing to the thoracic 4–5 vertebrae.)* It's about this wide. *(I hold up my fingers to show that it is about three inches wide.)* That is pretty big.

Client: Wow, yeah.

TZ: Practicing with the flow of the toroidal field is already helping the energy to get through a little bit more. Oh, you know, they *(my guides)* are saying that running your energy in this way will help you incorporate the energy between head and heart.

Client: Can you ask if that is what's giving me brain fog?

TZ: Yes . . . I am getting a great, big, giant *yes.*

Client: I thought I was becoming demented.

TZ: Now I see why it appeared like a big ring of energy, like a wreath. The energy flow has been so weak up your spine that it was not incorporating into your head. All this energy was outside of your head and not in your head.

Client: I get it! Even this morning, Tina, I thought . . . is there something in my spine blocking some kind of fluid going to my head? And that's why I have been feeling all nuts. This is amazing!

Medications and Supplements

At psychic fairs, I occasionally present as a speaker and offer fifteen-minute medical-intuitive sessions at my booth. I had just finished with a lighthearted, healthy client when the next person sat down in front of me, along with his girlfriend. I was overwhelmed with the sense of imminent death. His aura was a thick gray, and his skin tone matched his aura. I instantly saw in my mind's eye two outstretched hands heaping with pills and capsules. The hands shifted into fists and angrily struck each other.

I said to him, "You are taking huge amounts of supplements and many of them are fighting against each other."

His girlfriend hit him in the arm and declared, "I told you that you're taking too many supplements!"

"Yeah, yeah . . . okay," he responded.

I was lucky to see that same man about six months later at a psychic expo. He looked fantastic!

People seem to be taking more and more supplements and medications. Many people do not think supplements are the same as medication. Supplements are natural medications and are very potent. Natural substances are capable of creating huge alterations within the body. Taking supplements unsupervised can create negative symptoms, and in this case, illness and potential death. Teach your client to treat them respectfully.

The first time someone asked me to assess his medicines, I said of course, then immediately wondered how on earth I would ever receive information about pills.

"Please give me just a moment to ask my guides how to go about this in the best way," I said.

Dan, the client, waited quietly as I asked my specialists for the best way to do this. Spirit directed me to ask this man to slowly state the name of each medicine or supplement, and I was to watch and feel his energy as he listed them. I perceived different bodily reactions as he called out the name of each pill he was taking. One supplement caused his body to become fiery red, which signified a dramatic inflammatory response. Some were quite neutral, indicated by the lack of response within his energy field. Some brightened him with gorgeous iridescent colors, indicating a positive response. For some medications, I felt a sinking feeling in my own body, while others gave me a lifting sensation. I was elated to experience medical-intuitive information in such a different way.

Case Study:
Medications and Supplements Affecting Communication

This is an excerpt of a session with a woman who is taking medications and supplements. Many people treat themselves and have good results, while others treat themselves and have negative results. Receiving an intuitive symbol of the client's mouth often signals something ingested is causing a negative health situation.

Practice Experience:

Imagine you are the medical intuitive speaking the words in this transcript. Read it aloud or, if possible, with a study buddy, one taking part as the medical intuitive and one as the client. Practice this session as if you are actually giving these steps to someone who needs your guidance.

TZ: Let me tell you one other thing that just came in. I don't even know what to make of it yet. I saw you open your mouth and sticking your tongue way out, like we do at a doctor's appointment. You know when you say "ah" and the doctor looks into your mouth? Your tongue had a zigzagged crack down the length of it. Right down the center and length of your tongue. Then I saw it being stitched up. Where does that take you?

Client: Well, I originally thought of the image of a snake and then I had a vague feeling of increased communication or of being able to speak.

TZ: Yes, yes, that's what I am getting, or something about communication. The two are the same. There was a really deep zigzag cut, and it didn't go through your whole tongue. It did not give you a split tongue *(like a snake)* but it was a deep cut. Then I saw this just beautiful stitching and it being healed. The back of our throat is about expressing or struggling to express our particular individualized truth.

Client: Right.

TZ: Now one more thing. It feels like you are eating or taking a medication or a supplement that is not settling very well with you.

Client: Okay. Why you are saying that? I opened a vegetarian café in a flurry and at the same time came into what I think is menopause anxiety. I have been struggling for the first time in my life with pretty severe anxiety and depression. I have been taking . . . I could list the things I'm taking.

TZ: Yes, I often ask people to call off the names of what they are taking, but not too fast so I can intuitively check each one out.

Client: L-tyrosine.

TZ: That seems fine.

Client: Amino acid 5-HTP.

TZ: That actually feels good for you. You brightened up.

Client: A Chinese herbal menopause supplement.

TZ: There is a bit of a struggle about that one. Write down a struggle about that one.

Client: I am taking a natural progesterone cream.

TZ: That needs to be adjusted in some way. I felt a downward movement of energy, so a little bit less.

Client: Okay, I use it in the morning and at night.

TZ: Is it a prescription or is it on your own?

Client: No, it's on my own.

TZ: See about decreasing both doses just a little bit.

Client: When I get really flipped out, I take Ativan. It's an anti-anxiety pill. I have three others that I have taken for a long time.

TZ: Okay. Wait a minute. With the Ativan, I saw a snot-like substance coming out of your nose. That didn't feel very good. I am getting what you consider as anxiety is actually beautiful rushes of energy.

Client: Okay. I considered that before.

TZ: Excellent, excellent. Instead of tamping it down, allow it to rise up. I feel like you try to contain it. I also think the work we just did with your solar plexus is going to have a positive effect in what you consider anxiety. Now, go on with the others.

Client: Iodine.

TZ: Very bright, that looks very fine.

Client: Selenium.

TZ: That seems fine.

Client: A magnesium, calcium, potassium drink.

TZ: Is there zinc in any of those?

Client: Maybe, but I don't think so.

TZ: I am seeing that you should be taking zinc.

Client: Would you check herbal women's compound tincture?

TZ: That feels very good. In fact, I am seeing the image of two wires all tangled together, and they unwound and moved into alignment. So yes, that feels very positive to me. It will unwind you and assist you toward feeling more aligned.

Client: Okay.

(Engage the client to participate in their own process.)

TZ: See if it feels right to drop the Chinese herbal combination and switch to the herbal women's compound. Kind of take a minute and see what feels right to you.

Client: Well, I started taking a bunch of them together, but I've been wondering about that Chinese herbal supplement because it made me kind of crazy.

TZ: You already know stopping that will feel like you are being unwound. That will be very positive . . . unwound and realigned.

Client: I feel a little wound up. Actually, I feel manic almost. I knew something was doing that, but I was too afraid because it felt so much nicer than being totally depressed.

People are struggling to make the best choices and use their judgment correctly to build and maintain their health. You now have an intuitive method to assist people in those decisions. When your guides tell you the cause of an illness is prescriptions or supplements, and you intuitively assess each one with your client, you must be clear and direct. You also must insist that the client discuss any medication changes with their physician first. If you are not licensed to practice medicine and do not have a license to do so, you absolutely cannot direct a person to alter anything that a physician has ordered. Some medical intuitives take the extra step and have all their clients sign a form to address that they discuss everything with a physician first. If you feel that need, use a signed form to bring peace to your heart and mind. This level of peace will allow you to relax and receive intuitive information more readily without tension or fear.

Sometimes your intuition will overlook an illness or physical complaint from which a client states they suffer. In the following case study, I did not pick up any signs of my client's severe migraines. She had to tell me it was one of her struggles. When this happens, do not assume you have failed. Simply tell your client that Spirit did not sense it as a dominant factor and did not present it to you. Ask for permission to laser beam into that specific area of the body and confidently inform the client of anything you perceive.

Case Study:
Using Supplements as a Healing

This case includes healing toxins in the body through hydration and vitamins. Remain confident, ask for permission, check in with your guides, and laser beam into the specific area in question.

Practice Experience:

Imagine you are the medical intuitive speaking the words in this transcript. Read it aloud or, if possible, with a study buddy, one taking part as the medical intuitive and one as the client. Practice this session as if you are actually giving these steps to someone who needs your guidance.

TZ: I feel that you have some toxins in your body. I felt that from the moment we started our conversation.

Client: Could be, yeah. My body feels heavy. I'm not that big, but I always feel heavy. I'm a vegetarian. My diet, especially in the last seven years, has been very healthy, but before that it wasn't because I love to eat.

TZ: Okay, let me check why I'm getting toxins. Just a moment . . . Would you be willing to take B-12?

Client: I just started taking it recently!

TZ: Okay, very good. I feel like you are very depleted in the B vitamins, but especially B-12. If you would, go to a health food store for B-12 and a good quality supplement for detoxing your liver.

Client: Okay.

TZ: My guides are telling me that when you start taking these you will not feel good for a while because it will pull the toxins out of your liver and into your system to excrete. You are going to need to drink a lot of water to flush out your body. So, I think the B vitamins and getting rid of those toxins will bring a lighter feeling for your body. This is why you feel so heavy. I'm glad that you are taking the B-12.

Client: Yeah, I saw this doctor in May or June. He is a naturopathic doctor. He put me on the B-12 and B vitamins, and he also put me on those herbs for my liver and my digestive system.

TZ: Are you drinking a lot of water, fluids, and teas?

Client: I don't. I was good in taking those herbs for the first month. I felt better, but then in the last few months I got so dizzy, and I was very stressed. I was not so disciplined. I am not a big water drinker. I hardly drink water.

TZ: It's time now to feel so good about yourself that you will take care of yourself in better ways.

Client: Yes, I need to.

TZ: Please do, because I'm getting that you are toxic. If you go to real people (*myself and the naturopath*), we should be telling you very similar things. The naturopath told you the same things I have just picked up. So, please hear us. We cannot make you take care of yourself. After today, you are going to feel so good about yourself that you will want to take care of yourself!

Client: Okay, I will take care of myself.

(*Do not carry any worry about your clients home with you. It is not your burden to carry.*)

Food

Sometimes you may sense that a person's body is so inflamed it looks like it is on fire. Don't confuse this with anger, which looks similar. While anger is more muddy, inflammation due to food sensitivity feels light and very bright but not in a positive manner. Notice the location of the red fire. If it seems to be scattered throughout the person's body, you are probably perceiving an allergic reaction to either food or something else that was ingested. At this point, pause and ask your specialty guides for the cause.

Mary was calm and pleasant as she entered my office. After our greeting, I sent my laser beam toward her. I was instantly drawn down and into her small intestines. Rather than looking smooth and moist, I saw dry cracks and tiny divots as if the lining was eroding. This was the first time I had spotted this situation, so as always, I turned to my specialists for the cause. I heard the words "dairy," "gluten," and "leaky gut." A bit later in the session, "aloe vera juice" also leaped into my mind.

My personal theory explaining why people react so strongly to wheat and dairy, more than ever before in our history, is that grains have been genetically modified to the point that the human body no longer recognizes them as food. Dairy has been altered by antibiotics and growth hormones. The human body is trying to reject a foreign substance. The body's reactions to these changes are inflammation. For Mary's homework assignment, I told her to cut dairy and gluten from her diet. She was so miserable that she was willing to "experiment" with this change, as she called it.

Later, I asked a doctor friend about leaky gut and found that it is a term now used to describe this exact situation with the intestines. Allergies are the primary cause. This woman returned for another reading three months later and announced that she followed through with her diet change and felt healthier than she had in years.

Drugs

Most of us have had a friend or family member, or several, who use substances to some degree. I always tell this story in my medical intuitive workshop, but I will tell it here again.

The woman was near death when she walked into my office. How did I know so quickly? Her aura had dark, empty holes that tunneled down into her physical body so far that I could not see the bottom. The tunnels looked and smelled like rotten meat. They appeared in her head and throughout her entire body.

I looked into her eyes and said, "You are going to die soon."

She responded, "I thought so." She went on to tell me she had lost her home and her husband. The court declared she was no longer allowed to see her children. She was living in a run-down motel at the edge of the city with men who shared cocaine and heroin with her. At her request, we talked about her approaching death. My guides gently helped me understand that my role was simply to listen and be a witness for her story. No one had ever come to me near death due to substance abuse before, and no one has since.

I have perceived one common symptom among people who abuse substances, or anyone with an addiction: Their solar plexus appears to be empty, as if it has been used up. Their abdomen will feel quite cold, and will sometimes be dark brown or black, concave, and void of any color vibration. The client might not use the word "victim," but if you listen carefully, their words describe victimization. In energetic terms, they have lost all their personal power and their sense of self as an individual.

Healing Technique:
Negative Energy Caused by Substance Abuse

1. Describe the emptiness and its physical location in the person's body, such as how cold or dark it is.

2. Ask the client, "Where and when did you lose your empowerment?" Tell them to take the idea that instantly pops into their mind. Most of the time, they will share a current-life trauma. Sometimes they will become aware of a past-life trauma.

3. Guide the client to fill themselves up with the energy of the sun: breathe its warmth into their belly, push warmth along with a sparkling neon-yellow vibration into their abdomen. Do this with them so they feel they are not alone.

4. Ask the client to notice what they feel in the space that was previously empty. It will be warmer and fuller.

Injuries, Accidents, Surgeries

Not only do the choices you make to your body affect your

energetic field, but injuries, accidents, or surgeries, and the emotions surrounding them, can also cause negative effects such as a leak in one's energetic field. An energetic leak bubbles up like water coming out of a garden hose, or worse, a fireman's hose. You will perceive a leak rising up and away from an exact location in the body.

Leaks have two causes: a physical injury, such as a wound or even a past surgery; and emotional trauma. Physical trauma and our emotions regarding it are definitely interrelated. Emotional trauma is often a shock, and can have a physical impact on the human body as if one has been hit with a fist or a baseball bat. Energetic leaks caused by a shocking trauma seem to crash into the heart center or the solar plexus—the center of all emotions. The shock may also take away one's sense of empowerment, confidence, or personal identity. For instance, a betrayal will appear like a stab in the back that leaves a gaping hole in one's energy field. The death of a loved one will affect the chest at heart level, creating a concave or weakened place in the field.

The magnitude effect on one's energy field depends on how the individual responds to the event. Each person is so different. Someone who has had major surgery may show no outward evidence of trauma, while even a minor dental procedure can cause great emotional stress in someone else. One of the largest, gushing leaks I have witnessed came from a woman's lower jaw. When I described this to her, she said, "Oh yes, I had a tooth filled two weeks ago and it was a terrible experience."

I will now emphasize a fantastic teaching moment through the case of a client we will call Suzie.

Suzie sat in front of me looking puzzled, then denied that anything ever happened to the top of her head. I am sure I looked just as puzzled. When the medical intuitive spontaneously receives a piece of information and the client denies understanding any of it, do not waver. You received intuitive information, and it is accurate on some level for that person. Hold steadfast.

I responded gently but firmly that she was indeed leaking,

and we needed to address it because she was losing some of her life force and vitality through this area of her body. I went on with my observations throughout her body. Twenty minutes into the session, Suzie suddenly declared that she just remembered injuring the top of her head when she rose up too quickly under a machine in the factory where she works.

Sometimes the Treatment is More Vital than the Cause

What is disturbing to one person is not even memorable to another. An experience you would consider minor, someone else will consider harrowing. It is based on who we are, how we react, and what we react to. It is all about our thoughts and beliefs creating emotions.

Our mind is an energy field permeating every cell of the physical body. The intensity of positive or negative emotions then influence the body because the physical, mental, and emotional are truly all one. Sometimes your clients will deny emotional trauma. When this happens, do not waver. Sometimes the thinking mind puts a trauma aside as a way to protect. More often than not, your client will soon remember the hurtful event and will be surprised they had forgotten it.

For example, I was working with a sweet couple when a person in spirit came in quite strongly for the husband. The man in spirit clearly gave his first name and a piece of specific evidence. His wife squirmed in her seat as her husband kept saying that he had no idea who I was talking about. The wife could not take it any longer and yelled at him, "Your brother is here. It's your brother!" My client was blank and did not even recognize his own brother's name. Sometimes I don't receive information about the point of origin of the injury or illness but instead guidance for a healing treatment. The reason why this might happen is because the treatment is more vital than the cause.

For example, a woman came to me with issues in her right shoulder. She was not able to move it in any direction; it was frozen in place. I asked to receive the point of origin of her frozen right shoulder. Instead, I witnessed a spontaneous healing by Spirit—a psychic surgery. A silver, angelic hand reached down from the ceiling and provided a gentle surgical cut through the skin of her shoulder. The cut seemed somewhat superficial. I could not determine any depth to the incision at all. The silver hand reached in and pulled out a substance that looked like a hardened piece of gristle from a piece of meat. It was white, about two inches long and half an inch wide. The hand then released the gristle into the air. It lifted upward and faded from my sight. The hand then reappeared with golden thread and flawlessly sewed the incision closed with delicate stitches. All the while, my client was only aware of a profound sense of peace in the room and in her own body.

Months later, that same woman told me she never had problems with her shoulder again. This healing experience happened years ago, yet it is as vivid to me as I just described here. No matter how long we are medical intuitives, Spirit will continue to teach us in new and surprising ways.

We medical intuitives must be ready, able, and willing to go with the guidance of our specialists. A type of psychic surgery may happen in two different ways. You might suddenly begin thinking and feeling that you are to stretch your energetic hands toward your client and perform psychic surgery or an energetic manipulation or an extraction. You might also witness Spirit performing a surgery or manipulation on the client's behalf. Go with the flow.

Manipulation of the energetic body is another, more physically based option that will frequently have unbelievable results. Energetic manipulation of the physical body is an option if your spirit guides direct you to do so. The manipulation can be a surprise for you or, with guidance, it may be deliberately accomplished.

You may receive information to remove an energetic object from a person's body. You may find yourself reaching out with energetic hands to remove solidified objects such as scar tissue, knives, spears, or constricted objects such as tourniquets, ropes, or chains that might be embedded in the energetic bodies of humans.

If manipulation, psychic surgery, or the extraction of an object leaps into your mind, Spirit is guiding you to be the direct healer for that particular individual. Please ask for clear instructions and perform the energetic steps that Spirit gives you. We intuitives cannot make these things up. It is way beyond any imagination that most of us could ever have!

Healing Technique:
Psychic Surgery, Energetic Manipulations, Extractions

Remember, only provide a psychic surgery, energetic manipulation, or extraction if your specialty guides specifically direct you to do so, or you spontaneously sense it happening. Spirit will show you the exact steps you are to follow. Here are a few of the infinite possibilities Spirit may guide you to do:

1. Imagine your energetic hands gently penetrating your client's skin at the injured spot within the person's body.
2. Spirit will show you exactly what to do. For example, Spirit may tell you to . . .
   - Seal the leak by covering the bubbles leaking out of your client's body with your hands, like a Band-Aid or some type of wound dressing.
   - Energetically cut tough, gristle-like scar tissue out of a client's body.
   - Straighten a vertebra that has slipped out of place, or push the entire spinal cord into alignment.
   - Remove a cyst with your hand.
   - Smooth out a jagged or frayed tendon with your fingertips.
   - Remove an instrument from the energetic realm, such as an ancient sword, from the client's back.
   - Or, sometimes Spirit will heal the client for you.

3. When you remove anything from a physical or energetic human body, remember to fill the empty space with Love, Light, and perfect healing.

Please do not dismiss your personal healing capabilities by reducing this process to fantasy. Medical intuitives who truly accept the depth of their personal empowerment will achieve even more than the examples I describe above. Remember the quote from the Master Jesus? "You can do this and more."

Essential Points

- Sometimes the point of origin of an illness or struggle is something simple.

- Natural substances are capable of creating huge alterations within the body.

- Injuries, accidents, or surgeries, and the emotions surrounding them, can cause a leak in one's energy field.

- Only provide a psychic surgery, energetic manipulation, or extraction if your specialty guides specifically direct you to do so, or you can already sense it happening.

- Sometimes the treatment of an illness is more important than the cause.

Chapter 7

Thoughts and Emotions Causing Illness or Life Struggles

"If you feel down, unhappy, or don't seem to care . . . bring your soul back into this dimension and ground it to this reality."

—Raymon Grace

Remember, energy follows human thoughts. Each word within our thoughts and our requests has its own vibration and will attract things from the Universe that have a similar vibration. As you go throughout the days of your life, do it with the clearest awareness and intent. We are designed to be an important component of the Universe. Our bodies, our world, and our Universe becomes more positive, or more negative, based on thought energy.

In his book, *The Biology of Belief*, Dr. Bruce Lipton states: "Positive thoughts have a profound effect on behavior and genes, but only when they are in harmony with subconscious programming. And negative thoughts have an equally powerful effect. When we recognize how these positive and negative beliefs control our biology, we can use this knowledge to create lives filled with health and happiness."[6]

Here is how negative thoughts and emotions affect our lives.

Recovery

My sister has MS and has been in a motorized wheelchair for many

---

6 Bruce H. Lipton, *The Biology of Belief: Unleashing the Power of Consciousness, Matter, & Miracles*, (Carlsbad, CA: Hay House, 2016) xxviii.

years. Four days before Christmas, we decided to go to a movie. At her van, she stood for a moment holding on to the handle. As I followed the system we have to load her into the front seat, she screamed a bloodcurdling sound and fell backward into me. We both landed in the mud of her barnyard. She continued to scream and cry because the fragile, porous bone in her leg had fractured as she stood up.

Grief primarily congeals in our lungs. My sister went to the hospital for surgery and rehabilitation, and I went to bed for three weeks with bronchitis that became pneumonia. The moment my sister and I fell, I immediately knew her life would never be the same. I feared she would never make it alone at home while her beloved husband was at work. I was actually in just as bad condition as my sister, if not worse. It never occurred to my sister that she would not go home. Guess who recovered . . . my sister.

Auras

As a medical intuitive, you have many opportunities to teach clients that every word within their thoughts emits a vigorous signal to the body, which flows into every cell of our body. That vigorous signal then hurtles outward into what is known as the aura. Remember, negative emotions such as shame, guilt, fear, depression, and grief have a slow, thick, intense vibration. The traits of these emotions tend to become physical more quickly than other emotions. Their sluggishness congregates in certain areas of the human body, causing illness or disease.

For example, depression may tend to appear within the aura like a dark stocking cap on a person's head. Another example would be a grieving person who has lost someone or something very essential to them, sometimes within three to four months they will be diagnosed with a cyst or cancer. Some grieving people are so empty that you might find yourself looking past their rib cage into an empty cavern. It's as if their heart and lungs have disappeared.

Lying or deception will have a distinct appearance in someone's aura. I once stood with a young woman in the archway of my door. I was looking directly at her, but she was looking off to the side. She was saying all the right words in hopes of renting one of my apartments. She didn't realize that I was watching slimy, yellowish green-brown energy shooting out of her throat in all directions. She had no idea I could see that every word she said was a lie. She didn't get the apartment.

As an intuitive, I received a precise piece of information about that young woman and what she contributed to the cosmos. Liars contribute a stagnant energy to the world that appears like muddy swamp water. Picture that in your mind! As a medical intuitive, you not only assess someone for disease or struggles, you are also able to perceive the quality of each person's auric field and their lifestyle.

I once met with a woman who walked into my office with the energy and appearance of complete defeat. I saw the swampy green, yellow, brown aura encircling her. I almost opened my mouth to say that she was lying a great deal in her life. Thank goodness I caught myself. Instead I said, "People all around you are lying about you, aren't they?" She was shocked and broke into sobbing tears. She shared details of a group of people lying about her and taking her to court to sue her.

Can you see the difference between this client and the young woman who wanted to rent my apartment? The aura, the energy of the soul, tells its story. In the case of these two women, the liar is actively producing lies and the other is being lied about. Notice that earlier, I mentioned the movement of the swamp water energy was coming out of the liar's neck, while the woman who others lied about had swamp-colored energy all around her body. In the case of the latter example, the lying energy was not coming from her but was encircling her like a cloud. There was nothing shooting out of her. Be aware and learn from the energy field. If you notice the location, movement, and direction of energy within the aura, it will give you accurate intuitive information.

To finish the case of the woman who others lied about, I want to tell you what happened next. Spontaneously, without requesting healing assistance, a group of angelic spirits literally bolted into the session with scrub brushes and cleansed her until she twinkled and felt restored.

It is common for Spirit to offer an energetic homework assignment for people suffering from negative thoughts because of grief or depression. For example, Spirit may tell you to teach the client to breathe neon-green light into their heart and lungs in order to replenish their hope to go on living. Spirit may also guide you have the client say the words: "I now inhale bright, sparkling green as I take in a new breath of life." In this case, you are combining a specific vibration of energy with powerful words. Later on in their grieving process, you can teach them about the body-mind connection and emphasize that they have the ability to get in charge of their thinking.

Be prepared for your clients to tell you they do not know how to make their energy flow, or they cannot see any color in their mind. Simply tell them all they need to do is think about the steps, and the energy will follow their thoughts. For this example, tell them to think of the assigned color and imagine it is coming into their nose and mouth. They must imagine it entering into their chest, and they must use strong feelings to command that the color flows into their heart and lungs.

Allergies and Deficits

Negative thoughts and emotions can create deficits such as allergies, loss of hearing, or other ailments.

When we hear things we interpret as negative, especially if we hear it over and over again, it will have a tendency to decrease the energy of one or both ears. For example, there was a woman whose husband verbally yelled condescending words to her, put her down, and told her she was wrong, even in front of family and friends. This went on throughout their marriage of over fifty years. Over time, she had more and more trouble with her hearing until she became totally deaf to the point that not even hearing aids could help her. The body could not receive the verbal brutality any longer.

Case Study:
Thoughts and Emotions Causing Ear Pain

The following is an excerpt of a session where the person struggles with anger and repetitive negative thoughts that has subsequently caused ear pain. This was an opportunity to teach about the power of human thought.

Practice Experience:

Imagine you are the medical intuitive speaking the words in this transcript. Read it aloud or, if possible, with a study buddy, one taking part as the medical intuitive and one as the client. Practice this session as if you are actually giving these steps to someone who needs your guidance.

TZ: See what pops into your mind when I say this: There is anger rushing through you like a bolt of lightning.

Client: Well, yeah, I'm always angry. Oh, I am so angry all the time at the way this world's going. I'm always just so angry.

TZ: That is adding to the way the world is going.

Client: Huh?

TZ: Your anger is adding angry energy into the way the world is going.

Client: I know. I know it. Well, I don't mean the world like world events, or stuff like that.

TZ: Then what do you mean?

Client: I saw this commercial for—I know it's stupid, but for Victoria's Secret. These girls were parading around in their underwear with wings on, and I thought, *You're so stupid.* Why do you have this crap on TV, or do it at all? You know, it's that kind of stuff that just riles me up, and I know it's just hurting me, but I just react. So, maybe this will help that. I don't know. I got so mad.

TZ: Well, it seems you have an anti-girly thing going on.

Client: Yeah, there's that going on, but that's just one little tiny weeny example.

TZ: But it is a good example though.

Client: It's like, why do I let that bother me? It's not yours! You don't need to be involved in it! Why are you so angry? I wanted to see if we could talk to my subconscious and see if it has any negative contributions to some of this.

TZ: Well, I'll do that now and see what I get. But you already have a large red bolt coming from the left side of your head. It is anger, and it appears thicker than a writing pen. It is jabbing you like a big piece of hot wrought-iron into the left side of your head.

Client: Well, no wonder I'm mad.

TZ: It's there because you are already mad. It is not what is making you mad.

Client: Okay, okay. It's the energy of anger.

TZ: It is on the left side of your head, and it is about issues with females, and being too feminine, and the self-exploitation that many women are willing to do. You are trying to be logical, but you are so emotional. They are spikes of great emotion, but not all are anger. Some are simply surges of emotion.

Client: Sunday night I was sitting to read, and this horrible pain shot through my ear. I thought that thing was going to burst like it did several years ago. I lost all my balance and it was horrible.

TZ: What burst?

Client: The lymph sack inside the inner ear that causes balance. It took therapy to be able to walk again. It was a horrible pain that went down my neck to my shoulder.

TZ: Well, it does look inflamed a bit. I see a little tiny line of inflammation through there. I think you have a little infection. Let me see where it goes. It goes down the Eustachian tube. It goes down from there. I am not seeing that anything popped or burst. You're not all dizzy, or anything?

Client: No, it just scared me. I thought, oh God, I don't know how I would function.

TZ: There is a little red line of inflammation, and I am getting that your immune system is low. I see it like a tiny, little whitehead pimple. Talk to your doctor about taking something for your immune system to strengthen it. There are also supplements that will help build your immune system. *(Pause.)* I am getting that the underlying cause of your ear is that there is something in your life that you cannot hear any longer. Who is saying something that you don't want to hear?

Client: The students.

TZ: I am picking up that it is more about the other faculty you work with.

Client: The students are doing much better. We had a good time today.

TZ: Okay, do you hear your answer? It really is not your students. It is more the faculty who are verbally saying things that hit your ears in an energetic way. They are saying things that are hard for you to hear. As this goes on, it has lowered the energy in your right ear. I haven't even noticed anything about your left ear.

Client: And the right ear is my weak ear. The right ear had a major infection when I was a kid, then it exploded. This is the ear that goes cold and is the one that hurts. It's kind of weak anyway. We got lot of stuff today.

Negative emotions can also cause allergies. Here is a dramatic example: One evening a mother decided to give her two young children dinner rather than wait for their father, who was running late, to come home. As they ate their meal, someone came to the kitchen door. The mother found a policeman waiting for her. The policeman told her that her husband had been found dead. The mother collapsed on the floor, gasping for breath as her children watched.

After this event, both children became extremely allergic to the food they were eating at this particular dinner. They unconsciously connected their emotional trauma with the food they were eating the moment they heard their father was dead. After trying traditional medical techniques, the mother brought them to my center. After receiving acupuncture sessions with a licensed acupuncturist, using a technique called NAET (Nambudripad's Allergy Elimination Techniques), the children improved. Acupuncture is an ancient healing technique using tiny needles to stimulate energy flow. This particular acupuncture method is known to have healing responses for people suffering from allergies.

Sometimes our negative thoughts become reality. For example, a fifty-year-old client once told me she remembers sitting in the back seat of the family car at five years old. Her parents in the front seat were complaining about all their allergies and which symptoms they were having at the time. She distinctly remembered wishing she could have allergies just like her mother and father did. Guess what? She quickly became severely allergic to many foods and multiple plants in the environment. She did not have any allergies up until she had these particular thoughts. In this case, strong emotions of love and wanting to be like someone she loved created allergic reactions to the same things that her parents were allergic to.

You can use the following steps with a client who suffers from allergies caused by thoughts and traumatic memories. Most of the steps offered throughout this book are guidelines. This means the medical intuitive only guides the client to take particular steps while allowing the client to discover how the steps need to unfold for themselves. Do not tell them how to heal the situation. You are not the only one receiving wisdom. They, too, have the innate wisdom and guidance assisting them. They just need a boost to lead them toward their own self-healing abilities. Give them the boost by offering each step, but allow the individual to be guided by their own divine process.

Healing Technique:
Allergies Caused by Thoughts and Emotions

1. Ask the client to remember the moment they first became aware of having allergies. Even if it was in infancy, ask them to imagine going back to whatever age they feel they were.

2. Direct them to imagine their adult self going back in time to join their younger self. Emphasize that they cannot do this wrong and to allow whatever comes into their imagination.

3. Tell them to let it unfold like a daydream or a movie. Inform the client you will be quiet until they speak. They will often feel they should rush, so make sure you ask them to take their time. They will tell you when they feel they are with their younger self.

4. Instruct the client: "Make sure the younger you actually knows you are there with them." Then ask, "How can you tell they know you are there with them?"

5. Ask the adult and the younger self to notice everything around them and where they find themselves. (This helps the client settle into this new awareness.)

6. State: "Now talk it over with the younger you, and the two of you take all the negative emotions out of both of your bodies and give it back to wherever, or whomever, the negative emotions came from. Take out all the emotions from both of you and give everything back. Make sure you help the younger you to do this. Those negative emotions

are not yours to keep. You do not need to carry them any longer. I will be quiet until you speak."

7. Repeat all the dialogue in the previous step but substitute the word "allergies" in place of the phrase "negative emotions." Then state, "I will be quiet until you speak. Take your time."

8. When your client states they have done that, ask: "What happened and what did the negative emotions and the allergies look like when you released them?" Allow the client to describe their experience. Support them by telling them how real this is.

9. For the next step, direct the client by stating: "Now for a complete and permanent healing and release, take back everything that is positive for the younger you and the mature you. Take back all that is positive. Take back all that you gave away, and all that was taken from you, in that moment. Place it back inside both of you. Again, I will be quiet until you speak. Take your time."

10. After the client describes the experience, state: "I ask that the mature you and the younger you talk it over and see if there is anything else that needs to happen for a complete and permanent healing and release." (Take note of the power of the words "complete and permanent." Note that you are also encouraging the client to take any other steps necessary to release the allergies.)

Thought Forms

As thoughts and emotions replicate, their nonphysical energy becomes denser and more physical, and becomes what is often called a "thought form." The medical intuitive sees thought forms as a thick darkness either attached to the physical body, or hanging in the aura. It can also take formation as a dark bulk, like a leech, on someone's back. This congealed energy creates a glue-like constriction and restricts the natural flow of energy, limiting the body's ability to reenergize itself. This becomes the forerunner for an illness, especially in that particular area of the body.

A forty-five-year-old female client named Cindy walked into my office for her first medical-intuitive experience. The appearance of her first and second chakra caught my eye. A thick, brownish-black, cloud-like energy hung all around her lower torso. When we sat down, I informed her that I was already picking up some information and asked her for permission to look more deeply into her physical body. With her permission, I saw that this cloud was not only hanging in her aura but permeating her internal organs as well. I described exactly what I was perceiving. She was not surprised by my report. She later told me how completely shut down she was, emotionally and sexually. This "shut-down" of thought and emotion became the congealed form around her torso.

I asked my guides for our next course of action to create a complete healing for Cindy. They disclosed a precise homework assignment. Step by step, I asked Cindy to fill her first and second chakra with bright red-orange light, and imagine a deep warmth rising upward throughout her body. My guides told me to have her practice this for two to three minutes twice a day for two weeks. In the session, I practiced it with her and watched her energy change immediately.

At her request, I saw Cindy for six sessions. Every time she returned, I could see that nothing had changed for her. I informed her how her lower torso had not changed at all. She was honest and agreed that she had not taken the time to practice.

For a portion of every session, I taught Cindy about the mind-body-emotion connection. I informed her that she was apparently hesitant to get in charge of her own body and her own life and asked her to consider those thoughts. A month later, Cindy walked into my office for her sixth session. She was glowing in all the right places. I was so excited that I described her glow before she even sat down. Cindy replied, "Yes, I finally started doing my homework assignment!" Quite unconsciously, Cindy provided all of us with a profound validation in how real medical intuition truly is.

Spirit may direct you to give your client an energy assignment like this one. Do not agonize about it if a client does not follow through. If you find yourself thinking of a client and wondering if they have accomplished their homework, you are connected to some degree with their energy. Medical intuitive practitioners create a connection with clients during each session that vibrates with an intensity that does not happen in other relationships. If you find yourself worrying and fretting about a client, you are maintaining a degree of responsibility for them. Do not carry that responsibility with you. Teach them to how to be responsible for themselves.

Our thoughts construct our environment and influence our body's health or its destruction.

There is a saying: "We are what we eat." We need to also say: "We are what we think." And we really do become what we think.

Unresolved Memories

When there is an unresolved issue, memories and the thoughts that come with them will repeatedly rise into our awareness. Life is a continuation of day-by-day moments, events, decisions, and choices. Some are joyful, but some are painful and traumatic. As these memories emerge from our unconsciousness into our daily thoughts, emotions come with them. As negative memories, and the subsequent pain, repeatedly come into our awareness, negative energy builds up with an increasing intensity.

These negative memories cover a vast expanse of emotions, from agony to hatred to profound guilt. Secrets are hidden emotions of guilt, and hidden memories that carry an intense reverberation of negative energy. Unknown to many people, this repetition always offers us two choices: to take the appropriate steps toward healing, or to succumb to the heaviness of regret for the rest of our lives. If we keep choosing the latter, those painful moments will eat away at our lives and our bodies like cancer.

Secrets are unresolved moments in the past that we try to bury. Here is an example of how burying these unresolved moments can cause illness. A gentle, sullen woman came into my office and asked if she could lie down during the session rather than sit in the chair. I did happen to have a massage table in the room at that time, so I offered it to her. As I began the medical-intuitive assessment, I immediately envisioned black, finger-shaped forms throughout the right side of her head. I informed her as gently as possible. She responded by saying that she had been diagnosed with cancer of the brain. Without visible emotion, she informed me that I described the tumors exactly as the physicians explained them to her—dense fingers projecting throughout the right side of her brain.

Then she told me her story as if she already knew its correlation with her brain being eaten away. She was deeply in love with her husband of over forty years. However, during all those years, she maintained a sexual relationship with another man. She informed me that she had never told anyone her secret and asked that I keep the secret as well. I promised never to disclose her identity. She said she felt the greatest relief to release this burden to me. She died, only days after our time together, with her husband and many friends and family by her side. They will never know about her secret from me.

You, too, will also respectfully hold many secrets about your clients. The medical intuitive will hear many, many secrets. When someone shares their secrets you will know the cause of their illness, but you will also know that a healing has just begun. Confidentiality is a massive ethical concern for me. Never divulge your clients' names, locations, life issues, or secrets. It is not for us to tell their story without permission. One of the most important roles for the medical intuitive is to be the holder of many, many secrets. Trust must be the foundation for all your intuitive work.

Repetition of Life Patterns

We all have patterns that repeat throughout our lives. Someone may notice that many of their past boyfriends, and now their current husband, are just like their abusive father. Someone else may have a pattern of working in companies where they are not appreciated or recognized for their efforts. Another individual may find that when things go well, they wait for the shoe to drop. Examples of human patterns are infinite.

It is vital for us to recognize the life patterns of ourselves and that of our clients. Patterns will only develop, or persist, when we do not have a deeper sense of self-awareness. Sometimes people may blame others for getting caught up in patterns while being blind to their own patterns. Do not let your client fall into this trap! Keep them focused on how their own thoughts influence their own life patterns.

Sometimes a pattern forms in our lives because we are trying to heal ourselves, not everyone else. We create the pattern, and others simply begin to comply with you in the pattern. Life patterns are the Universe giving us opportunities again and again to advance our awareness so we can heal and release that particular burden forever.

In this case, the healing technique is for the client to understand three concepts: First, that the pattern exists in the first place. Second, these patterns are the reason they feel stuck in life. And third, these patterns can only resolve if they change their thinking and behavior. We "cannot see the forest for the trees" when it comes to our own struggles.

Physical Pain

Physical pain is another example of the potency of thought energy. Beneath that physical pain is always emotional pain, and beneath that emotional pain lie thought patterns. It is a layered effect: thoughts, emotion, and then physical pain.

Eric, a sixty-year-old man, described a chronic pain in his left hip down to his leg and into his foot. After receiving permission to look into the pain in his body, I called out to my specialists and asked for the point of origin of this man's pain. A scene rapidly developed within my mind's eye. I witnessed a physically abusive mother dominating a ten-year-old boy by striking him repeatedly and demeaning him verbally. I described the details of the scene as Eric's tears spilled down his cheeks. He said I just described a memory that he had always tried to forget. In short, his physical pain covered up the emotional pain from his childhood abuse.

When negative thoughts and emotions repeat over and over for years, it stimulates our body in a negative way. These specific thoughts and emotions began to congeal in Eric's body. In his case, it congealed in his left hip, leg, and foot, which makes perfect sense in the body-mind-emotion connection.

The left side of the human body represents female characteristics, or struggles with a female in our life. Hips represent the environment in which we grew up. Struggles and illness in the hip area are about the lack of stability. The body's legs and feet become ill when we do not have the ego, strength, or confidence to take the right steps forward in life. In other words, Eric's body directly simulated the pain and agony of his abusive past. That retention created constriction, congestion, and resistance in his physical body.

Negative memories that continue to rise up in our awareness signify unfinished business, or painful emotions that have not been resolved. Ignoring painful memories of our past only makes them more present, which then leads to a pressurized buildup of energy within the body, resulting in physical pain. Teach your clients about this unhealthy process and the consequences. Once a painful event is genuinely healed, the emotions associated with the memory become completely neutral.

Healing Technique:
Unresolved Issues

I asked my healing guides to show me the way to provide a complete and permanent healing for Eric. This is what Spirit directed me:

1. Tell your client to imagine sending his current self back to that specific moment and stand with his younger self.

2. Ask your client what they see and feel.

3. Tell your client to call in their own healing guides to join their younger self and current self in that exact painful moment.

4. Ask your client what they experience.

Take note that I did not tell Eric to specifically call in angels, nor did I direct him to ask them to surround his mother. Remember, during the healing portion of your session, steer your client in a certain direction but never tell them how to do it or what to experience. You may have a thought pop into your mind regarding the best way to create the healing moment, but get yourself out of the way. The client will describe a picturesque, compassionate, and benevolent moment that we healing practitioners could never come up with. Allow them to manifest their sacred moment. That moment will bring them the sense of empowerment and the ability to move into a sacred healing on their own.

Secondary Gain from Illness

Sometimes it is hard to understand, but a client who is ill or injured may receive a secondary gain from their illness. Look closely for the signs your client tells you, such as how busy they were before the illness struck them—the jobs they do for everyone in their life, or the multitude of daily tasks they completed. If you find yourself telling them you cannot believe they accomplished all these things for people, and you have no idea how they got it all done, your client is probably receiving a secondary gain by having a debilitating illness.

Intuitively, you may also find patterns of illness throughout this person's life, such as injuries or hospitalizations. As life goes on, this person has lost their vitality and their self-worth, and was completely drained until they were empty. The inability to say no and the drive to constantly care for everyone around them is the cause of their disabling illness. Their body has no choice but to say no for them. If they allow their body to heal, they assume they will be overwhelmed once again. If they remain ill, they never need to take on more tasks.

This person desperately yearns for peace and quiet. They yearn to refuse another task, or to take on more responsibilities, but they simply cannot admit the truth that they desperately want to say no. This is a subconscious decision to save themselves, but at the same time, not disappoint their loved ones. Illness helps them to avoid feeling a false sense of failure because they could not keep up. Up to this point, they are completely unconscious about any secondary gain. They are also subconsciously convinced that illness or injury is their only escape to get them off the hook.

Healing Technique:
Secondary Gain from Illness

1. In a gentle manner, ask if they tend to be people pleasers and have a difficult time saying no to people.

2. Inform your client they do not need to become more important than everyone else, but just equally as important. You will need to repeat this important piece of information again and again.

3. Inform them they are in charge of their thoughts and emotions. They can refuse to think negatively about themselves. They will be surprised when you inform them they can say no without making any excuses or explaining in any way. You will see a light go on in their eyes. A spark of new ideas just happened.

4. Ask them how they might take the first baby step in this process.

If the client struggles to admit they are taking on more than they can handle, they will not be able to take the first step toward recovery. For example, my client Emily hesitantly admitted she wanted to stop babysitting full time for her four grandchildren, who were all under the age of six. She was collapsing under the daily responsibility, but was terrified to admit this to her son and daughter-in-law. However, she did not realize she had escaped the daily duties of child rearing by becoming ill.

At this point, insisting that Emily tell her family the truth is a gigantic step that she will fail to accomplish. It is simply too scary. In this case, direct her to simply sit with you and find a tiny, doable step that she genuinely knows she can take. Your client will know exactly what that doable step is. Emily decided she could inform her family that she would like to care for the children four days a week instead of five. She had a large smile on her face when she discovered her first step. Accomplishing one tiny step after another brings success rather than failure.

Remember, sometimes you simply will not receive information regarding the point of origin of each illness, malady, disease, or struggle. You still have a healing option, one that comes up throughout the book, commonly called "dowsing." With the power of thought, you can send powerful healing to the exact point of origin. This dowsing technique is from Raymon Grace's dowsing training.

Where the blank is shown in the commands below, state the exact struggle, such as the pain in a client's right shoulder, their anger issues, etc. Focus on only one issue at a time. If you combine multiple concerns, the energy will be diffused and will not have the laser-beam effect. It is important to state each step and to feel these words as commands. Feel powerful as you state them in your mind, or out loud. Work with one step until it feels complete, or if you are using a pendulum, the step is complete when the pendulum stops. You then move on to the next step. Do the steps in the order that is stated below, and all in one sitting.

For deeply ingrained issues or illnesses, do all the steps every day until you notice the desired change. A good example took place with an energy worker I know. He had multiple severe allergies since childhood. He used these dowsing steps and repeated them every day for three weeks before he could tell a difference. Since his dowsing work, he is now completely relieved of the severe allergies.

Dowsing Steps

1. Completely scramble the point of origin of *(person's specific struggle)* on all levels and in all ways for *(person's full name)*.

2. Completely neutralize the point of origin of *(person's specific struggle)* on all levels and in all ways for *(person's full name)*.

3. Permanently and completely transform all scrambled and neutralized energy for *(person's full name)* into Divine Love and health.

Essential Points

- Negative thoughts control our biology.

- When conducting a healing, guide the client toward their own self-healing abilities and let them do the rest.

- If you agonize about whether a client has accomplished their homework, you are connected with their energy. Do not carry that responsibility with you.

- Our thoughts construct our environment and influence our body's health or its destruction.

- Thoughts influence emotion, and emotion influences physical pain.

Chapter 8

Relationships Causing Illness or Life Struggles

"Our minds influence the key activity of the brain, which then influences everything; perception, cognition, thoughts and feelings, personal relationships; they're all a projection of you."

—Deepak Chopra

Take a moment to consider the people in your life and the different behaviors and exchanges that present themselves within all types of relationships. While the observable behavior between people continues, there is much, much more happening on the energetic level. Some people take energy from others while others give their entire life essence away.

Children tend to grow up believing negative or positive comments directed at them is their truth. Very early on, children are convinced that the beliefs of their authority figures are truths. However, the beliefs of others are only repetitive thoughts that have built density over time. For example, children who listen to negative authority figures such as parents, grandparents, and teachers accept their negative and demeaning comments as truth. As children grow into adulthood they frequently struggle to create their own truths about themselves. Thoughts turn into beliefs, and beliefs become emotional. Thoughts and emotions are real, and they create powerful energy exchanges between people. What we say to each other, or think about each other, creates, builds, or diminishes our life essence.

Have you ever left a meeting with another individual and you were so drained that you wondered if you could even get to the next appointment? You desperately wanted to lie down for a nap. My definition of a vampire is a person who consciously or unconsciously taps into the solar plexus, or the subtle astral or etheric body, of an individual to pull energy from that person in order to fortify themselves. Vampire-type people function at a much lower level of awareness. They do not know or understand they, too, have the ability to build their own resources to sustain their body, mind, and soul. As a result, they attempt to capture some of the essence of people around them. They often drain the essence from animals, like their pets, as well.

Now consider Mother Teresa. She never relied on relationships to fortify her energy field. She was tapped into her toroidal field and made use of the energy of the Earth and the Universe. This woman walked among the multitudes, giving and giving some more. We, too, can give when our personal energy flows in balance with the Earth and the Universe. Remember, energy follows human thought. Training ourselves to deliberately run our toroidal field will maintain that balance. We can give and receive in our relationships when balance is maintained. We need this balance, and so do our relationships.

Case Study:
Relationships and Loss of Empowerment

The following case study illustrates a client's struggles with different types of relationships. Underneath these issues was the struggle to hold her own empowerment at home and at work. Physically, this woman had a congested throat chakra, auric field leaks, a hopeless and heavy heart, and a weakened solar plexus. During her session she received multiple homework assignments that correlated with her various struggles.

Practice Experience:
Imagine you are the medical intuitive speaking the words in this transcript. Read it aloud or, if possible, with a study buddy, one taking part as the

*medical intuitive and one as the client. Practice this session as if you are
actually giving these steps to someone who needs your guidance.*

TZ: (Suddenly coughing.) Well . . . I need to tell you that I haven't
been coughing at all this morning. When I get symptoms like
that during a session, I am really picking up some information
about you. It felt like you were just stabbed in the right side of
your neck. It felt like an ice pick, or something sharp jabbing
you.

Our throats are about either speaking up or expressing
who we really are, what our true thoughts are, what we really
feel in our hearts. What I get is that someone wants you to be
quiet; someone doesn't want to hear what you want to say.

When we struggle on the right side of our body, it is either
about what is considered to be male qualities of taking right
action, or it is about a male in your life. So, be aware of what
or who pops into your mind as I say these strange things to
you. I also need to say that I keep seeing a man's face with a
prominent nose and a mustache. He is coming into your energy
field so strongly that I can hardly see you. I've even asked this
person to step aside because I'm having a hard time getting to
you, and he is resistant. What are you getting from all of that?

Client: I think you are probably describing my husband.

TZ: His energy or his presence is coming between us. He is very
dominant or prominent in your life to the point that I'm having
a hard time getting past him to get to you. Does that make any
sense?

Client: Yes.

*(The only question an intuitive should ever ask is "Does that make
any sense to you?")*

TZ: Well, I have to say that he is sticking his nose into your business. I'm literally seeing his nose again and his face pushing

toward you, sticking his nose into your business. Which is kind of a strong thing to say about a husband, but I need to say that.

Client: Mhmm.

TZ: Now they're telling me to look at your heart, so may I look at your heart?

Client: Okay.

TZ: The very top of your physical heart has a darkened area, and that's where the primary arteries enter into the heart. It is quite low energy in a very specific area where the arteries come into the heart. There's also an emotional feeling of sinking and a heaviness of your heart.

Client: Mhmm. As far as I know, I don't have any physical health problems.

TZ: There's a heaviness and a sinking feeling in your heart. The word "hopeless" is coming in. We only go into hopelessness when we truly do not understand or believe that we have other options. A belief is only a thought that we think a lot. Whatever you believe can be changed. Nobody can really make you do anything. I don't want you to feel hopeless.

If you could hear the gentleness and the compassion that I hear in your voice, you would never be hopeless. You are such a good, good soul and a good person. It feels like you've lost track of that. Let me just check that if I may . . . I'm getting pulled back to a time in your life around the time you were in your twenties.

Client: Yes.

TZ: The deep sense of loss started when you were twenty years old. Does that make any sense to you?

Client: Yeah, I was married when I was twenty. There's one particular area that I'm having pain, and I've had pain for about two years. I didn't know if you could figure out where I'm having this pain.

(Notice that the client avoided discussing the relationship with her husband.)

TZ: Well . . . as you say that, I am pulled down into your belly.

Client: Hummm . . .

TZ: I'm seeing this is either around your belly button or right above it. You look like you've been punched in the gut.

Client: Hummm . . .

TZ: And that doesn't necessarily mean you were physically punched in the gut by something, or someone. It means you have taken an emotional hit, and it looks to me like you took the hit over and over and over again. It's actually very, very dark in comparison with your throat. Our energy field can have a leak *(due to a physical injury or an emotional event)*. A leak is often a trail of bubbles, and for you it is actually gushing—a gushing leak in the core of who you are as an individual. It is about our strength, our uniqueness as an individual. Do you hear that you're losing so much of your essence in your power center? It's our core of who we are. Everybody thinks the heart is probably the core of who we are, but really, energetically, it is within the solar plexus. Our solar plexus is about our individual thoughts, and it is where we sense things very uniquely as an individual. You have lost and are losing some of your individuality over and over again as if you are being punched in the gut.

Let me ask *(my guides)* what to do about this. *(Brief pause.)* My guides would like for you to put your hands on that area and imagine that you are putting a beautiful, beautiful Band-Aid over this leak. You're putting a coating of love for yourself over that area. They keep showing me a beautiful bright yellow, warm like the sun, because you're very cold in that area. You've lost so much energy and it has become cold. Your whole abdomen, literally from your groin up to your rib cage, lacks vitality. I want you to imagine the sun inside of you and filling you up with its warmth. So, imagine that for a minute and then tell me what you notice as you do that.

(The client just received her first homework assignment.)

Client: *(Coughs.)* I guess it makes me warmer and . . . I am more relaxed.

TZ: Please let yourself feel the emotions that I hear in your voice. Please let yourself, because as you are warming up, you are actually getting brighter, and then I got that jab in your neck again.

Client: Yeah.

TZ: It seems like a warning: don't do that, don't change, and don't fill yourself up with the sun. I hope you do it anyway though.

Client: *(Laughs and is tearful at the same time.)*

TZ: There's a reason why this is bringing emotions up . . .

Client: I do have a jab in the neck, but it's not on the right side.

TZ: Put your hands on that area and cover it over with a loving Band-Aid, whatever size it is, and then fill yourself up with the warm, warm sun. Do it once a day.

Look what we did here in less than a minute. It will help you rebuild your energy. Because you're getting pretty depleted in areas I've already mentioned. And there's something very important for you about this, or you wouldn't have the tears and the feelings that you just had. Now what direction do you want to go with the rest of our time we have together?

Client: I guess I've been looking for answers but not—I don't know—not knowing where to find them.

TZ: Well, what are some of the questions you're looking for answers to?

Client: What's causing the pain in my neck?

(Clients often struggle during a session. Thoughts and emotions come up that were tucked away a long time ago.)

TZ: I have described that the cause is not having freedom of speech in your life. It is about the inability to look in new directions. I tell you, you're a good person. What is the tiniest little thing that you could do for yourself that you haven't been doing? Tiny, tiny, itsy-bitsy.

Client: I'm trying to meditate. I've been trying to get started journaling.

TZ: Oh, excellent, excellent. I want you to make sure the journal is in a safe, secure place. And I'm saying that because that's what jumped into my awareness. Make sure you feel very confident of its privacy. Do you know how to meditate?

Client: I'm just trying it. I started reading a book called *Pain Free for Life*. It talks about meditating and journaling. Trying to tell your subconscious not to repress away so many things.

TZ: Well, that's exactly what is getting locked down in your neck and throat. I'm trying to say it in various ways. I went right there and I felt all this jabbing. The vertebras in your neck at C3 and C4 are too tight. The disc looks like it's become quite tight, and I would suspect you are getting some nerve pinching.

Client: So, what do you recommend for that?

(Protect yourself by consistently telling the client to consult their physician.)

TZ: My guides are telling me there are many, many emotions that are locked down and resistant in your neck. If you would unlock those emotions, it would give you a great deal of relief. Did you get this checked with the doctor? Did they want you to do surgery?

Client: No, no, it just came back fine.

TZ: Well, maybe physically it's fine, but . . . that's why I am picking up that surgery isn't going to affect it. It is your emotions trapped in that particular area of your body.

Client: In 2012 I took a position where I was working part time. That's another area where my guts tell me that I cannot do that. I don't know if you're seeing anything like that.

TZ: Let me see. I'm seeing there's a bright side to your job and a dark side. Because, in my mind's eye, literally it is cut right in half. I think there is a real bright area, and over here is a dark area that looks like a thistle or a thorn. It has sharp edges. It feels like either someone, or something, is not warm and fuzzy. Someone, or something, pokes at you or prickles you, and jabs at you.

There is a bright side to it too, but the bright side honestly is not as large as the dark. The dark feels sharp and jabs like a thistle. You could certainly resign from that position, but it doesn't feel right to go home and not have a job. The information I'm getting is for you to find something that nourishes you and would give to you as you give to it.

Client: Yeah.

TZ: I'm seeing you behind a desk or a reception area with people contact. I see you in an office, kind of like our office here. It's relaxed, it's gentle, and we try to make it feel more like a spa. I would say even a chiropractor's office is coming up.

Client: Hummm . . .

TZ: Even a holistic health area, or something like that, would nourish you as you help them.

Client: Can you see anything I should be doing that I'm not doing?

(Teach the client how to accomplish their homework. Watch as they practice and give feedback based on your perceptions.)

TZ: Well, you are not doing very much for yourself in positive ways. Our time together, at least in my head, has been about you caring for you and not carrying all this other responsibility in your neck and upper back. You are not at fault for what is going on. It takes two to tango. And each person (in a relationship) only has 50 percent of the relationship. Our 50 percent may look very different from the other person's. Someone, with their 50 percent, could be louder, nosier, grumpier, and the other person's 50 percent could be more quiet or sullen, but we still only have our 50 percent. You tend to want to take on 100 percent of everything. I'm seeing a big boulder on your back. So, I can think of all kinds of things for you to begin to do. Meditating would be great. I would ask you to only do two to five minutes, and don't try to sit for half an hour if you are not used to meditating.

You also have another homework assignment. Imagine your abdomen warming and put that "love Band-Aid" over the leak that has been gushing out of you. My guides say to do that once a day. You could do it before you get up in the morning, or you could go to sleep doing that in the evening.

Client: My chiropractor was very wise, and he's in his seventies. He said, "You just have to strengthen up your core because you're very weak there."

TZ: That's exactly what I have been saying to you. That is connected with the leak in your solar plexus.

Client: I've noticed for over a year that it seems like I can't strengthen that area.

TZ: My guides are asking you to do it energetically first with your hands over that area with a love Band-Aid, which kind of makes me giggle. I like it because I've never said it that way before. You fill yourself up with the sun by just dreaming that up or imagining it. If he (the chiropractor) gave you some core exercises to do, that would be phenomenal. Do you have any interest in yoga?

Client: The chiropractor I was speaking about asked me that too.

(When clients tell you they have heard the same information from other intuitives, explain when they go to real intuitives, we should be telling them similar information.)

TZ: See, I'm picking up chiropractor. I also said a little bit ago about working for a chiropractor or some healing-type office would also be of great benefit for you.

Client: Um.

TZ: But nobody can make you do this, Darlene. You know we all have choices.

Client: Yeah, but you get to a point where you have to make change.

TZ: You are energetically at the point that if you don't, you're going to become ill.

Client: Yeah.

TZ: I feel like I need to say this again. Your first steps of change should not be gigantic. Because if we make the first step too gigantic we can never do it. Break it down into tiny steps, like I'll do with my "love Band-Aid" after I fill myself with the sun today. Maybe do it three times today. See, that is a very, very powerful first step. You do not need the huge dramatic changes first because we cannot get there yet. It is completely up to you.

I would like you to take responsibility for yourself rather than so much responsibility for everybody else. I mean your husband and whoever else is out there. At least allow yourself to be as important as everybody else. Just equally important. I think you would also feel great just getting out of your current job.

Client: Yeah, it's very interesting how you know me, and you've totally pinned it.

Relationships May Imprison Us or Set Us Free

Relationships, or the lack of relationships, impact our lives in powerful ways. Relationships are much more than just the titles we give them. Some of the most powerful titles of relationships are parents, siblings, friends, family or coworkers. They are so much more than these titles. Relationships are complicated, intertwined energy patterns between complicated, energetic human beings. These interwoven connections are deeply affected by thoughts, emotions, and many misunderstandings that result in emotional conflicts between each person.

Unresolved misunderstandings are only one struggle among relationships. Thoughts create our reality in life to the point that our thoughts about something becomes a strong belief, which then becomes an absolute truth for that person. For most people, our emotions and beliefs are so dominant that they can no longer understand, or even perceive, that there are countless other perspectives.

Case Study:
We Create Our Own Imprisonment

This case study demonstrates how thoughts and emotions within a relationship lead to self-imprisonment.

Practice Experience:

Imagine you are the medical intuitive speaking the words in this transcript. Read it aloud or, if possible, with a study buddy, one taking part as the medical intuitive and one as the client. Practice this session as if you are actually giving these steps to someone who needs your guidance.

TZ: You have stress pushing at you; not pushing you down, but pushing at you. Even as I say that, I feel an ache and some pain in your chest. I feel that you have taken stress into your heart or your chest. Also, right in the center of your chest is this great big open flower that is just lovely. It is purple-pink and wide open. You are transforming into positive things. When I say these strange things, it is important for you to really notice who or what jumps into your mind very, very quickly. Altogether there are three primary things you want to work on. See if that feels true. I also see you with tears coming from your eyes.

Client: Okay, I have to say you're pretty right on with everything. I have been feeling sad for some reason. I feel very stressed out. I feel very emotional, even wanting to cry. I cannot explain it.

TZ: Tears are inside of you even if they are not coming out. Again, I feel like these stresses are coming *at* you. You're standing strong, but you are taking some hits, bam, bam, bam. I see energy shooting at you, and it's not positive. That's what I'm seeing.

Client: I will wake up in the middle of the night with pain all around the breast and even nodules.

TZ: As I listen to you, I am checking your energy field, and you didn't say which one but your left breast draws my attention and does not look as energetic. It has much lower energy than your right breast.

Client: Correct.

TZ: Okay. In the mind-body connection, our breasts represent more than just feeding babies. They are also about struggling to nurture ourselves. It is about not taking care of yourself as much as you should. That comes up in my awareness, and also a struggle with a female in your life. Who would that be?

Client: Well, you mentioned about those three concerns (*at the beginning of the session*). The funny thing is, one of my major concerns are about three women.

TZ: Thank you for that validation. Two of them seem more of a concern, and the third one is not so much.

Client: Yes.

TZ: Do you see how this connects? When I talked about issues with females, it is this emotion that is creating pain and nodules in your breasts.

Client: For the last five to six years, there is one woman who has caused a lot of pain and suffering for me. The sad part is that she is ill now with breast cancer. She was my ex's mother.

TZ: Okay. Do you see how these things are fitting together with your physical situation in your body? For some reason you believe the bad things she says about you. Why do you believe her? I want you to realize that what she thinks and believes are all about her struggles and have very little to do with you.

Client: I agree with what you say, and now I understand that whatever she said about me wasn't really true. She has really put me down, and she totally destroyed my self-esteem and everything. I have been getting much better since last year.

TZ: Hurting your self-esteem can only happen if you believe the things she says.

Client: Right.

TZ: My concern is that you believe her. Is that because you held her in high respect, or what is it?

Client: Yeah, that's a good question. I needed to put both of them (*her ex-partner and ex's mother*) up on a pedestal, and I looked up to them.

TZ: That tells me you do not feel equal to them.

Client: I felt like I had to take care of them and stuff, and obey them.

TZ: They are still affecting you, and its congealing in your breasts.

Client: Okay.

(*Finding the cause of the client's struggles begins here.*)

TZ: Give me a second, let me check something out. (*I ask my guides* *what needs to be done to heal this.)* They *(the three women)* are taking energy from you, but you are also giving away your energy to them. This is very low energy that I am seeing in your breasts, especially your left one, because you are participating with them to take your empowerment away.

Client: Okay, well, it does feel true . . . yeah. I mean, all these years I lived my life almost like a prisoner.

TZ: And how did that happen? In what way are you a prisoner?

Client: I wasn't allowed to go out or do anything without their company, and also I pretty much was cut off with communication with parents and friends. I made a call to my parents and my best friend, using a number without them knowing. Like I had to hide a lot of things. I couldn't do anything without their approval. I spent a lot of time in the kitchen; that's the only place where no one would bother me or disturb me.

TZ: This might be hard to hear, but I have to say this. As a grown woman, you had to participate with them in controlling you. In other words, you were not physically tied up or handcuffed or chained to the couch.

Client: No, it wasn't anything physical, but I had a lot of fear of them. I couldn't have any disagreement with them. It would always end up with huge fights or arguments, screaming and yelling and throwing things. I wasn't used to that kind of environment or lifestyle. My parents were very loving. It was total culture shock to me. So, I tried hard to work with whatever they asked me to do to avoid that kind of conflict.

TZ: Every time you did whatever you had to do to avoid the conflict, you were giving your energy away. This is the ache in your chest, and now pain and nodules in your breasts. It does not feel like you are still in this situation right now.

Client: No. I left. I ran away. I left on Christmas in 2015.

TZ: For them to take this control is like they were bullies in school that we see on TV. What no one ever talks about is that the bully actually feels horrible about themselves. The only way they can feel better about themselves is to push someone else down and down and down again. The bully takes the victim's energy away for their own use. Does that make sense?

Client: Yes, it does.

(The healing technique begins here.)

TZ: Would you be willing to imagine and picture in your mind your ex and the mother? Would that be okay? Can you see them or have a sense of them?

Client: Yeah, we could try that. I try to avoid thinking of them. It just causes a lot of fear and anxiety about them.

TZ: Pushing this away is why it's now in your breasts.

Client: Right.

TZ: I am asking you to bring them back into your mind, if you're willing. You don't have to. Now, is there especially one memory that is the most painful with them?

Client: There are too many.

TZ: Please know that it will feel terrible right now, but it will be very good for you and will help you. Now, here's what I want you to do. I want you to imagine pulling out of you all of their terribleness, all of their anger, all of their words. I want you to pull everything about them out of you right now. Just imagine pulling it out of you from head to toe, and especially from your breasts and your heart. I want you to imagine pulling, pulling, pulling, pulling. Take it out of you, and I want you to hand it back to them. Take your time and just see what it looks like as you start taking this stuff out of you, and just give it back to them. It does not matter what they do with it. It is their stuff. I will be quiet as you do this. Will that be okay?

Client: Okay.

TZ: All right, I'll be quiet now. Just take it out of you and give it back.

Client: *(A few minutes later.)* Yes, I did that.

(Assess the person to confirm that they have, or have not, removed all the negativity that is making them ill.)

TZ: Okay, tell me what it looked like or how you did it.

Client: I just pulled out all this stuff and handed it back to both of them, and it all seemed to be dark, greasy trash.

TZ: Now, would you go back inside and feel like you are walking around inside of yourself? I am getting that there is more. I am seeing it back behind your heart and also behind your breasts. Make sure you get every single piece of it and give it back.

Client: Okay. *(Long pause.)*

TZ: I can feel a difference now. So, you found more and took it out of you?

Client: Yes.

TZ: Yes, I feel that from you. No pressure on your heart now. It feels relaxed now.

Client: Yes.

TZ: Tell me what you gave back to them, and what did they do with it in your imagination?

Client: They seemed to be shocked.

TZ: Were they really? How do you know this?

Client: They seemed to be shocked. They think of themselves highly. They think of themselves as very spiritual and pure. They always said I am the one who had a lot of karma and evil.

TZ: Did you take that out of you too?

Client: Yes, I don't believe that anymore.

TZ: Excellent, excellent. When people cannot look at their own garbage, they always put it on somebody else. They were not about to look at their own karma, or their own learning or lack of learning, so they put it on you.

Okay, there are some other steps I would like you to do, and here it is. I want you to take back from both of them everything they took from you, and everything you gave away to them. I want you to take it back because it is not theirs to keep. I want you to bring it back to you through like a cleansing filter, like a beautiful cleaning, and pull everything out of them that is truly you and yours. You being a strong woman; you feeling good about yourself. Take back your confidence and your own strength. I will be quiet again, and make sure you take it all and get it back. It is not theirs.

Client: *(A few minutes later.)* Okay, I did that.

TZ: Excellent. What did that look like and feel like?

Client: I felt love, I felt stronger, and somehow I felt like I got bigger.

TZ: Yes, yes. That's because your energy is bigger. You are not down under your skin. Yes, when you have your full energy it goes out beyond your skin.

Client: Yeah, and they seemed to diminish. The funny thing is, I don't seem to be so fearful of them.

(Ask the person to take a moment to physically feel the changes they have created for themselves. This will lock in the positive changes on a physical, mental, and emotional level.)

TZ: Just sit there and notice and feel your strength somewhere in your body. Just take a moment and really feel that right now. Feel your bigness.

(Pause.)

Client: Okay.

TZ: What did you notice? There is no way to do it wrong. It's whatever your way is.

Client: I just feel the sensation.

TZ: Now, for some reason I need to ask you about the pedestals they were on. Are you still seeing them on a pedestal?

Client: No. They just disappeared in front of me.

(Describing their experiences accentuates the memory and the reality of it.)

TZ: Take a moment and look back over your history with them and see if it feels emotional or traumatic, or look back to see where the pedestals are at now.

Client: No, like I don't have any emotional sensation toward it.

TZ: Excellent! When we really heal a situation, it becomes neutral information. Just information in our history with no emotional impact anymore. See if this feels right to you. Take this bigger you, your confidence, your power, and go back into some of those memories and stand there in that strength and just notice what happens.

Client: *(A few minutes later.)* It seems like I feel much better about myself.

TZ: Yes, what happened when you went back in your strength? Whatever you noticed.

Client: I just noticed that I feel very warm and loved, and I feel very good about myself. I see myself with the positive characteristics rather than being very critical about myself.

(Report your intuitive observations to emphasize that their changes are real.)

TZ: I have been watching your energy field, and it has changed quite a bit. When I asked you to go back in those memories with all your empowerment and your confidence, you were quiet for quite a while. Your energy is just glowing now. You look so much better now. You have lots of yellows, oranges, and purples in your energy field. You really changed a great deal when you did this last step.

Client: Yeah, I feel different. I feel the energy around me is different.

Healing Technique:
Unhealthy Relationships, or the Loss of a Relationship

Over many years of private practice, I am constantly reminded that one of the most profound causes of illness or life struggles is the relationships between people. However, another cause is the loss of a person in an important relationship. So, you will be dealing with a wide range of positive and negative relationships. Be on the alert for both a loss of the dearest person in the client's life, or the most hated person in their life. You become the healer for your living client, and you will also suddenly have a deceased client. Both clients are just as alive as the other, and you are the healer for both sides of this relationship.

Another aspect of relationships causing illness is the client's lack of a meaningful relationship. In this case, you can discover the exact point of origin causing this client's struggle with creating relationships. Next you must guide the client into healing this moment, and opening up to receiving in the future.

There is an impressive spectrum of types and qualities of relationships between humans. One end of the spectrum is a lifelong, joy-filled connection to another person. The other end of the spectrum is a brutal relationship that seems more like a prison.

Here are the healing techniques for these multiple types of relationships:

1. Loss of a relationship with a loved one: Ask the client to feel the grief in their body. Ask where it is located and have them describe it to you. (For example, they might say it is a rock, log, or an empty hole.) Say to the client, "Let's learn everything about it." Tell the client to talk to the rock, log, or empty hole and ask the following questions:

- Why is it in that location?
- Walk around it. How large is it?
- What is it made of?
- What does it do for you?
- What does it want you to know?
- Is it positive or negative?
- What does it need to heal?

When the medical intuitive requests the client to ask a part of his body the key question, "What does it need to heal?" stay alert for the answer. Your job as a healer is to follow through with what it needs in order to heal. Ask your Divine and Sacred healers how to take the first step to accomplish the healing.

2. Never tell a client to leave a relationship unless they are in physical life-and-death danger. Instead, explore what the client can do to be more of themselves while in this relationship. For example, one of my clients told me she wanted to go to a yoga studio every Wednesday evening, but she could not. When I asked her, "Why don't you go?" she replied, "Because my husband insists that I cook his meal every single night, and then wants me to watch TV the remainder of the evening." I responded with, "I want you to notice that your husband seems to always get what he wants in his life. Now I want you to notice that you are not getting what you need in your life." What is the tiniest little step the client can actually accomplish? Becoming more of themselves while in the relationship is more powerful than leaving.

3. Never tell your clients they need to forgive. If the client is not ready, they will be negatively triggered by the word "forgiveness." Anger will take over, and as a result, the session cannot move beyond the client's anger. Please realize and remember that forgiveness is not a healing method. It is the very natural result of their deeply healed state of being.

Miasms

Some define a "miasm" as a "cloud or a fog" within the human. Miasms tend to cause physical symptoms rather than emotional struggles. You may receive this word from your spirit guide specialists as they point you toward the primary cause of your client's physical illness.

In Irvine Loudon's article, "A Brief History of Homeopathy," he describes Christian Friedrich Samuel Hahnemann's 1807 premise on "like cures like." Loudon summarizes Hahnemann's belief that "if a patient had an illness, it could be cured by giving a medicine which, if given to a healthy person, would produce similar symptoms of that same illness but to a slighter degree." In other words, the same medicine that can make healthy individual ill can cure a sick person who has similar symptoms.[7] Today, a commonly known example of this concept is the remedy for poisonous snake bites. The remedy is derived from the venom from that same type of poisonous snake.

Peter Morrell describes Hahnemann's discovery twenty-one years later when he identified three miasms that cause many chronic symptoms. These symptoms are now commonly known as autoimmune disorders. At that time he named the three miasms:

- Psora—Itching Miasm. Symptoms: intolerable itch, scaly dry skin, skin eruptions, toxicities, reaction to the environment, headaches, anxiety.

- Sycosis—Gonorrhea Miasm. Symptoms: sexual and urinary tract disorders, joint and mucus membrane disorders, allergies, warts, tumors, secretiveness, the hiding of weaknesses.

- Syphilis—Canker Miasm. Symptoms: ulcerations, tissue destruction, body/mind destruction, rigidity, psychological disorders.

---

7 Irvine Loudon, "A Brief History of Homeopathy," *JRSM: Journal of the Royal Society of Medicine* 9, no. 12 (2006): 607–610, accessed December 13, 2022, https://www.ncbi.nlm.nih.gov/pmc/articles/PMC1676328/.

Modern homeopathic medicine has identified another miasm:

- Tubercular Miasm—Symptoms: respiratory imbalance, anemia, offensive bodily discharges, bleeding gums, dissatisfaction, frequent changes.[8]

What is interesting for medical intuitives is that homeopathic medicine identifies a miasm as a "force" affecting an individual, but the individual does not actually have the disorder or illness. A miasm seems to be a type of energy signature, a thought form, or a force that is carried into one's current life.

I would summarize that a miasm is not based on an active disease process but rather an energetic force coming through our biological relationships within past lives as well as our current lives. This force has a tendency to exhibit traits of a disease. The body suffers with generalized chronic symptoms that constantly weaken certain organs or systems of the body. The individual, however, does not actually have the disease or disorder.

A friend of mine was informed by a trusted energy worker that she has a strong miasm for tuberculosis. She has always experienced weak lungs, and every winter she is in bed for up to three weeks with bronchitis, which eventually moves into pneumonia. All tests over the years have ruled out tuberculosis, and yet she had specific traits of it. The intuitive practitioner, not knowing her medical history, kept hearing the word "miasm," and then a minute later the word "tuberculosis." The intuitive's guides then told her to direct her client to take certain homeopathic remedies, medicinal mushrooms, and a more powerful vitamin mineral supplement, and to perform deep breathing exercises.

Healing Technique: Miasms

Miasms are somewhat similar to curses in that both are an energetic signature formation that follows an individual throughout

---

8 Peter Morrell, "Hahnemann's Miasm Theory and Miasm Remedies," last accessed December 13, 2022, http://www.homeoint.org/morrell/articles/pm_miasm.htm.

time and space. Use the Raymon Grace Dowsing Steps, which can be used to clear and heal many different situations or illnesses. You do not need a pendulum. The power of focused thought is required. Say them in the order that is stated below, and all in one sitting.

The Raymon Grace Dowsing Steps:

1. Ask for the original cause of the miasm.
2. Command: "Permanently scramble all negative miasms on all levels regarding *(person's full name)*."
3. Command: "Permanently neutralize all negative miasms on all levels regarding *(person's full name)*."
4. Command: "Completely transform all that has been scrambled and neutralized into Divine Love."

Essential Points

- Some people take energy from others while others give their entire life essence away.
- Relationships can either imprison us or set us free.
- Miasms tend to cause physical symptoms rather than emotional struggles.
- A miasm is described as a "force" affecting an individual, but the individual does not actually have the disorder or illness.

Chapter 9

Introduction to Nonphysical Entities
Causing Illness or Life Struggles

"We have found a strange footprint on the shores of the unknown."

—Arthur Eddington

As I prepared to write this book and especially these next three chapters, I became aware of six levels of negative interference that I have had experience with. These levels increase in severity from one to six. A lower level, however, can be just as intrusive to a living person as a higher level. I have organized chapters 10–12 with each chapter containing two levels with a similar severity of interference, and thus have the same healing technique. These healing techniques will be found at the end of each chapter.

The negative component of the nonphysical realm does exist, even if you would rather think it doesn't. I want to inform you of the variety of situations you may come across as a medical intuitive so you will be prepared for them. Study these three chapters and you will know how to handle yourself, your clients, and the negative aspects of the nonphysical world. You will discover how to provide healing in new and surprising ways.

This is a sensitive subject because of society's beliefs, philosophies, and religious trainings. It must be brought out into the light that nonphysical entities, especially the dark and deeply negative beings, are power-packed with emotion. If you are an energy worker offering any type of bodywork, you must be open to learning about negative spirits and entities that potentially affect your clients and will ultimately affect you.

I want you to be more prepared than I ever was. I want you to be educated, aware, and alert for all possibilities in the nonphysical realm of life. I want you to be ready for this level of awareness and know you can handle that awareness with a commanding attitude. If you have this education now, you will not be surprised and caught off guard when you perceive the "positive invisible world" and the "negative invisible world." You will think to yourself, "Oh, there it is. I have learned about this and I am prepared. I am capable of enjoying the positive and, at the same time, I am capable of facilitating healing steps when the negative is interfering. I am ready to help my physical clients and my nonphysical, nonhuman clients without any fear."

When fear surges though people, it is like a tidal wave of debilitating energy leaving us diminished and terribly jeopardized. Emotions such as guilt, shame, or remorse weaken areas in the human field. The nonhuman entity will become the bully, striking your most vulnerable point. Our weakest location is always obvious in our energetic field. The impaired area appears thin and vulnerable. That weakened area is like an open door that naturally draws the attention of negative beings.

The first time I presented this segment in my workshop inspired the advanced day of my workshop. I could not sleep the night before my presentation. That morning, trembling in front of a large class, I said, "We will begin today with the dark, but we will not end this day with the dark. We will end the day in Love, Light, and strength." I then began to teach about the strange, the weird, and the negative.

As I talked, the room became extraordinarily still. The students seemed immersed in my words. No one moved or became angry or ran out of the room as I expected. I continued on with my information in a neutral, matter-of-fact manner. The energy shifted when I said, "Many of you in this workshop are energy workers or professional intuitives. I know some of you have had similar experiences to those I have described. I can see that awareness in some of your eyes. My hope is that some of you will now share what you have perceived. If you do share, you will help validate the details I am teaching." Five students raised their hands to speak. They shared their own experiences with the strange, the weird, and the negative. The class then became eager to discuss this topic, and everyone began to breathe again.

Here is the key to your success as a medical intuitive: Negative beings have no power, energy, or love of their own, so they attempt to take it from others. You, as the medical intuitive, are the one in charge and in a powerful position to assist everyone and everything involved. Now I will give you two rules for conducting a medical-intuitive session with a client who is affected by a nonphysical entity:

Rule #1: I ask from this point forward that you now consider any level of an intrusive, interfering negative entity first and foremost as a *client*. Many times this "client" might be an unexpected surprise to you. This being is still a client who needs help and healing. This client, however, is also an obstructive interference for the living human client sitting in front of you. Both must be cared for with unconditional love. Both types of clients have come from Source. Everything from Source holds a spark of light. Even the negative and the dark beings come from the Creative Source of All. From the confused, unaware spirit person to the darkest of the dark, all have that same spark of Light and goodness. They have lost track of the Light, have forgotten, or do not feel they deserve it any longer.

Rule #2: Never chase a negative entity away, or try to get rid of them with hostile attacks similar to what you see with exorcisms on TV. Years and years ago, I too used to go at them with "guns a-blazing," but not anymore. I work with them as I do with any other client in need. Approach them with respect because of their strong abilities to interfere with human development. I also approach them knowing they, too, are struggling in ways that we humans cannot even conceive. If you approach them with the dazzling Light of the Divine Compassionate Source, it seems to catch them off guard. Please remember and utilize this new philosophy when you discover a negative nonphysical being.

Understanding negative beings as different levels of interference will provide you with a profound change in your concepts of the dark. Understanding negative entities as clients in need of relief will dramatically alter your beliefs in positive, life-changing ways. It is crucial that you keep the following truth in the forefront of your mind: Even the darkest of the dark entities came from the Greater Creator. The dark has forgotten, ignored, or become fearful of Source's Light. This Light is literally the spark of life energy and knowledge that springs from Source. The darkness and Light give us options for choices to make in developing our personal level of advancement and expansion.

When your client is affected with one or more negative types or levels of interference, you become the catalyst for change. And yes, there can be more than one entity involved with your client, and sometimes there may be many entities functioning at different levels. You may have the physical client in your office and many negative nonphysical entities at the same time. Just like people in the living, some are shy, quiet, and in hiding while others are aggressive and loud. Any and all negative beings that affect your client are simply in need of help as much as the physical client in your office. Accept this concept and you are on your way as an advanced medical intuitive.

Signals of Negative Interference

One day you might notice that an acquaintance, a client, a family member, or a friend is quite different since the last time you saw them. If that is the case, you may be detecting interferences by a negative entity. The differences can be subtle or radically different. Please understand that these differences are not always dark forces at work. The human client might have just discovered that an old friend died, but they are not ready to discuss it. They might be embarrassed to inform you they lost their job last week. Life changes can create mood changes, and can create different actions or behaviors too. It is not always "energetic bad guys." With permission, use your intuitive abilities to assess the individual's body and energy field to determine whether there is a negative influence.

When I look back over my earlier years of childhood and adolescence, I remember people who exhibited one or more of the following signals of negative interference. At that time, I was not aware that the spirit realm affected people in negative ways. As a child, my experiences with the spirit world were sometimes eerie but also a natural, positive part of my life. I had no idea that the spirit world included compassionate, selfless, loving beings and at the same time self-centered, egocentric beings with goals of power and destruction. Just like the physical world, the nonphysical world includes everything in between these extremes. The Bible states, "As above, so below."

Here is a list of some primary signals indicating that a negative influence is obstructing your client. Usually two or more signals will be noticed.

1. Statements such as:
   - "I have not felt right or well since I was at *(location)*."
   - "I feel weird all the time."
   - "I do not feel like myself."
   - "I feel like someone is behind me watching everything."
   - "I am having hideous dreams at night."
   - "I have gone to every specialist in the area and no one can find the reason for my illness."

2. The person is instantly healthy one day and radically ill the next.

3. Sudden dramatic changes in moral choices and decisions.

4. Change in personality, way of dressing, belligerent attitude, increased anger and irritability.

5. Sudden use of substances such as alcohol or marijuana when there is no history of substance abuse.

6. The person's face looks different. For example, their face seems too round or larger than normal. The eyes have a vacant look as if they are not engaged in the moment.

7. Changed voice.

8. Changes in sexual behavior.

9. Altered thinking and level of intelligence.

If the negative changes continue over a long period of time, then negative interference is likely.

Locating Negative Beings

I have not noticed any other book that discusses the proximity of a nonphysical being to the living individual. When you hone your skills to perceive details like this, you can clarify the degree of interference, the illness inflicting the person, and the organs or body systems this illness is affecting. An entity will tend to move around and present itself in various places. An entity may hover around the living person, or move in and out of their auric field. Some of the more antagonistic beings will appear between you and your client in an aggressive stance with an angry look on their face. Some beings will hover over to the side of the client while others will hide behind the person, peeking over their shoulders. Some entities appear glued to the client's skin, sometimes in a frantic, fearful posture as if it might be whisked away.

As discussed earlier in this book, beings can be connected by an energetic cord. The cording is usually connected to a certain chakra, a specific place in the body, or even a certain organ. Some spirit beings attach to the living person in a place that is symbolic or familiar to their damaging focus. For example, a negative spirit may tend to fasten to vertebrae 6–12 in the back of the victim. In the body-mind connection, victims tend to become vulnerable, and to medically struggle in that area of the body.

One day after my workshop, a young man approached me and asked if I would look at a photo of his dear friend. He went on to say that his friend was full of life and vitality one day, and was dying in a hospital the next. He said the physicians could not find any medical reason for his friend's illness.

I looked at the photo of a woman who appeared to be an athlete in running attire with a glow in her face and eyes. Instantly, a malicious male face rose up and enlarged itself, taking over the entire torso of this woman's body. Even I was startled. This being had completely taken over the woman's body and was consuming her.

There are different locations in which a negative spirit may reside when interfering in a human's life.

1. Drifting around the client in a specific environment, such as their workplace. It may also choose to follow the individual wherever they go throughout their day.

2. Energetically corded into the client. Notice the location of the cording to recognize the entity's goal.

   - The brain: to take control of the person's thoughts and ideas.

   - The heart: to leech energy from the person's emotions.

   - The solar plexus (just above the belly button): to drain the person's personal power.

   - The first or second chakras: sexual interest and to receive sensations.

3. Entering one's auric field at different levels.

4. Merging into a certain organ or section of the individual's body such as their back, neck, or shoulders.

5. Fully possessing someone and taking over their body, mind, and energy field.

I have been a clinical hypnotherapist specializing in past-life regressions for twenty-five years. I am also a certified practitioner through Michael Newton's Institute for Life Between Lives. Throughout my years facilitating past-life regressions and life between life regressions, I have witnessed negative forces causing distress, heartrending, harmful patterns in the lives of many people. Negative entities can be attached to a person in the living or in the spirit realm. They can affect a soul throughout lifetimes. When someone dies and leaves the physical body, that negative entity who has constantly interfered with their life moves right along with them into a nonphysical realm. The destructive negative spirit can affect that soul for many lives and many centuries with debilitating consequences.

It is also not unusual to find multiple undesirable beings connected in a type of network or organization, creating adverse situations with a soul, or even a group of souls, in the nonphysical realm. As a medical intuitive, you might discover that the living client sitting in your office may have a negative person in spirit attached to them. That negative spirit person may also have other spirits attached to them, and at the same time, those attachments may have another layer of attachments. You might try to picture this complicated network as plates stacked together, forming layers upon layers.

Occasionally, my regression clients would describe a negative being staying with them and harming them for multiple lives. Destructive entities, at any of the last four of the six levels, do not worry about killing their host. When the host dies, they seem to take one of two options: They disconnect and move to other victims, or they continue to stay with the deceased person whom they physically destroyed. This leeching effect has no limits of physicality, time, or space.

The nonphysical realm is just as complicated as the physical realm, with just as many complicated relationships. Do not be afraid to come across complicated, scary things with your clients. We tend to receive clients that we are ready for.

In order to teach intuitives how to best help those affected by negative interference, I have organized the next three chapters to depict nonphysical energy and entities in six levels of intensity and interference:

- Chapter 10
  - Level 1: Negative Thought Forms
  - Level 2: People in Spirit: Confused and Afraid
- Chapter 11
  - Level 3: People in Spirit: Angry and Possessive
  - Level 4: People in Spirit: Vicious, Hateful, Deliberate
- Chapter 12
  - Level 5: Nonhuman Entities
  - Level 6: The Darkest Entities

Essential Points

- Negative beings have no power, energy, or love of their own, so they attempt to take it from others.
- Even the darkest of the dark entities came from the Greater Creator.
- Perceive all nonphysical entities first as a client in need.
- Never chase a negative entity away, or be hostile toward them.
- If a person appears quite different since the last time you saw them, you may be detecting interferences by a negative entity.
- An entity that is affecting a human client will tend to move around and present itself in various places.

Chapter 10

Nonphysical Entities Causing Illness
or Life Struggles

Levels 1 and 2

Levels 1 and 2 of nonphysical entities are similar but at the same time so different. Negative thought forms are congealed negative energy that has built up over time. Thought forms are not entities. Confused and afraid individuals are entities. I place these together in this level based on one important detail: Thought forms and confused deceased people are able to create illness, but there is no deliberate intention to cause harm.

Level 1: Negative Thought Forms

Negative thought forms are not actual entities. Thought forms are not and never have been living people, nor are they deceased people. I place thought forms in their own level because they are a destructive form of nonphysical interference. Thoughts and beliefs can create exaggerated negative emotions. Those negative emotions can then create more negative thoughts, each building onto the other. To create negative thought forms, one must first be a negative person who constantly focuses on thoughts that are pessimistic, downbeat, depressing, disapproving, discouraging, and self-critical. These thoughts, beliefs, and emotions have a slow, thick, and sluggish frequency.

The density of this vibration eventually produces a more compressed, gelatinous phenomenon. It actually becomes a "thing." My sense is that it is not a living thing, but it does grow over time and weighs on the individual's energy field. So, in addition to a draining entity, it is a massive, burdensome physical object that weakens the human due to its weight and the emotions that contribute to its bulk.

On top of that, the repetition of negative thoughts and subsequent gloomy emotions weaken the human field. That vibration will attract similar frequencies from other people but also from any environment they move through. So, the form tends to grow bulkier. Intuitives will frequently observe this thing as a black blob and, interestingly enough, the black blob will almost always form on the individual's shoulders and back—thus the phrase, "Carrying the weight of the world on their shoulders."

The medical intuitive must teach the client that their gloomy disposition, thoughts, and emotions are profoundly hindering their life. Inform them that scientific research has shown that human thoughts are powerful, and that the thoughts of the scientists themselves have altered the outcome of their own research projects. Tell your clients they are the only ones who can get in charge of their thoughts and emotions. When they feel they are a victim to their thoughts, I always announce to them, "If you are not in charge of your own thoughts and emotions, then who is in charge of them and who is really in charge of you?" I will also inform my client of some books that will help them to understand the body, mind, emotion connection, including the following books found in the Recommended Resources section at the end of this book:

- *Heal Your Body* by Louise Hay
- *The Amazing Power of Deliberate Intent: Living the Art of Allowing* by Esther Hicks and Jerry Hicks
- *The Energy Healing Experiments: Science Reveals Our Natural Power to Heal* by Gary Schwartz, PhD.

After sharing these new ideas with your client, ask them to give you a moment to call out to your specialty healing guides. Ask your guides to show you how to remove the thought form and completely heal the client. Intuitively call out to the purest of pure healing specialists from the Light to heal this negative formation, this person, their thoughts, and their emotions. Ask the client to call out for assistance at the same time that you call out on their behalf. The healing possibilities your guides will show you and your client cannot even be numbered—there are so many options. I witnessed a healing where the angelic realm actually came in with brushes and literally scrubbed the client's brain, and scrubbed away the thought form that had solidified on the person's body. This is only one possibility of a healing that you may witness.

Level 2: People in Spirit: Confused and Afraid

Many deceased people create struggles, conflicts, and even illness in living humans. However, the deceased people who are confused and fearful do not do this deliberately. They, in fact, have no idea they have any effect on living people because their level of awareness is so diminished.

I sat in stillness as my client sobbed. Her husband had passed on two months ago. I gently asked that she allow herself to cry, so she continued to cry. When she felt calmer, she asked if I could make contact with her husband.

"I already see him standing next to a stove in a kitchen," I said.

She burst out in loud sobs that physically rocked her body. When she was able to calm herself again, she said, "He loved to cook!"

Mediumship is a natural and essential part of a medical intuitive's work. Sometimes people in spirit cause illness within your client, and sometimes they create a rewarding, therapeutic experience. It is paramount that you quickly sense if the person in spirit is causing illness or attempting to comfort your client. Whichever it is, you now have two clients: a client in the physical realm of life and a client in the nonphysical realm of life. Both are alive and real, and both need something in that moment.

Inform your client whatever, or whoever, you perceive

without judgment. I almost made a judgment that, especially in this circumstance, a man would not focus on a stove, when it was actually a powerful signal between them. She knew immediately that he was present for her. He meant no harm. In fact, he came with love in his heart for his distraught wife. In a situation like this, you are not just a translator. You are also a communicator, a friend, and a gentle witness for a precious moment between two people that is intense and extraordinary. Slow down and give your physical client time to imprint this moment in their memory. You do not need to talk every minute. Silence is precious while the three of you are together. Get comfortable with short periods of silence as part of the healing environment.

The mediumship portion of your work is not always tearful and solemn. I had one deceased family member who blasted into the session doing nonstop jumping jacks. The client laughed and said, "Oh, when he was alive he was always doing jumping jacks!"

Another person in spirit came to the session with many dogs and a large smile on his face. I remember a young woman who died of an aggressive breast cancer but arrived at her own funeral describing to me how happy she was in the spirit realm as her energy field shimmered with brilliant sparkles.

Here is a personal example of happy deceased people coming to me over a period of a few nights. After I went to bed and covered up with blankets, a nicely dressed man appeared as only a Southern gentleman could. He sat down in the wicker chair in my bedroom. I could see him and his stately demeanor, and I could hear the creaks that only wicker furniture can make.

One night I finally said, "Who are you?"

He quickly looked at me and clearly gave his name.

I then asked him why he was here.

He telepathically responded, in a matter-of-fact voice, "Well, all the spirit activity in your house drew my attention here."

"You are a stranger to me and you're in a woman's bedroom. That is not appropriate!" I responded.

He apologized in a gentleman-like way and off he went. He has never returned.

I have another personal example showing that most spirits are just living their life in the nonphysical realm without thought of maltreatment. I woke one night and found a male spirit, who looked like the well-known actor Nathan Lane, quietly sitting at the foot of my bed. He paid no attention to me. He sat looking out as if deep in thought.

I calmly asked him why he was sitting on my bed.

He answered that he was not sure why he was there.

I asked him to think about it and look back to what brought him here.

After a brief pause, he responded, "I followed that girl from a hotel I was staying at, and I followed her to this house." (He specifically named the hotel, but I will not disclose the name in this book.)

I told him it was not appropriate for him to be sitting on the bed of a woman he does not know. He instantly disappeared before I could suggest transitioning into Source.

Case Study:
Confused People in Spirit Causing Anguish and Pain

This brief excerpt demonstrates how people in spirit can be pushy and demanding. When they behave this way, they are demonstrating how unaware and needy they are at that moment. Keep in mind that a spirit person is still a real person with real needs. This unaware spirit person was causing long-term anguish that had already created a great deal of physical pain for the client throughout her back and ribcage and would have eventually led to disease.

Practice Experience:

Imagine you are the medical intuitive speaking the words in this transcript. Read it aloud or, if possible, with a study buddy, one taking part as the medical intuitive and one as the client. Practice this session as if you are actually giving these steps to someone who needs your guidance.

TZ: You suddenly have two entities that come in very strongly ... two beings on each side of you. One is a glowing orangey-peachy color, and the other one over here is a blue-green vibration. Now they appear as strong as I see you sitting there.

Client: Wow.

TZ: Somebody else came in, a third entity right here in between us, right in front of you, and he has a mustache.

Client: No one I know had one from my past.

TZ: Well, he says he's your father.

Client: The last two years before he died is when I saw him last, and he didn't have one, and he didn't have one when I was a child.

TZ: He is showing me a mustache. Usually, men who do have mustaches are really proud of it and they always show it to me.

Client: Can you ask him if he is the father I had in this life?

TZ: Yes. He doesn't want to be missed. It is important for him that you know he is here and that is why he popped in right in front of me.

Client: And he would.

TZ: He is telling me he wants to make amends.

Client: I have talked with him I don't know how many times. When he shows up in my house he smells like cigarettes. I have forgiven him. I have blessed him. I have his picture on the table with Mom. I don't know what more I can do to convince him.

TZ: Well, I don't know why you think he needs convincing. You seem to think you have to do something. He is not saying you need to do anything.

Client: Oh!

TZ: It is about him making amends.

Client: I see. Okay.

TZ: He is very focused on making amends. He says it will be beneficial for his development, and he hopes it would be for yours also.

Client: Okay. Well, it's okay with me if he does that.

TZ: It is interesting that right away you thought you had to do something.

Client: Well, it's like a two-way street. He is looking for forgiveness, and then he wants to make amends, and I thought, "I have done that!"

TZ: Well, he doesn't feel like he has done it all completely enough.

Client: I see.

TZ: So, it is all about him. It's all about his own stuff.

Client: Okay.

TZ: Is there anything you wanted me to check out with him?

Client: Well, I've got two questions for you, Dad. One, is it you who comes in and presents yourself as cigarette smoke in the house? Because somebody is doing that.

TZ: I heard a big "yes." He knows you'll recognize that.

Client: Yes. And what is your plan for making amends so I can recognize it?

TZ: "Lightheartedness for both of us." He said that before you even got the full question out.

Client: Okay.

TZ: "Lightheartedness for both of us." He also just said it will probably surprise you that he even knows the word "lightheartedness."

Client: For me, he was always giggling and laughing, and he was making light of everything. It was my opinion of him. Things he shouldn't have made light of, he did. I needed a father who was strong and stood beside me, and I would like that now.

TZ: Honest, he says, "I don't think I am there yet, but I'm trying and I'm working toward it. I am not there yet."

Client: Yes, I understand that. *(Talking to her father)* That's something you can work toward.

TZ: Is there anything else with the two of you? I am hearing "nope" on his part, but what about you?

Client: Are you still hanging out with Mom?

TZ: He is showing me he is coming and going, and that there is an awareness of each other. They are not hanging out together at this time, but there is an awareness. They pass each other sometimes and they are aware.

Client: I don't have anything else.

I sat quietly with my dearest friend and his dying father. Gary needed a break, so I told him to go ahead to the cafeteria and I would stay with his father while he was gone. I promised I would call him if he needed to rush back. Gary's father had been unresponsive for many days, so I thought checking in with him intuitively might be helpful. I hoped to discover if he needed anything from us, or if he needed to say or do anything. I closed my eyes and sent my energy outward when instantly a spirit being appeared between us and physically pushed me back into the chair.

The spirit guide clearly demanded, "Do not interfere!"

I apologized and held my energy to myself so I wouldn't overstep my bounds again. I informed Gary about the event, and we both wondered what that was about.

The next day, Gary and I sat together at his father's bedside. I finally had to speak up.

"There is a young man standing on the other side of your father's bed," I said to Gary. "He has been staring at your father for a long time now, but he is not saying anything." I described the man in spirit to Gary in detail.

He responded, "My father's heart transplant was donated by a young male of that exact description!"

There was something very special going on in this particular death transformation. The young male spirit was not causing harm. In fact, his presence seemed extraordinarily special but also complex. I feel deeply that I received that powerful "Do not interfere!" due to the heart both of them shared. While I could not hear any spoken words, it seemed as if a private conversation was going on between an old man, who held the spirit person's heart in his chest, and the young man who gave it away over twenty-five years ago.

Every word within a thought attracts or repels nonphysical energy. Since that is the case, we humans must understand that the power of our thoughts may also have negative consequences with entities of the nonphysical realm. People are always inadvertently summoning nonphysical beings, especially when they "channel" entities. Psychics who channel are usually allowing nonphysical beings to step into their physical body and speak using their vocal cords. In his book *Healing Lost Souls*, William J. Baldwin describes the following:

> "It has been fashionable among New Age enthusiasts to attempt to channel some higher power who will use the voice of a willing person to speak 'words of wisdom.' Some use the terminology 'for my highest good' when calling for a spirit to channel through them. In essence, this welcomes a discarnate entity, the host granting permission to be used.
>
> "The identifiers such as 'master' and 'teacher' and qualifiers such as 'for my highest good,' may be claimed by the malevolent entities as their own identifications, qualities, or attributes. They lie. Unfortunately, some opportunistic entities who respond to this invitation refuse to leave at the end of a channeling session."[9]

---

9 William J. Baldwin, *Healing Lost Souls* (Newburyport, MA: Hampton Roads Publishing).

Please hear the warning in Baldwin's quote above. The misuse of our words is an open invitation for beings to attach to us or interfere with us on a deeper level. Choose your words and thoughts wisely when calling out to the cosmos. Consider using precise words and phrases, such as in the name of Christ, in the name of Almighty God, in the name of the Holy Spirit, the Holiest of the Holy, the Light of Source, the Compassionate Heart Light, Sacred Light of All, held in the Light, the most Sacred of All, the highest divinity, pure, hallowed, consecrated, ultimate good, divine.

Case Study:
Children in Spirit

This case study demonstrates how a deceased person can inadvertently cause illness. It also describes how living children are usually comfortable with deceased children. Notice that the parents are not really my clients. My true clients are a child in the living and a child in spirit.

My client's parents asked me to come into their home because they thought spirits were interfering with their four-year-old son, Eric. I let them know I could work with them, their child, and their home from a distance. We did not need to meet in the physical location of their home. I did ask them to say their street address out loud to me. I went into a light meditative state and projected my energy toward the "feeling" of that address. In general, I find that if I simply send my energy outward in that laser-beam way, I will feel a pull in a certain direction and I just go with the pull. When I arrive at the home, I go in, "look" around, and receive information through all my senses.

In this case, before I intuitively entered the house, I became aware of a child who called herself Rosie. Rosie did not like that I was approaching her, or her house, so I immediately stopped moving forward. I honored her as a real person because she was still a real person and a very young child. I introduced myself and asked if it was okay to talk to her. She did not readily respond, so I waited. I finally felt the sensation of "yes," which felt like the air around me lifted upward. I also felt her send me the feeling of relief.

When Rosie agreed to talk to me, she became my client. Once the nonphysical being agrees to become your client, you move forward in the session just like you would for a person sitting in your office.

Rosie sent me an image showing that she fell down a deep, open well. Her body instantly died, but her spirit showed me that her parents found her at the bottom of the well. As they looked down into the well, her spirit body looked up at them. She then initiated the interaction with me telepathically.

Practice Experience:

Imagine you are the medical intuitive speaking the words in this transcript. Read it aloud or, if possible, with a study buddy, one taking part as the medical intuitive and one as the client. Practice this session as if you are actually giving these steps to someone who needs your guidance.

Rosie: Everything changes.

TZ: Show me your room. Has your room changed?

Rosie: I have to share *all* the time!

TZ: What do you and Eric do all day?

(I suddenly see an image rather than her words sent telepathically. She shows me that she sits on the floor and plays with toys.)

TZ: Do you like Eric's parents?

(Again she answers me with an image, this time of Eric's mother standing at the kitchen sink. Rosie watches her.)

TZ: Do you ever hurt the other kids?

(Rosie looks surprised and confused, so I do not think she means any harm.)

TZ: Where are your parents?

(Rosie shows me again that she is down at the bottom of a well, or a very deep hole, and she is looking up at her parents. She sees them at the top looking down at her.)

TZ: Did you fall down a big hole and get hurt?

(I receive sensations of a deep pressure against the base of her throat and pain in her abdomen.)

TZ: Do you want to go to see your parents?

Rosie: I'm afraid to leave my house and yard.

TZ: Oh, okay. For now, would you be willing to be more kind to your playmate and stop moving things around in the house?

Rosie: We both do it!

TZ: Okay. Can I come back some time?

(Rosie sends me a "knowing" of yes. She doesn't think she has a choice since I am a grown-up.)

Later that day, I realized I did not get directives from my guides to assist Rosie in making her transformation to the Light. I did not question my guides and thought I knew better. I told Eric's parents to speak to Rosie frequently as if they can see her, and give her firm but kind directions. I told them that I sense she will comply with them. They have openly communicated with Rosie, and the strange activities in the house have stopped.

After reading this brief sample, notice if you have a "rule" that states you must go to the physical location of your clients' home or business. You can certainly continue to travel to homes and businesses if that feels right to you, but you will soon find that you do not have time to do home visits, and it is not necessary to do so. Take a moment right now to notice if it seems like you must be inside a home to accomplish your work. Assess yourself right now. Does it seem like a rule and, if so, does that rule still feel right for you now? If it feels troublesome, please take this moment to push past that rule. It is your intuitive abilities that travel effortlessly across time and space. Your physical body does not need to.

I received a call from an exhausted mother of a three-year-old. She hoped I could help her and her son. I expected her to describe some terrible illness or disease, but instead the young mother told me her son is too happy. His happiness, as she put it, really was not the best for him. Every night, her three-year-old stayed up most of the night laughing and playing. She described his exhaustion but also added that her son is "sick all the time." If this behavior continued, the little boy would probably become more critically ill.

Before I intuitively check in with children, I ask them for permission no matter their age. I also inform the parents that I must ask their child for permission before I proceed. I tell the parents that if their child says no, I have to honor their choice. Most parents will push you to ignore the child's refusal. If the child does refuse the help, which would be very unusual, I quickly check for interfering negative forces that are much more aggressive than the child's quieter soul energy. In this case, I received a big "yes" from this enthusiastic three-year-old boy.

Young children tend to communicate through images rather than verbal information. When I sent my laser beam out to the three-year-old boy, I received a visual of a female child who appeared to be about the boy's age. Together they showed me how they sit in the boy's bedroom and throw toys at each other. I heard them laughing and saw toys flying. I was chuckling too until I noticed an energetic cord connecting them together. The child in spirit was very playful, but at the same time she was drawing energy from my three-year-old client. This explained why the mother reported that he became sick all the time. While the midnight hours playing were taxing, the cording was funneling his energy away. This jovial little spirit-child was unintentionally pulling on her playmate's life essence.

I received all this information in just a few split seconds of my initial check-in. When I shared this first piece of intuitive information, the mother gasped for air. She said her son had a female twin who did not live. We were both covered with goose bumps.

Generally, a spirit person who has yet to make their transformation into the Light is aware of nothing but the burdens that plagued them in the physical realm. They are simply full of their own unresolved issues from a past life and the recent life they just left. Most of the time, the spirit person does not realize they are affecting your client in any way (We will talk about spirit people deliberately harming a living person in chapter 11). They are confused or holding on to emotions, sensations, or personal possessions they had in the physical realm. Some spirit people may continue to crave the feelings of drugs or alcohol, while others unknowingly carry the vibration of the disease that caused their death.

People in spirit who have not made their transition into the Light will appear more like a physical person. As a result, they usually appear more solid or dense and often feel gloomy or somewhat depressed. The vibrations of the disease, drugs, or unresolved conflicts that the spirit person is clinging to can transfer to a living individual. For example, if the spirit person was in the depth of depression at the time of their death, they will be drawn to a living person who is also depressed. The frequency of depression will become even more established for both of them. This detrimental relationship may cause the living individual to become depressed to the point of suicide. Here is another situation in which a living person was dramatically affected by a spirit person:

A spiritually aware friend of mine told me about the death of a family member. At the moment of death, Nancy, another distraught family member, threw herself over the top of the dying person. Even as early as the funeral, Nancy seemed very different to the family. She became very involved with the belongings of the dead family member. She asked if she could have the clothes of the deceased and began wearing them right away. Her mannerisms changed, closely resembling the family member whom they had just lost. Three months later, Nancy became ill with the same disease that caused the death of their family member. In this true story, the deceased person probably had no idea she had just died and slipped into another human body. Undoubtedly, she was simply trying to be herself.

The death transition is a sacred moment that can always be shared together. As you hold the hand of your loved one, do not become afraid of this happening to you. Continue to be an integral part of this blessed experience, but do not interfere with the soul's transition. The alive and vibrant soul energy, beyond a doubt, is rising upward and out of the physical body at the time of death. Give them room to rise up to the Blessed Light. This is such an important yet unknown point that I now discuss this event in my workshops so that others can pass on this valuable piece of information.

We have choices after death just like we have choices in the physical realm. Many spirit people know they are in a nonphysical form but are afraid to go on to the Light or feel they do not deserve a place there, so they make the choice to remain here. When they do this, they may clutch onto the first person they come across, or a familiar environment. More frequently, they affix to a person who emotionally or physically feels similar to what the spirit person is feeling. The spirit person will often link into an area of the living person's body that is significant to the cause of their own death, or to their old lifestyle. A twenty-three-year-old female college-student client offers a perfect example.

Amber walked into my office for her intuitive mentoring session. She informed me that she had severe symptoms of a sexually transmitted disease. Amber said she had been to her doctor repeatedly, but despite her obvious physical symptoms, all tests came back negative. Amber also admitted to feeling depressed and having suicidal thoughts. She told me her grades were going down and she was losing her high grade point average.

Some clients will go on to say they have seen every medical specialist in the area or have even been tested in famous medical clinics to no avail. When clients tell you they have had many medical tests with many doctors and no one finds anything medically wrong, you are hearing typical signs of negative nonphysical-spirit interference. Take the next step and check their body and energy field for some level of entity interference.

The second that Amber asked me to scan her field, I saw the spirit form of a beautiful young blonde woman standing behind her. I now had two clients. This young woman in spirit showed me many bars and many men. She revealed her internal battles in her shortened life of alcohol, men, and a great deal of sex. After sharing this information with Amber, I told her I was going to ask the blonde woman some questions, and I wanted Amber to accept any thoughts or images that jumped into her awareness and then share the information with me.

I asked the young woman why she was holding on to Amber, and if she realized she was making Amber ill. She told Amber she had no idea she was affecting Amber's health in any way. She saw Amber walk into a bar that she considered her hangout and rushed up to Amber with the intent of making a new friend. I asked the spirit person how long she had been with Amber, and she said about three months. That is when my client's mouth fell open with surprise. She informed me she was in a bar about three months ago, and that was when her sexually transmitted disease symptoms began. Amber had not felt well since.

I directed my thoughts and questions out loud again to the spirit person, strongly emphasizing she was making her host ill. I reminded her that she was an entirely separate and different person from this host. I told her she deserved to succeed and flourish. I asked the spirit person and my client to help me call in spirit guides who are perfect in assisting this young woman in her transition. I did so, then paused to allow the client and the spirit time to participate. I then asked how many guides came to help. I heard them both say "three."

I asked, on the spirit person's behalf, for specialty guides to come to the spirit person and assist her to release the hold and to move beyond the Earth plane. In a strong but kind voice, I directed the spirit to turn and focus all her attention on the guides. I asked her if she could feel their love. Without responding to my question, she lifted up and away with them. At the same time, I asked Amber to deliberately feel the spirit disconnecting and to send the spirit out of her body. Two weeks later, Amber walked in with a smile and said the painful symptoms had completely left her within twenty-four hours.

Case Study:
Getting in Charge of the Spirit People Around You

This case has it all. It begins with medical and emotional inform-ation regarding this client. The focus then changes to fear of her mediumship abilities. We then become aware of the need to help release a person in spirit who is negatively affecting the living client. This session includes teaching as well as healing for both the spirit and the client.

Practice Experience:
Imagine you are the medical intuitive speaking the words in this transcript. Read it aloud or, if possible, with a study buddy, one taking part as the medical intuitive and one as the client. Practice this session as if you are actually giving these steps to someone who needs your guidance.

TZ: When I look at your energy field, instantly, there is very low energy around your neck and your throat, and it signifies that you're holding back, or holding something down. When I see it this way, it signifies suppressing your individual expression and not speaking your personal truth. It could be very simple things like you are in the mood for seafood and the other person wants to go for pizza, or something simple like that.

Client: Yes.

TZ: Okay, that makes sense to you? It can even be little things, or big things like not sharing something with your partner. This area has low energy, but every once in a while a bunch of anger comes rushing out of you. You are holding back, holding back, then like a pressure cooker, you blow.

Client: Yeah.

TZ: Now it *(anger)* is blowing out of the left side of your neck and throat, and then the left side of your body. The left side of our bodies tends to be about characteristics of being female, or issues concerning a female in your life. And then it kind of blows out in that direction. Okay. I'm just checking with my guides. I need to ask you to let people know what you're thinking or feeling. No one will fall over when you do it. I don't see people falling over. If anything, you feel pretty private. Whenever I *(intuitively)* ask you if it is okay to look at your thyroid, a privacy keeps popping up around you. I cannot get past it, and no psychic can get through it either. Is it okay to let me in to check out your throat?

Client: Yes.

TZ: There is somebody telling you they don't know you very well because of this privacy thing. You are hesitant to share your deeper thoughts. Somebody feels like they do not know you. They are in your recent past or your current life. Now, all that being said, I am pulled down to your entire lower intestinal tract.

Client: Okay.

TZ: I think I'm going to need to talk about your female organs and large intestine. I also need to ask . . . do you feel like your heart jumps a little bit?

Client: Yeah, it's been doing it a lot more recently. I didn't know if it was anxiety.

(Give the information to them before they tell you anything. This will boost your credibility.)

TZ: Don't tell me anything else you think it would be. Let me see your intestine and then we'll go to your heart . . . Now, in your intestine, there are red lines of irritation. Let's look at your colon. It, too, is a little bit inflamed. Would you say that you have problems with constipation and then diarrhea?

Client: Yeah.

TZ: Well, there is a little bit of ballooning. That is how I can tell you get constipated. It's a little too wide in one place, and it's lost some of its elasticity. I'm hearing *(from spirit)* to take a little bit of aloe vera juice.

Client: Okay.

TZ: It will be very soothing for your entire intestinal tract. I see you taking just a tablespoon, and if that is too much, just cut back to a teaspoonful.

Let's go back to your heart. I want to check that out while it's still jumping around. Did you actually feel it jump around at the same time I said that I felt it?

Client: It's doing it right now.

TZ: Give it a little more time here. Has anyone ever said you have a murmur?

Client: Not that I know of.

TZ: Okay. I want you to check this out with your doctor. You might have a little bit of a murmur too. I don't hear it, but I see it. It's not to worry about. It feels like you may be depleted of magnesium and potassium. It feels like you are dehydrated. Are you dehydrated? Do you drink very much fluid?

Client: Coffee.

TZ: Do you know that coffee is a diuretic? It actually makes you go to the bathroom. That is why my mouth is getting drier and drier. That is my signal that you are dehydrated. Again, you are low on potassium and magnesium. It looks like you may even be low in sodium. You can take all these in individual capsules, but if you get a good mineral supplement with all those minerals, you can take one of those. It would help you.

Let's see if there is anything more with the organ of your heart. You know that old saying, when life gives you lemons make lemonade? You have been doing that, only you are making a butterfly out of some life situations. You are trying to rise up. I actually see this butterfly developing energetically around your heart. So, that tells me you are trying to take a painful situation and actually learn from it. That is fitting, isn't it?

Client: Yes.

TZ: I can see your emotion about it. You are really doing it, or I couldn't see it show up like this butterfly. I see it even though you are a bit hidden. You have been hidden and not speaking some of your truth to somebody in your recent past. I see him standing over there. *(I point to a place in the room.)*

Client: Well, I had a falling out with my dad about four years ago, and I haven't spoken to him since. It was a bad fight. I've been feeling like I'm ready to move past that now. I also could see things that other people could not see.

(This client just transitioned from her intuitive abilities to her fear of it.)

TZ: Well, maybe it *(her intuitive abilities)* wasn't positive for you.

Client: It scared me a lot. So, my family—my mom, my grandma, and I—did a ceremony so I wouldn't see stuff until I was ready. And I feel like I've been trying to see. Maybe that is the hidden part. I have been trying to block it out, and maybe it's kind of coming to me now.

TZ: It feels like you are closed down. Every time I check something out for you, I feel like I need to ask for permission again and again. You are hidden. You are closed up for whatever reason. It could have been their ceremony. Let me check and see what I get about that. *(Pause.)* I get something around seven years old. They are telling me that through your mom's eyes, or your eyes, there was a battle between the good and the bad, the dark forces and the bright, like Harry Potter. Does that make sense to you? What about seven years old stands out to you?

Client: Well, that probably would have been when we did it *(the ceremony)*. I was seven.

TZ: Okay, yes.

Client: I would see different things, like airplanes or something. My daughter is two and a half, and she is starting to see airplanes in her room. And I didn't even know she knew what an airplane was. She says it's always white and it has wings. I think that's what brought it up, because she is seeing things like me. People's voices are yelling at me too.

TZ: Do you want to keep this tapped down, keep this contained? You are very contained.

Client: Part of me doesn't. It scares me.

TZ: You keep validating the things I say to you. Do you see auras and things like that?

Client: I haven't in a while. When I was little I used to.

TZ: Sure. Most little kids do. Kids will draw their cat green and the teacher will say, "Your cats are not green." Kids then begin to think, "Oh, okay. I must be wrong."

Client: Yeah. The problem I'm having right now is that there is so much chatter in my head I can't hear my own guidance. I feel like I can't hear my guidance over my own thoughts. Or maybe I can't tell the difference between the two.

(Always incorporate teaching your clients to take charge of their energy.)

TZ: Yes, I'd agree with that. So, who is doing all the yelling at you? Does it feel like lots of different people? Does it feel like it is coming from a guide? What does it feel like?

Client: It feels like different people.

TZ: One of the things I teach people is to get in charge of all the spirit people around us and to get in charge of our own energy field, to be more in command of it. A friend of mine opened up to all this and he was actually bombarded. I mean bombarded. Everybody was yelling at him. I want you to tell them *(the talkative spirit people)* to get in line and come to you one at a time. I want you to create some rules. Whatever rules you want.

I'll just share one of my rules. Because I have a foot in the physical world and one in the nonphysical world twenty-four hours a day, spirit people contact me quite frequently. I internally say to them, "I have to sleep at night. I am going to bed. I am still in the physical realm and I need my sleep. Everybody out of here and be quiet until morning, and then I can speak with you." People in spirit are still real people too, and because of that, they will do what you ask them to do. So, what might be your rules or guidelines if you open up to this? What do you want as guidelines for yourself and for people in spirit?

Client: Probably one at a time. Because a lot of times, like yesterday, it was yelling and there was an old woman waving a blue flag. There was so much yelling I couldn't really make sense of anything.

TZ: Exactly. Tell them this does not make any sense to you, so knock it off. Tell them you want them to all line up one at a time. This could be your first guideline you give to them. So, you are already getting a lot of information. I do think this is about you being hidden. You are trying to keep it closed down in your throat too . . . try not to speak about it.

Client: Yes.

TZ: Yes, yes, yes! What else might be a guideline for you? I'll tell you another one of mine. I don't want to see anyone when I get up to go to the bathroom at night. I think it's creepy.

Client: *(Laughing.)*

TZ: I love talking about this stuff. They *(spirit people)* know this is one of my guidelines. I have never seen anybody when I go to the bathroom. They know it is one of my guidelines.

Client: That's why, when I was little, I was so scared.

TZ: Yes. You were not in charge.

Client: I have a terrible fear of being by myself, and my husband travels a lot for work. I've had anxiety attacks because I'm so afraid I'm going to see something. I've made it more fear-based.

TZ: Yes. It's because you did not know you can be in charge of it. And they will comply because they are still real people. They are just so eager to connect with people who are mediums. We intuitives stand out like a big candle to people in spirit. They know they can tell their story to you, you can hear them, and you can see them. Get in charge. Jot down your rules and repeat them in the morning, and repeat them when your husband leaves on one of his trips. Feel that you are in charge of this. State the rules as a command.

Client: Yeah, I've never really looked at it that way before.

TZ: It's imperative that you do.

Client: Okay.

TZ: Especially because you are bombarded. Now, remember that you told me you and your child are seeing airplanes? I'm seeing into your child's room right now and I am seeing fairies, not airplanes. They are real too. I am seeing little Tinkerbell-type fairies. Very bright and jumping around. When you said that around seven years old your mom and grandma felt like a battle with dark and light was going on? Where does that take you in your memories?

Client: Part of what scared me was that my grandma's an intuitive and palm reader. Part of what scared me is, she had a friend who had a very hard life and the friend came to stay with us. My grandma lived with us and the friend came to stay with us too. Then my grandma got demons. She couldn't sleep at night. They would shake her bed and we found piles of . . . I don't know what.

TZ: You mean stuff you couldn't identify?

Client: Yes. I don't know what it was. But she had a really hard time with these demons. She found somebody who got rid of them.

TZ: I want you to know that I checked in with you when you were around seven years old. My guides gave me some information. I saw a dark human form back behind you. Then a gigantic, beautiful, glowing angelic form. I was told and shown that there was a great battle between the Dark and the Light, but the Light was much bigger and more powerful. Please hear that. Now, depending on what direction you want to go with your time here, we can talk about what to do with the dark, because it exists.

Client: Okay.

TZ: I can help you out instantly. About 99 percent of the time, what is called "demons" or "evil" is really just people in the spirit realm. Their body has died and they are messed up, sleepy, or groggy. Some were nasty people when they were here on Earth. They are sometimes confused from doing drugs. They still feel drugged even though they have left their body. So, 99 percent of the time it is just dead people who are very messed up.

Now, if you can really hang on to the information I have given you, the fear will subside. Give spirit people instructions like I do. Talk with them and work with them. We can actually help them.

Client: Some of the darkness around me, I might be doing to myself. Is that what you're saying? You see it?

TZ: Yes, I see it.

Client: Okay.

TZ: But please hear the rest of it. The dark form is right here, but the bright form is four feet above your head and much more powerful than the dark. Say more about what you know about this dark form.

(You are now the medical intuitive for your client and also for the person in spirit.)

Client: Well, is this from when I was seven or would this be in the now?

TZ: Oh, that's a good question. Let me ask . . . I keep hearing now, now, now. It feels kind of agitated. You have been calling for help, have you not?

Client: Yes, I have.

TZ: The help is there. They are keeping it *(the dark form)* under control, or contained or something. It's not gone.

Client: Well, about two or three months ago, I got this strange sensation in my head, and I immediately knew it was something weird. I've had headaches, and I thought I may be having an aneurysm or something. I called my husband just because it was the strangest thing I have ever felt. The whole way to the hospital I'm thinking I am going to die. I don't know why, it was just this strange sensation. I had a CAT scan and an MRI.

TZ: They didn't find anything, did they?

Client: No. I had convinced myself that I had MS. I'm normally not a crier and I just sat around crying. I felt a darkness come over me, and all of a sudden I started telling my husband I'm going to die soon. He tells me to snap out of this. I feel like maybe there's darkness around me because I have scared myself into thinking I'm going to die.

TZ: Well, terror and fear is a very strong vibration, and it draws people in spirit who are still living in that realm. When we die, we don't become angels and things like that. We pretty much pass on as who we are and with the current level of awareness. So, people who had a terrible life pass on with that same low level of awareness. They hang around, with little awareness, instead of moving on. Now, do you remember I said it is right behind you? You already know it is corded into your head?

Client: Well, it doesn't surprise me at all.

(*Remember, energetic cording into someone's head is about controlling the person who is alive.*)

TZ: Okay, let's do something about this. It will just feel like you're dreaming it up, but I'm going to ask it questions. You listen and tell me what it answers, and how it answers. It has allowed for us to be aware of it and for me to see it. I'm going to ask it if it knows itself as male or female. Just see how it answers and tell me what you get.

Client: "Female."

TZ: I'm wondering . . . Are you still aware of your name? Would you tell us your name?

Client: "Angela" . . . "Angelina," maybe?

TZ: Angelina, are you aware that you are not in the physical world anymore? Do you realize your body has actually died?

Client: "Yes."

TZ: Okay. What drew you to my client? How is it that you became of aware of her?

Client: "Anger."

TZ: Okay. So are you saying, Angelina, that you were angry in life?

Client: "Yes."

TZ: Do you have a sense of how long you've been around my client?

Client: "Two years."

TZ: Do you think, Angelina, that you might be the reason for my client's strange feelings in her head and the pain?

Client: "No."

TZ: You're not really aware of it, then. What do you get from hanging out with her? What happens?

(Now a surprising turn of events happens.)

Client: I keep hearing "guidance." That doesn't make sense.

TZ: Okay, tell us more about what you mean by guidance?

Client: "Guiding her to her path."

TZ: Angelina, I want you to notice if you are the very large light being behind my client, or are you actually the smaller shorter darker figure?

Client: "Light."

TZ: Well, Angelina, are you aware of the dark figure who apparently is not speaking?

Client: "Yes."

TZ: Are you trying to help my client in regard to that dark figure?

Client: "Yes."

TZ: Angelina, have you been in human form yourself in the past, or are you from a different realm?

Client: "No, I have not been human."

TZ: Would you consider yourself to be from the angelic realm?

Client: "Yes."

TZ: I'm wondering if you would help us out with the dark figure, who so far has been quiet?

Client: "Yes."

TZ: Let's ask the dark figure to show itself and see what it gets by connecting in with my client.

Client: The letter T. That's all I'm getting.

TZ: So, the dark figure . . . are you telling us your name is T?

Client: "Tony."

TZ: Thank you, Tony. Well, Tony, are you aware that we have been talking with the angel that's around you?

Client: "Yes."

TZ: How long have you been aware of that?

Client: "Four months."

TZ: Okay. And how is it that you came to this person?

Client: "Destruction."

TZ: Tony, are you aware that you do not have a physical body at this time?

Client: "No."

TZ: Is it something about destruction in your own life, Tony?

Client: "Yes."

TZ: Okay, that makes sense. Thank you. Do you, Tony, have any awareness of affecting my client in a negative way?

Client: "Yes."

TZ: I'm wondering . . . do you realize you really are a separate being in and of yourself, and that you are actually male connected into a female in the living?

Client: "No."

TZ: Okay, I want you, in your own way, Tony, to start noticing that you are actually a totally different and separate being in and of yourself, and just notice it. I'm going to ask my client to notice how she is also separate. And Tony, I want to ask you to realize that you have not moved on to the Light and that you actually do not have your own physical body right now.

Client: "No."

TZ: Okay, so you are not aware of that? You are actually connected in with a female body when you are male.

Client: I don't hear anything.

TZ: What I'm picking up, Tony, is that you are thinking about and considering it. Tell my client if that is accurate.

Client: "Yes."

TZ: I am glad you are thinking about it. I am wondering if you believe me. Do you know that there is a much, much better life for you to live and grow that has nothing to do with my client?

Client: "Yes."

TZ: Okay. I'm calling in now on your behalf, Tony, specialists who are coming in right now to assist you in this transition and to keep you very, very safe; to keep you very, very intact; and to help you to completely leave my client. I want you to start paying more attention to your specialists than to me. In other words, turn it over to your specialists and notice them. I want you to count and tell us how many specialty guides you are aware of right now.

Client: "Seven."

TZ: Excellent, very good, very good. I want you to notice the feel of them too. There is no scariness about them. They do specialize in assisting people like you. See what you notice about them.

Client: He says, "White, white light."

TZ: Notice that the more you pay attention to them, the better you feel. Just take your time. I am asking them to make sure every element, every fragment, every tendril that is really of you releases now out of my client. So you have your full transformation . . . feeling lighter and lighter, more and more wonderful. *(To my client)* And I am asking you to say out loud whatever you are aware of. Just check it out for yourself and see what you are aware of.

Client: I feel like there is white circling me. I feel like my head is pulled back a little bit.

TZ: I am calling in specialists just to make sure that every single element of Tony goes with Tony.

Tony. And Tony, turn it over to this love. In fact, I'm wondering if you notice the love yet, Tony?

Client: "Yes."

TZ: Very good. And just the lifting up and lifting away in a complete, very, very clean release, up and out. Tony, turn it over to your specialists. *(To the client)* I ask you to call in your own specialists to clean out every remnant, every tendril, just cleansing you, cleansing you, very clean and clear, light, and bright. And what are you *(the client)* noticing now about that?

Client: I feel lighter.

TZ: Okay, really allow the healing specialists to come in and completely heal you. I need to keep saying the word "clean," just healing and cleaning. I want you to notice any distance between you and Tony now. See what you notice about that.

Client: I feel like he is moving away.

TZ: Yes, he is. Pulling out, just pulling out everything that is him. And Tony, pay more and more attention to the Light and Love from all the specialists who are there for you. I want you to notice feeling much more alive as you continue on.

(Involving the client keeps them from remaining a victim.)

TZ: *(To the client)* I'm particularly noticing your thoracic vertebrae 4 and 5, which is straight through from your spine to your heart. I want you to let healing guides come in and clean up your heart and vertebrae 4 and 5. Insist that the healers cleanse the back of your head, and inside of your head, and to fill your head with Light and Love and compassion . . . very soothing. I want you to let me know when you feel like it's complete. Make sure that all aspects of that separate being are completely gone. Trust yourself as you notice.

Client: *(Long pause.)* Okay.

TZ: Excellent. Filling you up, keeping you safe, Light, and Love, and opening your eyes when it feels just right to you. *(Pause.)* Where are your thoughts going?

Client: I feel a lot lighter.

TZ: I'll bet.

Client: I feel like I can breathe a little bit easier.

TZ: The air in the room is lighter.

Client: I feel like maybe I've known that he was there but didn't want to admit it.

TZ: Yes, you did.

Client: I didn't want to acknowledge it because I was afraid of what it was.

TZ: So, hopefully you can really reframe what used to be fearful about this stuff. People in spirit are almost always just messed-up people who are hanging on for dear life because they do not know what else to do. He could have been a lot nastier and I would have still done the same thing. He could have been a demon-like thing and, energetically, I would still do the same process.

Client: Okay.

(Bring the session back full circle to address the original issue.)

TZ: I ask you to use your imagination right now, and pretend you are in the house by yourself and your husband is on a trip.

Client: I see, when I close my eyes, a white outline of somebody but it has wings.

TZ: Yes. Ask it if it is Angelina, I think was her name.

Client: "Yes."

TZ: Excellent. I also want you to be the boss and to give commands in a loving way. You need to get in charge. Tell them *(people in spirit)* what you want them to do. If you want everybody to leave the house, then tell them that. They will do it. Make sure you do not send Angelina out of the house though.

Client: Okay.

TZ: Our words are very, very important. If we give vague commands, then we get back vague responses. If we stay very precise, precise things will happen. Our words are full of energy. Listen to this recording again and again. I think you will hear yourself say something, or I may say something that will be important. Get in charge. Start today when you go home.

Client: Okay.

My guides did not tell me to address the energetic cord between Tony and my client. Apparently, that was not a primary focus in healing this situation, but it would need to be addressed in the near future. Sometimes the specific removal of energetic cords is a critical factor in the healing experience. Cords can exist not only between a needy spirit person and an individual in the physical, but also between two or more physically alive people as well.

Healing Technique Levels 1–2:
Negative Thought Forms and Confused or
Afraid People in Spirit

1. Tell the client you will ask the spirit person/thought form questions, but they are to receive the spirit's answers and tell you what thoughts leap into their minds. This engages the client with their own healing process.

2. Ask the person in spirit questions to create a sense of relationship with them. This engages the spirit person in their own recovery. As your living client receives the spirit's information, the living client will realize the cause of their own struggles and what led the spirit person to connect with them in the first place.

3. Call in Divine and Sacred guides who specialize in transformation of this spirit person.

4. After a brief pause, now direct the spirit person to count the specialists who have come for them. This engages the spirit but also begins their own sense of making positive choices and feeling empowered.

5. Direct the spirit person to feel the love emanating from these guides and to turn their care over to the guides.

6. Your living client must consciously and completely release the spirit that has been affecting them. Ask them to actively send the spirit person out of their body and energy field. (Many clients will selfishly refuse to send the spirit away. Do not accept this. Tell them they are interfering with the transformation the spirit person absolutely deserves.)

7. When something leaves, the medical intuitive as well as the client always need to request the most compassionate Light, Love, and healing to come in and fill every single space and place where the spirit used to be. This is a powerful key for permanent healing.

8. Invite a specialty guide who excels in cleaning and clearing to create the ideal cleansing filter for you to return through to maintain perfect health for you.

9. Deliberately and consciously pull your energetic laser beam back from the client and the experience through the filter. You may feel the filter, or you may actually see it working. You can assist yourself by inhaling and imagining each inhalation pulls your energy back to you through that filter.

10. At the same time, command: "I now bring me—and only me—back to myself, clean and clear through a perfect filter provided for me by my Divine cleansing specialist."

Essential Points

- Negative thought forms are not actual living entities but are burdensome physical objects that are destructive to the human.

- Your clients are the only ones who can get in charge of their thoughts and emotions.

- It is paramount that you quickly sense if the person in spirit is causing illness or attempting to comfort your client.

- Inform your client whatever, or whomever, you perceive without judgment.

- We humans must understand that the power of our thoughts may have negative consequences with entities of the nonphysical realm.

- Once the nonphysical being agrees to become your client, you move forward in the session just like you would for a person sitting in your office.

- It is your intuitive abilities that travel effortlessly across time and space. Your physical body does not need to.

- Young children tend to communicate through images rather than verbal information.

- The vibrations of the disease, drugs, or unresolved conflicts that the spirit person is clinging to can transfer to a living individual.

- When you are with a loved one who is dying, do not interfere with the soul's transition.

- When clients tell you they have had many medical tests with many doctors and no one finds anything medically wrong, you are hearing typical signs of negative nonphysical-spirit interference.

- Get in charge of your own energy field and all the spirit people around you.

Chapter 11

Nonphysical Entities Causing Illness or Life Struggles: Levels 3 and 4

Level 3: People in Spirit: Angry and Possessive

Again, for teaching purposes, I am describing people in spirit by the levels of interference they create with living people. Chapter 9 described the confused and afraid people in spirit as well as the heavy burden of negative thought forms. This chapter describes people in spirit who are angry and possessive. The primary difference between these two groups is their high level of negative emotions. But even worse, angry and possessive people in spirit deliberately interfere with living humans.

These are the individuals who living people usually declare are trapped on Earth. The living people who declare this are generally on ghost-chasing television shows and often yell out challenging remarks, trying to provoke spirit people. It also makes any reaction from spirit people seem that it must certainly be evil or satanic. While all that is going on, I often perceive a male or female spirit person who is just trying to keep their house or precious possessions for themselves. They might be worried that someone will find money they had stashed while in the living. Yes, they are full of emotion and powerful concentrations of focused thought. The fact that energy follows thought still holds true in the nonphysical sphere. "As above, so below."

If this level of spirit people are trapped, it is because they have trapped themselves within their own thought and emotional processes. Their focus may revolve around a certain person, an emotional event, an object, a building, or even a sensation such as drugs or alcohol. Fear or guilt of facing God will bring a halt to a person's evolution as well. I do not see this as necessarily trapped, but they certainly do seem to be focused on the Earth plane because of the intensity of their emotions and thoughts. They are people who also function at a low level of conscious awareness.

I walked into my waiting room looking for Karen, who was scheduled for my next appointment. I found four people in the waiting room and did not see Karen until I looked again. She appeared so different that I hadn't recognized her at first glance. Karen's body, especially her face, seemed too large, round, and puffy. In my office, she dropped down into the chair. She declared she had been irritable and was planning to drop out of college because she was sick of it. As she talked, I continued to be drawn to her face. It was distorted with irritability, self-hatred, hopelessness, and anger.

I asked her if I could watch her energy field as she continued to describe her recent life. I closed my eyes to block out any distractions. An older man stood behind her, wearing black leathers with biker club symbols on the jacket and a bandanna holding back his long, gray hair. He stood with his arms folded across his wide chest, scowling at me. I described all this to her and explained he was the cause of all her recent changes. Karen was surprised but believed me and wanted to get rid of him.

I told her it would be wise to find out why he had attached to her in the first place, and for how long. She agreed, and the biker spirit person agreed at the same time. He was attracted to her when she walked into a bar that he considered home. He was trying to continue on with life as he knew it. He knew he had died but was afraid to move on from the bar. He did not know what to expect if he left that familiar environment. He had led a hard, aggressive life and felt he did not deserve to go to heaven. He knew about women and liked the feel of dominating them, so off he went to control Karen. His hostile belligerency eclipsed Karen's kind manner and her goal of a college degree. He stood so closely within her energy field that his assertive controlling traits were entangled with Karen's. He was so enmeshed in her energetic essence that she was actually beginning to resemble his physical traits.

The biker man was not the devil or satanic. Despite his fearsome persona, he was afraid he did not deserve to go to the Light due to his life of aggression, knife fights, drugs, drinking, and living on the wild side. He was attempting to hang on to something resembling his former life rather than facing the unknown. This man's negative life held a heavy, dense vibration and was pulling Karen down into it. While this interference by a person in spirit is common, it certainly is not nourishing or positive for the living human and, in general, there is at least a draining effect on your client, and in this case, Karen was also losing her values and personal identity.

Case Study:
Giving Away One's Empowerment to a Spirit Person

I had just informed my client that far back in her past she had completely lost her sense of self. It left her powerless, and even today she was emotionally raw as if the situation had happened recently.

I then asked her, "What instantly jumps into your mind when I ask you this? When and how did you lose your sense of self? Please do not censor your answer."

She said her ex-husband abandoned her forty years ago with a toddler while she was pregnant with their second child. She added that her ex-husband died two years ago. She and her two adult children were at his side as he passed. My client went on to tell me that she never told her children she had divorced him.

This woman's emotions still felt openly raw to me, as if her husband's affair happened last week and not forty years ago.

"It also feels to me that one particular memory keeps coming up in your mind more than any other," I continued. I asked her to go back to that memory and give him back his responsibility. I told her to literally take out of her body anything that was truly his.

"You do not need to carry his junk or mess from his actions any longer," I said. "It is his to have and to learn from."

There was a long period of silence as she took this weighty energy out of her field. I then asked her to take back from him all that he took from her, and to take back to herself all that she gave away to him.

As she began to take her own empowerment back into herself, I clearly saw a man's shadowy form take a step forward as he walked right out of this woman's body. I had no perception prior to that moment that he had been living within her body and her energy field. I questioned my guides, who informed me that her ex-husband could no longer stay connected to her because she was instantly strengthening her own self-love and self-respect while doing this healing technique. He had to leave her because she no longer held the same subservient vibration he needed. I noticed he simply stood about three feet in front of her as if he did not know what else to do. I called in specialists for him to guide his transition into the Light.

In this case, the man deliberately chose to remain in a situation he helped create. In other words, rather than moving forward in his own development, he stayed within his ex-wife's field where he felt comfort and familiarity. He was also constantly drawing energy from her and keeping her forever in a raw state of emotion. My client's weakened field allowed this man to continue his abuse of her. He continued the ultimate abandonment and betrayal until this healing practically ejected him from her body and energy field. She immediately looked younger and refreshed.

Case Study:
Angry and Possessive Spirit People Affecting Breathing

This case study provides actual dialogue clearly demonstrating specific steps to release and heal everyone involved. The study provides different ways to address clients and spirit beings who are reluctant to release their connection. This session is longer than other cases. It begins with two clients: a mother and her thirteen-year-old son, Adam. Both are energetically aware people. Both are aware of some type of negative influence in Adam's life. It became evident during the session that there was more than one entity involved.

Practice Experience:

Imagine you are the medical intuitive speaking the words in this transcript. Read it aloud or, if possible, with a study buddy, one taking part as the medical intuitive and one as the client. Practice this session as if you are actually giving these steps to someone who needs your guidance.

TZ: Do not tell me anything about yourself, if that is okay. I will close my eyes and open my eyes a whole bunch. I close my eyes so I can just see your energy. All right, so let me sit in quiet for just a minute while I check in with you. I am looking around, going from head to toe. Around your head I see red shooting lines, for lack of another word, especially on the left side of your head and a little bit on the right side of your head also. There is not a lot of energy in your head or your throat area. Give me a second and let me look there also. There is too much energy coming out of your heart. It is leaking out of you from your back, behind your heart. Your lungs are also a bit diminished. I keep hearing "inflammation." There is inflammation going on inside of you and inside your head.

(Asking for permission throughout the session allows the client to relax and open up.)

TZ: You both nodded *(Adam and his mother).* What I see between your brain and your skull is inflammation. May I look at your whole spinal cord and your whole back? Just let me look. Well, your entire spinal column looks inflamed also. Has this been your normal way of breathing?

(Adam did not seem to breathe for long periods of time and then suddenly gasps for breath making loud gulping sounds.)

Client: For about two months. Two months is when it all started. *(Gasping for breath.)*

(A sudden onset of strange symptoms may be a red flag that the person is affected by negative interference to some degree.)

Mother: It really intensified, but it's really been going on since the fourth grade.

TZ: I have a whole gang of helpers here. You know, guides and angels. Let me check with them . . . Do you remember around fourth grade if there were some really hurtful moments that happened?

Mom: *(Speaking to her son)* You can say whatever.

Client: Well, when it first started I always kind of blamed Dad because that is when everyone passed away and stuff.

Mom: Quite a few people died that year.

Client: But I can remember since I was little, my dad is kind of angry. He's not physically abusive but he's pretty emotionally abusive, and that's been kind of hard on me. That's the only time that it *(constant loud, gasping breaths)* got worse that I can remember.

TZ: I am getting people with a lot of emotion, and that's kind of what you are saying too. I said you have a big leak in your chest. We do not want to be leaking. It is like a tire on a car; we don't want the tire to be leaking. So, does it actually feel like you have a hard time getting the air into your lungs?

Client: It's just different from when it started.

TZ: I don't doubt it. My angels are saying you are struggling to move forward in life. Whenever we take a breath, it is a signal to our body that we are going to take our next breath of life. We are going to keep living and keep going on. So, tell me what comes up in your mind when I say that.

(Helping mother and client to connect emotional events with the client's physical reaction of constantly gasping for breath.)

Client: I think that's true because sometimes it hurts just to walk, so that make sense. I really can't keep going like this.

TZ: Yes, that is a better way to put it. I am getting that there is a giant amount of emotion that is causing this. Okay? That's one thing. Let me check here for something else. With all the people who you lost during that time, it seems like those people were family.

Client: There were a couple of family members and a really close family friend, and that was really hard for me.

TZ: Who was it?

Mom: An uncle and then our family friend. Right before she passed away, we lost our horse and then we lost our dog.

TZ: I saw you bending over in sadness. Did you literally bend over in sadness? Did you have funerals?

Mom: We did for the dog and then we went to their funerals.

TZ: Did you bend over, like the casket? I just see you bending over in such deep sadness.

(Just then I saw a dark form enter into the client as he bent over something. I did not want to bring up dark forms so early into the session. I was waiting to see if the client or his mother mentioned any level of awareness about negative beings.)

Client: I don't necessarily remember because I was only ten, and I was blaming this on my dad when it started.

Mom: It was just sudden too. Our dog was run over by a car and she was just gone.

TZ: Before all that happened four years ago, you didn't have these struggles then.

Client: I used to be more like a bubbly kid. Then just in the last four years, I've been really kind of quiet, and it's just been really hard. I was outgoing and stuff, and then I started to get fearful of stuff and all that. You know what I realize though? I had that really bad presence and stuff.

Mom: *(Speaking to her son.)* Do you want to tell her about that?

(I now know that the client and his mother are aware of negative beings.)

TZ: Yes, I was hoping you would.

Client: I remember feeling kind of scary and evil things around me, and that was a couple of months ago.

Mom: Yeah.

TZ: Okay. I want you to know that you cannot get too weird for me, okay? This is not weird for me. It is probably weird for you two, but it is not weird for me.

(This statement always encourages people to speak freely about their conscious awareness of negative interference in their lives.)

Mom: He is really open to all this.

TZ: When I saw you *(client)* leaning over something, I also saw a dark thing come into you. Let me ask my guides and see what we might do.

Client: I feel it, I guess. *(Uncontrollable tears.)* I feel like it's always right behind me. And I like—*(More tears.)*

TZ: Do you know that I specialize in this kind of thing? Okay?

Client: I don't think it's crazy. I think it's really cool because for, like, all this time for the past four years I thought I was a dummy for having these things in my head. So, I like that different view on it.

TZ: I see the dark form on your back, even.

Client: Yes!

(Now I engage the client to participate with his own healing. Remember, this client is only thirteen years old.)

TZ: Okay. Would you be willing, if I asked it questions, would you listen and tell me what it says? Just let it have a voice. And you tell me?

Client: *(To his mother.)* Is that okay for me to do?

TZ: *(To client's mother.)* Is that okay?

Mom: *(In an excited voice)* Yes!

TZ: Just go with whatever jumps into your head. I am going to ask it questions, and just say whatever the first thing is that pops into your head. I am going to ask it first if it is a human. I want to know if you are human or are you something else?

Client: I got, "Something else."

TZ: Okay. If you are something else, when did you actually find Adam the first time? How long ago?

Client: I just say what comes into my head?

TZ: Absolutely the first thing.

Client: "Six months ago."

TZ: What attracted you to Adam more than other people? Why come to Adam?

Client: I don't get anything.

TZ: Don't try so hard because it is that being that is talking, so just let it talk. Tell Adam: is it because you don't want us to know, or maybe you don't know what attracted you?

Client: It doesn't know.

TZ: That happens sometimes. I hear that with people. Okay. Do you have a name even though you say you are not human?

Client: You want me to tell you what came in my head?

TZ: Yes

Client: "Sarah."

TZ: Yeah, okay, Sarah. So, Sarah, so are you a female human?

Client: It was more female.

TZ: Sarah, have you ever connected in with any other kids before?

Client: "Yes."

TZ: What are kids about for you?

Client: I don't know why it would say that, but it's like a guidance thing.

(Once communication with an entity is established, focus on how different and separate the client and the entity really are. It is time for everyone involved to have a better life. Focus on and emphasize their differences.)

TZ: Sarah, are you aware that you are actually a separate thing from Adam?

Client: I feel like a lot of times it's on my back or something.

TZ: I am asking Sarah, "Do you know that you are not a thirteen-year-old male?

Client: "Yeah."

TZ: Okay. Sarah, tell Adam where you are connecting into his body.

Client: "Heart."

TZ: Adam, remember when I said you have got a lot of energy coming out of your heart? Okay, Sarah, is there any other place in Adam's body that you are attached?

Client: I got my "heart" and "mind."

TZ: Okay, all right, okay. Sarah, what are you getting out of connecting in with Adam? What do you get out of it?

Client: I get that it's trying to complete something, but I didn't get that at first.

TZ: Sarah and Adam, I want you both to notice that you two are two different things, okay? So, I want you both to feel very separate.

Client: I feel like there is another thing. I know there's another thing.

TZ: There usually is more than one being. So, that doesn't surprise me. You might be surprised.

Client: Its name is John and it is a human.

TZ: So, John is speaking up now. Let's talk to John for a bit. John, how long have you been with Adam?

Client: "Three years."

TZ: Okay, John, do you know that you are not a thirteen-year-old male?

Client: "Yeah."

TZ: Okay. John, how old are you?

Client: "Thirty."

TZ: John, do you know that you do not have a physical body anymore?

Client: "Uh-huh."

TZ: John, I want you to realize you are a thirty-year-old man and that you are separate from a thirteen-year-old male. And Adam, I want you to feel and know you are separate from him. And just start to feel that. No right way or wrong way. And John, I am calling in some angels and guides to help you to come out of Adam. You are a male; you are a separate being. I want you to look around and tell Adam how many guides or angels have come to help you.

Client: "Eight."

TZ: Okay.

Client: When we've been talking to John, Sarah feels like she is on my back or something. When we are talking to him, I feel it a lot right here *(points to his head)*.

TZ: John, tell Adam how you died.

Client: "Car accident."

TZ: And where were you injured in your own body, John?

Client: "Head."

TZ: John, I am asking you to really look at your eight angels because you were very clear that there are eight of them. I want you to let them help you because they specialize in helping people, like you, to release out of Adam. You are not a thirteen-year-old boy. You are a very, very separate thirty-year-old man.

Client: I feel like he wants to go, but he is worried, but says he wants to go.

TZ: They do get worried sometimes.

Client: I really feel pain when he is talking. *(Points at his head again.)*

(Be assertive and direct both clients, the living one and the nonphysical one, to take each step you ask them to take. Tell them again they are to follow your directives.)

TZ: Yes. He was really injured there in his car wreck. Okay, John, I want you to know that you are doing harm to Adam, and it is time for you to release out of him because your specialists have come to help you. They specialize in males who have been in car wrecks, and they are there to help you. No judgment.

Client: I feel like I'm going to fall down. I don't know why.

TZ: Now, Adam, you have to be willing to let him go too. He is a thirty-year-old man. He needs to go.

(Many clients do not want the entity to leave. Do not argue with the living or the deceased clients. Insist they are both being harmed and they must do this for each other.)

Client: I feel like he wants me to do something.

TZ: I am telling you what to do. He doesn't know what to do. That is why he has been attached to you. He doesn't know what to do. So, I want you to let him disconnect and let him go on his way. They are going to take care of him. He is already lifting up and out of you.

Client: Oh! I can feel it. I know it's just what's meant to be.

TZ: John, I want you to pay more attention to your angels. I want you to pay attention to the specialists that have come to help you. Pay more attention to them than to me.

Client: *(Upset.)*

TZ: It is okay. They are just disconnecting. It is all right. Are you letting him disconnect?

Client: He said he's not in me anymore, but there is like a cord or something.

(Continue to give strong directives.)

TZ: John, I want every bit of you to come out of Adam and the angels will show you the brightest, brightest light and that is the direction you are to go. Follow the most love and the brightest light of all. John, just let them hold you and come out of Adam and go to the brightest, brightest light of all.

Client: I feel the other one *(Sarah)* really on me right now.

(Tell the client what you are perceiving during the process to validate their experience.)

TZ: Yes. We will get to Sarah next. I have not forgotten her. Just let John go. And all that energy about him will pull out of your head, your stomach, and your throat. The angels are holding him, rocking him, giving him comfort. Just lifting up and out of you. He is heading toward this giant feeling of love. He is feeling a lot better and he is into the process now.

(The healing process shifts from the person in spirit to the client. When something has left the client, something divine must fill that space. There can never be a void within your client.)

TZ: Now Adam, I want you to help me call in some healers for you and to fill up every place inside of you where John used to be. I am calling in healing specialists to fill all those places with Light and Love in your head, your throat, your heart, your belly, and I want you to pay more attention to that right now. They want you to look for a bright sparkly color that is filling you up in all those places where he used to be. They are removing all that memory and all that sensation and all those feelings right out of you, Adam.

Client: I feel better, and I do feel kind of like a weight is gone.

TZ: He was kind of heavy to lug around, wasn't he? He was kind of messed up. I saw him lay down in the angel's arms and they rocked him. I got goose bumps.

(Help your client to feel more normal and validate their experience as reality.)

TZ: He was more physical, wasn't he? You are making total sense. I want you to know that you make so much sense to me. You are very aware, okay? There are not many people who you could say these things too. This is very normal to me. Do you understand that?

Client: Yeah.

TZ: Okay. I want Sarah to know I am a specialist to help her also, because it is not best for her to stay connected with you either. Okay. Now she has different specialists and I am calling them in right now. Sarah, how many specialists have come to help you?

Client: "Two." I'm actually getting more human stuff from her. She is twenty-eight and blonde, and she had two kids.

TZ: When she told us her name was Sarah I thought she was human.

Client: I just feel like she doesn't want to bother me anymore.

TZ: Sarah, is Adam getting this correct? The information about Sarah. Were you twenty-eight and did you have two kids? Tell Adam if he is understanding you correctly.

Client: She said that's right. She said she lost a baby. I don't know why.

TZ: Sarah, are you afraid to move on and afraid to leave Adam?

Client: She is having trouble leaving.

TZ: They always have trouble leaving. That is why they hook onto people. They are very troubled. Sarah, I am wondering if you know you are dead and you do not have a physical body right now?

Client: She said she had complications with the surgery and she knows she's dead, but she can't accept it.

(Adam has been taking loud gasps of breath every few minutes for months now. His loud gasping was going on throughout this session.)

TZ: Oh, that makes sense. Sarah, do you realize you are interfering with Adam's whole life? You are interfering with Adam's body, with Adam's breathing, and with his life. Do you know that you are having a negative effect on him? Sarah, you are not a thirteen-year-old male. You are a twenty-eight-year-old woman. It is time for you to join your baby. I am getting that you are still trying to feel alive through Adam. But Sarah, it is time for you to stop negatively affecting Adam. And it is time for you to let go of Adam's breathing. It is not keeping you alive and it is hindering Adam. So, I want you to let go of his breathing first of all.

Client: She won't let go.

TZ: She will. She is just working on it. Both of you are kind of scared right now. I think you are more scared right now than you were with releasing John.

Client: She feels like a real negative thing. He was almost kind of a comforting thing but he needed to go.

TZ: And Sarah is not a bad woman either. She was just into her life. Adam, this pattern of you gasping for breath is really a pattern she had while dying.

Client: Do you mean she is causing this?

TZ: Yes, she is causing it. She is still reliving her breath through you. I am asking her and you to let her release, just like you did with John. Let's just practice, Sarah and Adam together. There is no rush at all.

(Clients and negative beings will resist change. Use the client's name as well as the spirit person's name repeatedly to emphasize your directives.)

Client: She's having a hard time going, but she said okay.

TZ: My guides and her guides are telling me they want you two to practice releasing the struggle with your breathing. I want you two to practice. Go slowly. They want you two to practice just noticing that but very, very slowly.

Sarah, I want you to pull out of Adam with the help of your guides. I want you to pull out of this breathing pattern so Adam can breathe normally again. Sarah, I want you to look and pay more attention to your two specialty guides that have come to help you. I want you to pay more attention to them because they know what you should do next. Let them comfort you, Sarah, because you have a better life ahead of you than this existence of being hooked onto Adam. There is much more for both you and Adam. Just pulling that breathing struggle out of you now, Adam.

Okay. I am feeling her coming out of your chest and your lungs. You two are starting that separation, and you know what? I am covered with goose bumps, and that always means we are really doing something good here.

Make sure you bless her and tell her it is time to go, and it is time for you to breathe normally again. I want you to notice that your healing angels, Adam, are showing you how to breathe normally again. You need to relearn it right now.

Adam, your own healers are telling me they want you to pay more attention to them now. They are giving your breathing back to you, but you have got to work with them. How many do you see? I want you to notice them.

(Shift their focus to the specialty guides and less on you as the release takes place.)

Client: Three. I got a good feeling they're all here and real.

TZ: This is real. They are real. I am seeing them put their wings, or arms, or hands on you.

Client: A hug. They are hugging me right now.

(Increase the client's participation in their own healing process.)

TZ: Let's ask them what they need to do next for your breathing to be normal. Just ask them and tell me and your mom what they are saying or doing. Ask if you are supposed to just soak in their love.

Client: I feel like it's getting easier already.

TZ: Now that you're breathing normally now, just soak up this love that is coming in.

Client: I feel much more comfort because people have been trying to make me stop breathing like that.

TZ: Yes, I bet they have been.

Mom: He is breathing easier now.

(All three of us are breathing deeply together.)

TZ: They are telling me they are removing the unhealthy breathing pattern. You are extremely psychic. You being super psychic actually left you wide open. Everybody was able to connect into you.

Mom: It's so amazing to see him breathe through his nose!

(Teaching about one's energy field begins here.)

TZ: *(To Adam)* I want you to imagine God's Light. In your heart area, I want you to deliberately direct that light to get bigger and bigger and bigger and fill you until you shine out. Let it get real sparkly, real bright. Let it shine out through every inch of your skin, and don't forget your backside. Your energy is getting bigger and bigger, and fuller and fuller. It is very calm and very bright. Can you picture that?

Client: I feel like it's a little more difficult to have light, but I imagine a yellow, purple light everywhere. I am so glad I can breathe through my nose. I'm not panicky.

TZ: There is no reason to panic now.

Mom: He has always said, "There is something that is not me that's causing me to do this."

TZ: *(To client's mother)* Look at his eyes. His eyes are alive. Adam, you are more alive!

Level 4: People in Spirit: Vicious, Hateful, and Deliberate

Many practitioners believe nonphysical beings at this level are nonhuman demons. I want to point out that deceased humans might feel or look like nonhuman entities when, in fact, they are very human. These deceased humans have lived one or more violent, vicious, and even murderous lives. They will usually appear to you in a blackened human form.

My house sits back off the road. I looked out my kitchen window at about seven on a Friday evening. A car had stopped on the road in front of my house. It remained there for quite some time. I finally looked through binoculars toward the car. Four men sat in the car, and one of them looked back at me through his binoculars. Our eyes met. He dropped the binoculars, yelled something, and the car spun its wheels and took off.

My family felt fear. Our rural area is known for methamphetamine production. We knew we were being evaluated for a potential robbery. Fear in the house continued to increase throughout the weekend.

Sunday night around midnight, a family member came to my bedroom door and called out, "You have got to do something with the house. There are sounds of banging, knocking, popping, and the walls sound like wood is splitting inside of them."

"Well, we must have an unhappy spirit here," I responded. "Give me some time to wake up and I will scan the house to see what is going on."

I sat up in bed and sent my energy all around the upstairs, scanning for a presence, but found nothing. So I sent my energy down the stairs into all the rooms there. I looked in the two bedrooms—nothing there. I moved my intuitive sensors into a back storage room, piled high with camping supplies, and there he stood in the dark corner. He felt threatening and scary. Before I could project my thoughts to him, he informed me just how bad he was. He sent images of murdering people, raping women— proudly showing me his long history of violence.

I stood my ground, giving him time to tell me who he was. I

asked him why he had come to my home. He said he loved the fear, and that brought him here. I told him I was sorry he had such a horrible childhood and a horrible life. I said, "It does not matter what you have done in the past. You still have a spark of God's Light inside of your heart."

Defiantly, he sneered and laughed at me, then showed me more images of his cruelty and bloodshed.

This went on for quite some time. As he projected more of his memories toward me, I deliberately empowered my toroidal field, but not in fear and never once reacting to him. I was enhancing my own powerful Light of Source.

When he finished that last barrage of images from his horrid life, I continued in my matter-of-fact voice, strongly saying, "Look down inside of your chest. You will see and feel that portion of you is of God."

I was quite surprised when he looked down at his chest. When he raised his head to sneer at me again, I said, "I have already called in guides who specialize in people who are in relentless pain like you are. Look around right now and tell me how many have come for you."

He really did turn his head to look into the completely dark room around him. "Six," he answered.

I responded by saying, "I will be quiet now because they are telling me they want to speak with you." I became quiet and watched for what seemed to be a long time. Commanding representatives from the angelic realm encircled him. Tears fell down his face and his energy softened. The six angels reached out for him. He leaned into their arms, folded his body into a fetal position, and they carried him away.

Terrifying, hateful, brutal people in spirit are still just people. They are more damaged and broken than we could ever be in this life. If you reach out to the humanity within them, you will find a vulnerability that opens the doorway to transmute the ugly negativity into Light. But if you go into fear, the bully within them will rise up in an alarming way and strike your weakest spot. Fear always weakens our energetic field and our body.

This is why I keep discussing the toroidal field and the steps to enrich and bolster our most natural defense. That defense is not a crystal bubble around us, nor armor like the knights wore long ago. The truth of our safety is our ability to invigorate our personal electromagnetic aliveness: refined, delicate luminosity, standing on behalf of Source. When you accomplish this enriched aliveness, "bad-guy" spirit people will soften and melt before you.

Case Study:
Vicious Spirits Causing Cancer

I looked into her lungs and saw a darkened area in the lower lobe of her right lung. She said I was correct. A medical professional had told her the cancerous lesion was located there. I continued to go deeper into the darkness inside her lung, but I did not perceive cancer in my usual way. I did, however, see a human-type face, and when it realized that I found him it opened its enormous mouth and showed long, fang-like teeth dripping with thick drool. I was not surprised to see an entity, but I was surprised when it turned away from me as if it were shy.

I softened my voice and said to my client, "You have a negative being in your lung and it is causing this cancer."

Try to believe me when I tell you what happened next. She whispered, "I have been aware of it since childhood."

She went on to describe a female spirit who used to "bother" her. The spirit was very sad and depressed, and my client said she also felt unhappy when the female spirit was around her. She had not seen the spirit person since she was a child, but she always knew it was with her. I believe she no longer visualized it because the being no longer hovered around her but had merged into her body.

I followed the same steps as in the transcribed session with Adam and his mother. I told my client I would ask the female spirit some questions and wanted her to listen for the spirit's response. I asked my client to accept the most instant word, or words, that leaped into her mind, and tell me the answers she received. I asked this particular being questions such as:

- "How long have you been with my client?"
- "Are you human like my client?" (If it is not human, the technique for the darkest nonhuman entities will apply.)
- "What name do you go by?"
- "Do you know that you are a separate being from my client?"
- "Do you know there is a better life for you to live than being attached to my client?"

I then called in my specialty guides, and asked the spirit being to look for them and tell us how many had come to help her. I focused on describing their differences out loud so the living and the deceased both heard those differences. I repeated the spirit's name and that they were to lift up and away with guides who specialized in transformations, and I knew exactly what they needed to heal. Then, of course, it needed to give itself over to the loving into the Light.

Keep in mind that you do not want to focus on getting to know the entity. The point of interacting with them is to make a communicative connection. Once that is established and you are getting responses, you shift the focus to emphasize how living and spirit are different from each other. Keep stating that life like this is not beneficial for either of them. Then describe how the client and entity can release each other now. More often than not, one or both of them will be hesitant to allow that change. Be persistent and resolute with both of them that life and health is threatened in this relationship, but life after the separation offers fulfillment and love.

Healing Technique

Levels 3–4: Angry, Possessive, Vicious, Hateful, and Deliberate People in Spirit

1. Inform the client they have a negative spirit person interfering with them. You can describe the spirit to them. Clients can often identify who they are.

2. If the negative spirit controls the client to refuse consent to remove the entity, ignore it and continue giving instructions.

3. Ask the spirit person questions, and tell the client to listen to the spirit's responses and tell you what they are. This engages the client in their own healing process. Here are a few examples of questions to ask the spirit entity:

   - How long have you been connected to the client?
   - What drew you to this person?
   - What goal do you have by staying connected?
   - How many other people are you connected to right now?
   - How is this connection not working for you any longer?
   - Have you forgotten that you are a separate human being from this human?

4. Move on in conversation, emphasizing how separate and different the spirit entity is with statements or questions such as:

   - If they are different genders, emphasize that difference.
   - Do you know that you can never become your own self while attached to this human?
   - This is not a good life for you to remain with this human.
   - You cannot be happy or become who you are meant to be.

- You will be forgotten by everyone if you remain attached to this human.

5. If the spirit person refuses to talk, state that they must be uncomfortable with what you are saying and that they do not want to answer. This will encourage responses to resume.

6. Tell the spirit person you have already called in specialty guides from the Compassionate Source just for them. Direct the spirit to count the guides that have come and to feel their love. Tell the spirit person the specialty guides do not care how terrible the entity thinks they are. The guides can only feel love for them, no matter what they have done.

7. Describe aloud how both the client and the spirit person are now separating away from each other. Repeatedly state how this is best for them both.

8. Throughout this session, internally ask guides to completely extract all levels of these negative entities from your client.

9. Ask the client to participate and allow the release to happen. Tell the client to declare, "I completely and permanently release this spirit person and anyone who is associated with you now. Go with the specialists who are here for you."

10. Describe out loud to your client how you, as the medical intuitive, are perceiving the separation that is happening.

11. Ask your specialists to remove the being and take it to the best place for its highest transformation into Light, Compassion, and Love.

12. Call in your Purest Healing Specialists of the Light to cleanse every single space and place where negativity used to be. Request immediate special healing that is best for this client and this situation. Command that a complete and permanent healing and cleansing happen now.

13. Ask the client to accept the healing and to tell you when the healing is complete. Tell them you will be quiet until they speak.

14. Ask the client to describe their experience during the healing. This will help the client remember the details.

15. Invite a specialty guide who excels in cleaning and clearing to create the ideal cleansing filter for you to return through to maintain perfect health for you. Deliberately and consciously pull your energetic laser beam back from the client and the experience through the filter. You may feel, or actually see, the filter working. You can assist yourself by inhaling and imagining each inhalation pulls your energy back to you through that filter.

16. Command: "I now bring me, and only me, back to myself, clean and clear through a perfect filter provided for me by my Divine cleansing specialist."

Essential Points

- Angry and possessive people in spirit deliberately interfere with living humans.

- The fact that energy follows thought still holds true in the nonphysical sphere.

- Angry and possessive people in spirit have trapped themselves within their own thought and emotional processes.

- Spirit people are full of emotion and powerful concentrations of focused thought.

- When removing an angry or possessive person in spirit, focus on their differences from the client.

- Terrifying, hateful, brutal people in spirit are still just people.

- Fear always weakens our energetic field and our body.

- Negative spirit people will soften and melt before you when you invigorate your personal enriched aliveness.

- When interacting with an entity, do not focus on getting to know them but instead to make a communicative connection.

- Many people will refuse to let you to remove a negative spirit. This is the negative spirit in control.

Chapter 12

Nonphysical Entities Causing Illness or Life Struggles: Levels 5 and 6

Nonhuman beings truly do exist, which is only one of the reasons that the nonphysical realms are so complex and multifaceted. Not all entities are negative and trying to do harm. Many are also of the natural realms of the Earth such as fairies, leprechauns, and elves. This chapter focuses on beings that cause illness or life struggles for living humans as well as deceased humans. They do come in scary forms, shapes, sizes, but all are a dark shade of color with very little or no light. Ugly and dark never means powerful. They have little, if any, intellect and they are weak and extremely needy. Why else would they need to attach and interfere with human beings? Again, these two levels of entities deliberately interfere with humans.

Level 5: Nonhuman Entities

Over the many years as an intuitive practitioner, I have witnessed a wide variety of surprisingly ugly entities of all types from monstrous, to insect-like, to robotic-like entities. The more negative they are, the more they try to hide from you. They hide because they are weak and needy. You are the powerful being because you are full of Love and Light.

A dedicated mentoring client emailed me the following experience she had with nonhuman entities and how the more negative often hide while the less negative might show themselves first:

> I want to share a brief follow-up after completing my home-work today. I reviewed the steps for removing nonhuman and

dark entities FIRST. I powered up differently today—I followed the new sequence of commands and included each color from the rainbow. And I LOVE IT. It felt much more protective, and I felt more in control and calm as a result.

When I commanded them to encapsulate the nonhuman beings with my client, I found there were three in hiding. None of them seemed to be interested in leaving. They were quite a cruel bunch. For the first time, I felt like I knew exactly what each of them looked like. The three in hiding had fang-looking teeth; one definitely had creepy-looking horns, but I knew they were just the clients I had to help today.

I took my time with these beings. I asked them questions just like you guide us to do. I learned they've been with this person most of her life. They were attracted to her by her mother. I was shown a person her mother interacts with (someone who calls themselves a medium) who drew them in initially. I believe this person may be well aware that these nonhuman entities are attaching to her clients.

These beings wanted to spread misery and negativity through my client. I explained to them that none of them can progress for their own development in this way. As I explained, I could tell they understood because their ugliness started to fade away. I watched the horns sink and the energy become less like they were hanging on to the client with a death grip. I felt them start to let go.

I had them count the specialist guides who came to help, focused on the Love, and reminded them I am an expert at helping beings just like them. It took a little while, but I patiently waited while they separated. Then I filled ALL that space with Divine Love and healing for my client.

I love powering up this new way! *(See chapter 2—Protection that Works with the Negative.)* When I truly tuned in, I realized I can see and observe much more than I think I admit to myself. I also noticed I felt calm, confident, and in control of the Divine and Sacred Team. I did not get anxious during this work. I just stayed focused and collected.

This might be a stretch for many readers, but other types of entities inhabit the Universe—more than we humans can even imagine. When creation happened, it was apparently, extremely creative! Once again, way beyond what even we intuitives can imagine. Just when I think I have intuitively perceived it all, I come across another entity I have never seen before. There is much more going on in life than physical and nonphysical human beings.

Scientists had no idea single-cell organisms existed until the microscope was developed. When each scientist looked through their first microscope, the world expanded in shocking ways. In the same surprising manner, people who open up their natural intuitive abilities become acutely aware of the extensive and surprising realms of life we all live in, breathe in, and walk through. The mass population of humanity, however, has no awareness that anything exists beyond what their physical eyes see. In real life, surprises are truly everywhere!

Nonhuman beings exist, but not all are threatening or harmful. Some nonhuman entities are ornery and mischievous but do not intend direct harm. Some beings are part of the natural world of Earth while others are a natural part of other dimensions, other planets, and other universes. We are not alone and never have been.

When I was in Ireland, I stood with a group of people looking at a waterfall. Some people were chattering about everyday topics and some were soaking up the beauty of the environment. With a giant smile on my face, I watched the "little people." They scampered from rock to rock and then they jumped into the rocks. One of the rocks smiled back at me. Then suddenly many of the rocks smiled at me. The rocks changed form, adjusting to the different individuals that were jumping into them. The little people within the rocks smiled and laughed as some of their friends ran on top of them. This was the first time I had ever experienced what must have been leprechauns.

Fairies, gnomes, satyrs, and elves—just to name a few—exist in human folklore because intuitives were able to perceive these beings. This is not about insanity or psychosis. Intuitives live with one foot in the physical world and one foot in the nonphysical. Intuitives understand that we humans are not alone. Other beings exist and are very much alive. When an individual unlocks their instinctive intuitive senses, other realms of life are unlocked as well. Consider the first scientist who looked into the first microscope and realized there was an "invisible world" that others were not aware of. Some of the invisible organisms are positive and others, like viruses and some bacteria, are negative. This experience on the Earth planet is structured with both the positive and the negative. We face those two experiences every day of our lives, and every day we make our choices based on our level of advancement.

My first nonhuman experience occurred very early in my life. I had no understanding, training, or experience when I decided to send love to a disturbed friend of the family. I sat in meditation for a few moments, picturing this person in my mind. I filled myself with love and projected it outward toward that person. The second the love frequency reached that individual, their body blew open and an enraged looking gremlin-type entity flung itself at me and across the 1,500 miles between us. I had heard about blasting negativity with white light. That is the only tool I had, so that is what I did as it hurled itself at me. It shattered into tiny particles that lifted upward. I was hysterical with fear because I was not prepared. You will be prepared.

Years later, I was a newly trained Reiki practitioner working with one of my first clients. She seemed deeply relaxed, and I was feeling profound sensations of love waving through me. I was a vessel of love and my client was soaking in the healing energy. I moved my hands from this woman's upper chest to her abdomen and felt a rumbling. Energetically, her entire abdomen split open and a similar type of gremlin leaped out of the client's body and onto the floor. I was momentarily paralyzed as it ran around the room with an ear-piercing shriek.

My only tool in my toolbox at that time was the beam of white light. The light hit the being and it, too, broke up into tiny particles that slowly floated up and out through the ceiling. I had not moved a muscle as this took place. I still had my hot hands on her abdomen. I pulled myself together and completed a full-body session. I whispered to her that she could sit up when it felt right.

Her eyes popped open with a startled look, and she said, "What just happened in my stomach!"

I could not tell her what I just experienced. Always being honest, however, I told her that she released a large amount of negativity that had been building up. She said she knew something released from her body.

I want you to be a prepared medical intuitive, ready for anything at any time and in any form. I later saw some of these alarming nonhuman forms in TV ads for horror movies and on book covers. My guess is that the creators of the horror movies and books have some conscious or unconscious knowledge of these fearsome creatures from other realms.

I will try to describe the forms I have personally witnessed as well as what other healers have shared with me. Many of us have discovered leech-like black blobs hanging on or around other people's bodies. You may perceive enlarged human faces that take over the entire length of a person. Some entities will frequently show themselves as monsters. Monsters tend to come in a variety of shapes and forms. You might see them with mouths wide open, fangs dripping with strings of drool. They will all have creepy flaming red eyes. I do not look into those red eyes and I do not react to them either. It is just part of their show. Other daunting forms you might discover are clusters of slithering snakes, huge black spiders, bats, black dragons, swarms of ant-like insects, trolls, gargoyles, and even beings that look like Gollum in the movie *Lord of the Rings*. Some will show flaming red eyes without any visible body, or crooked and knotted hands with long claws, or will be a type of lizard or other reptile. Any of these forms may leap at you unexpectedly. If you have done the preparation I have described throughout this book, you will already be prepared and protected, and they cannot reach you. Your Light from Sacred Source is too brilliantly bright and more powerful than they can ever be.

I have placed extraterrestrials within this category of non-physical intrusive entities. I have met many people over the years who are aware of ET interference in their lives, and many more who had no idea this type of entity was real, let alone personally affecting them. Here is a quote from William Baldwin, PhD, in *Healing Lost Souls*.

"Attached ETs may be lost, marooned, or retired here on the Earth. Some ETs are here on scientific expeditions, much as human scientists explore jungles, oceans, and remote places on this globe. Some claim to use the eyes and ears of humans, as they do not have the proper apparatus to perceive this reality. Many of them cannot interpret the band of the electromagnetic spectrum that is seen as color, nor can they interpret sound waves.

"Extraterrestrials express various reasons for being here, but have no compunction about the invasion, or hesitation in the violation of one's free will. Basically, there is no concern for personal sovereignty."[10]

I was deeply involved in the healing portion of my client's session. I had only begun to send him Reiki energy when I intuitively witnessed metallic-looking clamps rising up from his spine. Each of the four clamps seemed to slowly release their grip, disconnecting one at a time from four different vertebrae. At that time, I had no idea why I was visualizing that release. As the clamps lifted away, I was startled when four faces of the aliens commonly called "the Greys" appeared right in front of my face. They were indeed gray with large black eyes that were void of any emotion. Once again, I had no training in how to deal with this type of intrusion. I blasted all four of them with the Reiki

---

10 William J. Baldwin, *Healing Lost Souls: Releasing Unwanted Spirits from Your Energy Body* (Newburyport, MA: Hampton Roads Publishing, 2003).

frequency of compassionate Love and Light. They backed off and faded from sight.

This client already knew that his life was compromised by invasive extraterrestrials. Once again, I was surprised that people usually have some degree of knowledge about their struggles with energetic beings. And once again, I was not prepared to experience these beings, let alone know how to handle a healing situation involving them. In the end, I always discover that any type of dark energy forces simply cannot tolerate the intense electrical vibration of true, compassionate Love and Light. So, when in doubt about what to do, send waves of true, compassionate Love and brilliant white Light. Do not go into fear, no matter what category of negative beings you are facing.

My friend Tom had a serpent tail wrapped all around his physical body. I intuitively scanned the length of the serpent and found its tail piercing his physical heart. It had stabbed him in the heart, then spiraled around his chest to hold on to him. I did not expect a dragon-type serpent piercing this man's heart and crushing his chest and lungs.

A few weeks later, Tom's closest friend and colleague passed on. Tom asked me to check in with the spirit of his friend to see how his transition was going. First, I asked his friend, who had passed on, for permission to approach him. I felt the man in spirit give me a "yes." As I approached him with my laser beam of sensors, I sensed a deep struggle. I again asked permission to scan his essence to determine the cause of his struggle. Instantly, that same serpent appeared, but this time its tail was not embedded into his heart. It was plunged into the energetic head and brain of this man in spirit. When I reported this to Tom, he told me his friend had died of a brain tumor.

In this case, neither man was aware of the destructive being damaging, and even destroying, their lives, in one case causing a death. In both circumstances, I pulled my energy back and called out to the Universe for sacred spirit guides to come forth. I asked for guides who specialized with this type of entity to take it to the appropriate place for its highest transformation into Light and Love. I watched as the specialists silently interacted with the serpent. It released both its victims and lifted away with the spirit guides surrounding it.

Please note: The serpent entity did not release the man after death but continued on with him into the spirit realm.

Case Study:
Removal of Multiple Types of Negative Interference

The following transcription is an excerpt from a session with twenty-eight-year-old Cindy. I did not include the first part of her session because I walked her through the steps of working with and building her own toroidal field, which was presented earlier in this book. The remainder of this transcription describes the removal and clearing for Level 2: Confused and Afraid People in Spirit, and Level 5: Nonhuman Beings. Over five entities were involved in this healing: two adult humans, an infant female, and a nonhuman being. I could sense a fifth entity, but I could not clearly identify it because it did not have the dark, heavy level of dense energy.

Practice Experience:

Imagine you are the medical intuitive speaking the words in this transcript. Read it aloud or, if possible, with a study buddy, one taking part as the medical intuitive and one as the client. Practice this session as if you are actually giving these steps to someone who needs your guidance.

Client: I feel more solid, or something like that.

TZ: The whole point of deliberately running our energy field is so we are not so porous.

Client: Yes, sometimes I just feel like Swiss cheese.

TZ: I think that Swiss-cheese feeling comes from being so psychic like you are. But we do not have to be so vulnerable to be intuitive. We do not need to be so affected by anything negative. We can fill up our body, our space, and our energy field with nothing but the best and the most positive. The negative spirit attachments are now getting uncomfortable about the positive energy work you have just done for yourself.

Client: Mhmm.

TZ: Now I would like to talk to the beings (the client already identified a total of five beings attached to her) that are there, and I would like you to listen to what they say as they answer my questions.

Client: One of them is standing out to me because it seems to be the strongest. It causes pain wherever it touches me. Real pain.

TZ: So, you mean real physical pain?

Client: Yes.

TZ: Okay. Let's ask him and the other four if they can sense the energy-protective work you just did for yourself.

Client: Yes, they say they are feeling it.

TZ: I am wondering if it is not as comfortable to be hanging out with Cindy as it used to. Is that true?

Client: Yes, and I feel energy from them in my feet, and it is trying to dissipate and move away from me.

TZ: Are all of you one gender or another? Do you identify yourselves as male or female?

Client: The main one says it is male. The others are one female and the others male. The other males seem weaker too. One female and one male are just along for the ride.

TZ: Okay. Did the five of you used to have a physical body?

Client: I hear "yes."

TZ: Do you all realize you have not had your own body for quite some time?

Client: I think some of them don't know. They seem confused. I am seeing them in like a hierarchy. Like one knows but the others do not know.

TZ: Yes. That is common. I want all of you to know that even though you do not have a body you still have a soul and heart. You still have a heart of Light no matter where you are or who you are. I am asking you now to look inside of yourself . . . into your own Light. Your Light is very separate from Cindy's Light. (Long pause.) What do they say about that?

Client: Well, it's like they know, but this one here doesn't want them to do it.

TZ: Yes. Well, he is in charge.

Client: They won't do it unless you make them.

TZ: So, are they all seeing their heart Light?

Client: Yes, but they don't know what to do with it.

TZ: What about the main entity, the one who seems to be the director?

Client: He is just so black . . . so black.

TZ: I am asking this to the director. How long have you been with Cindy?

Client: I hear "twenty years." That is just so weird! That is when I was so suicidal and all the weird psychic stuff started happening and my abilities opened up. That is just crazy! That is the point when all this started for me! When I was a kid, I had stuff happen to me and I started feeling and sensing more things. It was right around the age of eight. It was like the door opened. I had weird visions when I went to bed, like killing babies, and baby bodies were rotten. It was a very weird time for me because I didn't know what was happening to me.

TZ: Yes, that makes complete sense. I am asking this question to the one who is directing. Are you aware that you feel you are male but you are now in the female body of Cindy?

Client: He says that does not make any difference to him.

TZ: That is quite all right. That's all right. Do you, the director, know that even though you are so black and so dark that everything has a Light?

(Long pause.)

Client: I just think he enjoys being dark. It serves him and is working for him.

TZ: Yes, of course he does. Director, I think you have known this for a long time . . . for a very long time.

Client: I think his feelings toward me just turned. Back in the beginning I think he liked me, but over time all of a sudden it changed. He says, "Now I'm going to kill you."

TZ: Well, let's ask him. Is Cindy describing this accurately?

Client: Well, he wasn't attacking me back then.

TZ: Make sure you let him speak and do not speak for him. Let him speak.

Client: Okay. But it is not like he is really speaking. It is more like feelings he is sending me.

TZ: Sure. Okay. That makes total sense.

Client: So, at some point it was okay to change.

TZ: I'm asking the director: how are the others involved that are with you?

Client: He just uses them. He is a kidnapper. It's like he is holding a gun to someone's head and says, "Let's do this so I can have more."

TZ: So, director, are you noticing that Cindy is one being, you are one being, and the other four are also separate beings from Cindy?

Client: I just got the word "obsession." Like it has become habitual.

TZ: All right. Is Cindy understanding this correctly?

Client: Yep. He wants and likes the attention.

TZ: Well, there is even more attention for you *(the director)* and the other four. I want you all to look up and around you. I have been calling in compassion specialists who want you to be even more of yourselves. These specialists want to show you all that you are more than just a glob hanging on to Cindy. You haven't been able to live your fullness while hanging on to Cindy.

Client: He is a blob, but the other ones I see are humans. They have faces but he is a black blob.

TZ: All right. In that case, I am inviting in a different type of specialist that can give you the type of attention you love, but a different kind of attention. They are going to show you exactly what you really need and want. I want you to notice the special ones who have come to assist you, and I am telling the other four to look at the different specialists who are for them.

(Long pause.)

Client: It's like the four are gathering and talking. They are mingling with their specialists.

TZ: Yes, they are talking it over.

Client: I see the subtle ones. They are male and female, a couple. At first they felt like they should not be doing this with us. *(The client is referring to the releasement that is happening.)* But now they feel it is right.

TZ: I am now addressing this couple. You have not had a full life while staying with the director and with Cindy. There is a glorious and special place. Notice the guidance from your own guardians. They are here to help you. Do not even notice me and Cindy anymore. Pay close attention to the compassionate beings that have been waiting for you both. They have just been waiting. You are now lifting and lifting up and out of Cindy . . . up, out, and away from Cindy.

Client: This is weird. They came right up my legs and shot out of me.

TZ: Very fine. Now I am addressing the other two. You have your own specialists who have come to help you.

Client: I am seeing a baby . . . a female. She doesn't want to be left behind. She wants to go with the other two.

TZ: Oh, okay. I am now asking her own safe-keepers just to hold her in their arms and help her lift out and away.

Client: Now I am feeling other beings. One right here *(motions next to her)* and there is one in each of my feet.

TZ: Yes, there are other specialists for them too. You all are now lifting up and out of Cindy with your specialty guides. Now I am directing all the attention to the director. The black blob.

Client: He seems very neutral now.

TZ: Excellent . . . Hear me now *(to the spirit guide specialists)*, I request guides who specialize in beings like the director. Place it in a powerful bubble of brilliant white Light that encircles him completely. Make this Light very tight around him. Take him to the perfect place for his loving transformation.

(I took this step for two reasons. Its level of interference frequently caused suicidal thoughts. It was also resistant to the previous steps of release. Cindy and this being were entrenched together and had been for many years.)

Client: I can see him rising out of me.

TZ: I call out for the compassionate warriors of the Light of Source to encapsulate any and all beings that are connected to, or affiliated with, this being . . . the entire network encircled by the Light of Source. I request on its behalf and the behalf of Cindy, that it all be taken now to the exact place for the entire hierarchy to be permanently transformed into the Light from Source. Right now, completely remove it and all tendrils, all roots, and all aspects of it from Cindy, now and forever. Lift it up and out of Cindy immediately, now without delay. And Cindy, you are now to release it all from you completely and permanently, now and forever. *(Long pause.)* I call out to the cleansers to clear and clean out all remnants, all residue of the negative or dark forces. *(Long pause.)* I now call out to the most perfect healers from the greatest, brightest Light of All and fill every space and place where the negative and the dark used to be. Cleanse and clear Cindy on any and all levels of her being, now and forever. *(Very long pause.)*

Client: I can feel it all happening.

TZ: You are walking out of here with many specialty beings to assist you, Cindy.

Client: I feel buzzed. Everything is crystal clear . . . crystal clear.

TZ: You are actually sparkly!

Client: I feel sparkly!

Notice there are many steps and many specific commands throughout the healing of Level 5 entities. Do not allow this to be confusing. Continue to call in Divine and Sacred specialists for each type and each level of being you are perceiving. In fact, go back through this dialogue and notice the common sense of each step. Notice that the more levels of interference you discover, the more powerful and clear commands you must create. You are the commander of the healing. The negative beings and the Divine and Sacred beings will all follow your commands.

Level 6: The Darkest Entities

You might be wondering at this point, "How could these levels get any worse?" This level does encompass what many people call evil, devil, wicked, demonic, dark forces, or Satan. You will rarely, if ever, come across this level of entity, but please realize it does exist. If you work intuitively with law enforcement, you may discover this level of being in those dramatic situations. You must understand and know, right now, that this entity is not human and probably never has been. Still consider it as interference in a person's life. It would be rare, and even unlikely, that anyone with this level of being would show up as your client in the first place. The only time that might be possible is when the dark force first enters the human person, and the interference is at its beginning stage.

This darkest of negativity is different in a few ways. Even if a person is affected by entities from some, or all, the levels stated above, they can still have a dark-force entity within them. While entities from other levels are more likely to show themselves to you during a medical-intuitive session, the darkest negative entities will very rarely show themselves to you. This level is more deeply hidden and seems to have more deliberate control of its mission of destruction. That being said, you must hold on to the knowledge that this entity is still just a suffering being. That suffering being still must be considered one of your clients who, even more desperately, needs relief, healing, and release into the Light. Hear and absorb my words about this: The dark entity is simply another client along with the human client sitting in front of you.

There may literally be layers of beings interfering within your human client. The ones you readily perceive are often the least of the client's problems. They are frequently lost people in spirit who are eager to accept your help and guidance, so they quickly and willingly show themselves. They are definitely adding to the client's problems and ill health, but they are often not the only beings involved. The darkest beings are usually deeper, quieter, and more entrenched than other layers of entities.

The darkest being, slowly or quickly, takes control and alters the individual's actions. They eventually cause the person to become violent—killing, raping, or stealing from others without any remorse. They will destroy the living human, then move along with the soul at the time of death only to return into the next incarnation with that same soul. Assassins for hire, terrorists, serial killers, and monarchs who order genocide fall into this category.

Entities in Level 6 have not lived as humans. They are from other realms or worlds that really do exist. Sometimes they will appear for a moment in an exaggerated human form, but they have never been human. They might also show themselves, for a few moments, as a deceased loved one, but they cannot seem to conceal the red or black, blank eyes of a dark being. All of them will attempt to frighten you because fear makes you immediately vulnerable to them. Remember, fear collapses the fine frequency of the Divine Source. Generally, they want to scare you off so you stop interfering with their life's work or the assignment they think they are performing. They will appear in different scary forms. These forms may be true to what they are, or they may be taking a certain form just to frighten you.

All dark, negative forces at any level, interfere with love. That interference may affect an individual's ability to love themselves, their family, their spouse, their country, and so on. In his book *Spirit Releasement Therapy*, William Baldwin states:

"Individually and collectively in groups, they are ordered to cause as much pain, suffering, disruption, chaos, damage, destruction, and death as possible to as many humans as possible. They thrive on the pain of human suffering. They interfere with any and every form of love. This includes self-esteem in the individual, conjugal love for couples, and familiar love and respect. Disruption of family unity is a primary assignment and a major accomplishment. They attempt to interfere with projects and institutions which can advance or improve the human condition."[11]

Always realize, remember, and deeply believe this. The dark entities at any level have four major disadvantages:

1. They are fighting against the more powerful, energetic, divine frequency of Love and Sacred Source Light.

---

11 William Baldwin, *Spirit Releasement Therapy: A Technique Manual* (London: Headline Publishing, 1995).

2. They have completely forgotten their own original Light of Sacred Source. No matter how tiny it is, that Light eternally resides within their own essence. All the darkest entities have the Light but have not recognized it for centuries or more.

3. They live in fear of being punished if they stop their devious work.

4. They desperately need us. We are in charge of the client and their healing needs, but at the same time, we are also in charge of guiding the bleakest, most dismal, darkest of dark beings back into the Brightest of Holy Light.

I also agree with Dr. Baldwin that a dark entity seldom works alone. There is often an organized group that affects not only your client but many other people at the same time. The greatest outcome of your healing work with an individual is facilitating the removal and transformation of an entire system of interconnected dark forces and all the human beings suffering from their interference. You are able to accomplish the healing transformation for an entire system of negativity that begins with one client who sits before you in your office.

Notice how the healing steps for these two exceedingly negative categories of entities are different from the steps for the other levels of interference.

Healing Technique Levels 5–6:
Nonhuman Entities and the Darkest Entities

You have just perceived a nonhuman being or the darkest entity. You have studied this. We have talked about it. You are ready now. Follow these steps:

1. Feel no fear. Ugly does not mean powerful. It only means ugly. When you sense these two levels, stop your assessment immediately. Electrify your energy field and body with rainbows and a violet flame throughout you and

all around you, shining stars inside of every cell of who you are, and shimmering golden energy. Generate a fierce, powerful sense of yourself, and know you are defiant with that fierce attitude of invincibility. You are deliberately in charge because you are the true meaning of Light Worker, purposefully emanating tidal waves of Love, Compassion, and the Sacred Light of the Holy Source.

2. Immediately pull your laser beam back to yourself by your thoughts and by inhaling, through which you can create the sensation of pulling your laser beam back to your body.

3. Command: "Divine, Sacred healers who specialize in transmuting negative energy, completely and permanently transmute all negative energy coming at me into pure Divine, Sacred, golden healing energy."

4. Command: "I invoke Sacred Specialists from Source Light to instantly and completely encapsulate (or wrap) *all* the dark beings in a warm, loving blanket of Pure Sacred Protective Light."

5. Other commands to use:

"I, *(full name)*, completely and permanently reject, repel, and revoke ALL negative entities and all dark-force energy from me and my clients in all ways and on ALL levels! Keep me out of this and keep me safe!"

"I, *(full name)*, am invincible and unassailable to all negativity on all levels. Only the divine, compassionate, loving Light of Source fills my mind, my body, my soul, my higher self, and my spirit."

"The Purest Healing and Cleansing Guides from Source, instantly create the perfect cleansing filter for me, and I pull all my energy back to me."

6. Inform the client of negativity attached to them, but never describe it. Do not scare them. Fear will constrict the client's

energy, and that constriction clamps down on the being too. This is the opposite response you want to achieve.

7. Many people will say they do not want it removed. That is the negative entity in control of the client. Strongly inform them, "I am the specialist now in this process. You are not in charge. I am in charge now, and the healing will continue for everyone involved."

8. Ask the client to listen for the being's answers to your questions. Do not let the dark being ask you questions. You are in charge and the only one who asks questions. Here are some examples of these questions:

   - How long have you been connected to this human?

   - What drew you, and why did you connect with this particular human? (*You are looking for vulnerable characteristics, actions, or an event that allowed the dark being to attach to the client.*)

   - What do you get from interfering with this human?

   - How many levels like you are connected to this human? (*There is often an entire network and hierarchy. Learn the full extent of dark forces. All need to be released by the end of the session.*)

   - Do you have a director or leader? (*You want to include all levels of dark forces that are involved for them to be released as well.*)

   - How many humans total are you connected to right now? (*Often, many other humans are interlaced with a dark force. All affected humans in this particular network must be included in the release and healing.*)

   - Have you forgotten where you originated?

9. Intuitively command: "I invoke Sacred Specialists from Source Light to immediately encapsulate and contain the dark beings with Pure Sacred Protective Light. Extract

all negative/dark-force commanders, managers, and all beings within their network."

10. Ask the client how many specialists have come to remove the entities. *(This engages the client in the healing process.)*

11. Intuitively command: "I invoke Sacred Specialists from Source Light to immediately surround and contain the dark beings and the entire network, including any commanders, with Pure Sacred Protective Light immediately. Take every one of them to the best place for their complete and highest transformation into Love and Light." *(Keep repeating this command as necessary for each level of the hierarchy.)*

12. Repeatedly tell the client and the dark entities that they are separating and becoming individuals.

13. Direct the client to actively reject and push the negative entity out of their body, mind, soul, and spirit.

14. Intuitively call in healing guide specialists to completely remove all layers, all tendrils, and all sludge from the client now.

15. You and the client ask that Pure Light and compassionate Love immediately fill every single space and place where the negative used to be. *(When something is removed, something positive must fill the empty space, or the negative will rush back in.)*

16. Ask the client to allow the healing and inform you when the healing is complete. Be quiet until the client speaks.

I give William Baldwin credit for a certain step that I have added in my releasement process. Because of him, I incorporate the bubble, or blanket, of Light encapsulating the negative being, and any network involved, completely and tightly. This is a safety measure, but it also expedites the release. I have not used this step when human spirits are interfering because, since they are human beings, I want kindness to prevail. I use the bubble for attached thought forms if I am guided by Spirit to do so.

Breaking My Own Rule

By now, you know it is imperative you ask for permission before working intuitively with any client. Ask for permission from an infant, a child, an adult, someone in a coma, everyone, no matter the age of that client or their life situation. Asking permission and honoring a "no" assures we intuitives that we are not crossing the line between initiating healing, guided by the Holy Light of Source, and initiating control over another human, which will lead us to the negative shadows.

There is only one exception to this rule, and that is when the entities are so aggressive and intrusive that the living person cannot give you permission to extract them. When you ask permission to remove the entity and the client refuses you, it is actually the negative intruder that is refusing you. The negative being does not want to accept what is about to happen. Negative beings can feel your positive presence before the client even gets to your office. The client will frequently tell you they had a difficult time trying to get to the appointment. The entities will try to impede or sabotage the session in any way possible. It desperately wants to remain attached to the client. If a negative entity works hard to avoid you, realize there is an underlying message in the entity's behavior: that they are aware of the power of the transforming Light of Source that vibrates from us medical intuitives. It is vital that you participate in all the protective steps in Chapter 2. Those steps are real and will take care of you. Repeat them on a daily basis for your personal energetic hygiene. Negative entities are terribly afraid of you and the healing that is about to happen. No matter how ugly or intimidating they are, please imprint this in your mind now: The negative entities are extremely fearful of you as the healer. The more you understand and accept this truth, the more invincible you really are.

Our thought energy is powerful and becoming more powerful as medical intuitives. We must be extremely careful with our word choice, especially when we use commands. The only time I use the words "forever," "permanent," or "eternity" is in two situations.

The first situation in which those intense and potent words should be used in healings is when I extract or assist the transformation of dark energy. In these situations, state the following:

"I now request the specialists for this particular being to carry it to the appropriate realm for its permanent transformation into the Light forever."

The second, and only other, situation in which these three words are appropriate to use is for the healing of your living client. In this case, use this command:

"I now request that the most perfect healing guides for (name of living person/client) permanently fill every single space and place where the negative used to be; fill with God's Compassion, Love, and Light for eternity."

You may certainly replace "God" with "Source" or "the Creator," etc. It is imperative that you are sincerely comfortable with every word within your command, so make adjustments if necessary.

Essential Points

- Nonhuman beings exist, but not all are threatening or harmful.
- Some of the invisible organisms are positive and others are negative.
- Ugly does not mean a nonhuman entity is more powerful. It only means they are ugly.
- The darkest entities are not human and probably never have been.
- Remember to see the darkest entities as simply another client.
- While entities from other levels are more likely to show themselves to you, the darkest negative entities will very rarely do this.

- Lower-level entities are often not the only beings involved in a client's illness.

- The darkest entities cause a living person to become violent without any remorse.

- Fear collapses the fine frequency of the divine Source.

- All the darkest entities have the Light but have not recognized it for centuries or more.

- A dark entity seldom works alone.

- Inform the client of negativity attached to them, but never describe it.

Chapter 13

The Environment Causing Illness or Life Struggles

We tend to think of the environment as the earth around us. Our environment shifts as we move throughout our day. For example, our environment might begin in the kitchen, then move to our yard, then a car, an intersection we drive through, the shop we stop by, or the hospital where we visit a loved one. Our environment is anywhere we are located at the moment.

One of my mentoring clients, who excels as a medical intuitive, thought she was about to provide a medical-intuitive session focusing on her client's physical body. However, when she commanded her guides to show her the exact point of origin causing the client's medical conditions, the following instantly happened:

"I did some work for a lady last week remotely, and while tuning into her I was told *(by her guides)* to look at the land the house is built on. There was a big *(energetic)* crack in the ground, and there was a soldier standing at the end of the crack. So, I called on a guide to come forward to help, and I was amazed.

"A pure white, glowing staircase appeared from the crack. All these souls started walking out. He *(the soldier)* was standing there watching, holding his gun. He was wearing a red tunic with gold buttons, a tall black hat with gold on it, and the gun had like a bell at the end of it. Then the last two souls came out. They turned around, and it looked like they were pulling a rope to bring the steps up. As they pulled the steps up, the crack sealed. They all proceeded to a lovely arched door that had a baby-blue-coloured light. The soldier then looked back at me and saluted, then he went towards the door.

"I later asked for feedback from the lady, and she said she couldn't believe the difference, as it seemed to happen within the hour of me doing it. What an amazing experience! I was going to do a medical-intuitive reading with her, and as I said before, you never know where you'll go or what you'll see. A healing took place for many there . . . Still amazes me!"

More and more, I have noticed the environment frequently causing physical illness. Then I noticed the environment is also the cause of emotional struggles such as anxiety, nightmares, depression, and many other symptoms. In the case above, spirit people in the environment interfered with this client's physical health. This environment was inundated with the human emotions of spirit people, who were lingering above and beneath the ground of this woman's property.

Your environment is not just where you live. It is not only the structure of the house or apartment you live in but also the land it is on. It includes your workplace, where you go for fun, your journey down the road between one place to another, an intersection, a railroad crossing, or even an airplane. Your location creates your environment. I have driven past auto wrecks that have negatively affected me on an emotional level and on a spiritual level at the exact same time. For weeks, the spirit of a young male about seventeen or eighteen years old would appear in the passenger seat of my car as I drove home from work. He told me his name was Bobby and he died at the spot where his parents placed the cross. The next day, I looked more closely at the cross along the side of the road. This cross marked the exact place where he died in an automobile wreck and, indeed, the name "Bobby" was etched into it.

Later that week, I was driving down that same road and saw a tall, thin male walk across the road at that same spot. When I got to that wide-open place in the road, no one was physically there.

Because I have been a medium ever since I can remember, neither that man nor that section of the road negatively affected me. However, someone who drives through that same area every day might pick up the intense density of emotions that were lingering at the site of that automobile wreck.

Here is one example of spirit people potentially causing emotional or physical illness in living people through a certain environment. Robert Moss, author of *Sidewalk Oracles*, describes what he saw with his "inner senses" just as he was about to begin teaching his workshop.

> "It was not really a surprise when I noticed through my inner senses that we had been joined by the spirits of several hundred men in blue and gray, soldiers killed on both sides in the American Civil War who had apparently remained close to the place where their bodies had fallen. I requested their senior officers to step forward. I suggested to them that they were welcome to audit our class but that it was primarily intended for the living who had joined our circle and that I would be grateful if they would remain outside our perimeter and maintain good order."[12]

Based on their uniforms, those spirit people have been there for a very long time. I want to point out that, in Robert Moss's example, those soldiers in battle mode could have been the primary underlying cause of conflict among the staff and attendees at that retreat center. Their presence could keep up an agitated, argumentative feeling to the grounds and the buildings, and no one would ever figure that out unless they lived at an intuitive level of life.

Again, I want to emphasize that spirit people are focused on a certain environment because of the powerful negative emotions that surround it. When those negative emotions build over time and affect living people, they too add to the energy of the old conflict of war. Notice how Moss simply discussed things with

---

12 Robert Moss, *Sidewalk Oracles* (Novato, CA: New World Library, 2015), 60.

the leaders in a matter-of-fact dialogue. They seemed to agree. But notice that, at least in his book, he did not do a healing and release for those souls. Please always communicate in a back-and-forth dialogue in a matter-of-fact manner. Do not add to the trauma or the drama with your own emotions. And as always, never chase deceased people away. They are real people who need help to heal and release the emotions that locked them into that environment.

Jade Osera, an excellent mentoring client in Australia, shared her environmental experiences.

"I was advised by my guides many years ago . . . heal the land and the people will heal! It feels very important for people to have access to this information. I have lived in many areas around Australia and often become aware of past massacres and long-forgotten atrocities that have taken place here. Just as you write (in *Advanced Medical Intuition*), a lot of souls are often stuck because of shock, anger, and a feeling of not wanting to give up their land. I was once at a lake and became aware that I was shot in the arm with an energetic spear. I then noticed lots of indigenous male spirits in the trees, spearing the people around me, who remained oblivious, swimming and having family fun.

"I continued to see similar indigenous energy in the local areas. One day I was watching an energy print of a massacre of innocent indigenous families. Then, as I was watching the enactments from the land, a spirit made himself known to me. He said he was a gatekeeper for the area, and he shouted at me, 'Go away, witch!' I told him I was of the Light like him, and I showed him my Light. I said, 'Look at my energy. I want to help you.' He disappeared only to show up a day later with hundreds of indigenous souls at my house. I felt a little overwhelmed by this, as I had never crossed over such a large amount. I then assisted fifty at a time to go into the Light.

"The next time this happened unexpectedly, I was at a nature spot when a tribal leader appeared to me. As he talked, spirit people from everywhere started to appear. A big eight-pointed star appeared above the area and collected all the spirits. I was covered in goose bumps. The energy felt so calm and peaceful, I was moved to tears. When he spoke through me in another language, I understood what he was saying. The energies were shifting on Earth, and it was time to return home now."

As you can see in Jade's experiences, it is not only troubled deceased people who create negative thought forms in certain environments, but living people as well. Over time, negative thoughts will accumulate in certain locations. Every time a living person has a heavy negative thought and its subsequent emotion, the energy of it accumulates in that same space over time.

Another client, Jane, provides a case study demonstrating how the environment may be the primary cause of illness. This case also offers you an unusual example of Spirit giving an energetic healing assignment *before* I was given the cause. In my experience, this was quite different from other sessions. It is a perfect example showing how the medical intuitive must always be ready for the unexpected.

Jane sat down and immediately informed me she had multiple physical concerns. I held up my hand to interrupt her and insisted she remain silent as I perceived the information from her energy field and physical body. She was surprised but agreed.

Both of her lungs had round, fibrous nodules throughout, but they were heavier in her left lung. I asked my guides what would give the most complete healing for her lungs. They showed me my client was to imagine filling her lungs with the most beautiful shade of neon green. I walked her through the steps to imagine breathing in the green color. As she followed my directions, I began to feel quite nauseated. At the same time, I also realized the room was filling up with a heavy, musky smell of flowers. The smell was so intense I thought I would pass out. The thick smell decreased as Jane continued to practice her energy treatment.

I described everything I experienced: that a powerful smell of flowers had engulfed us to the point I was becoming ill, and that this floral smell was releasing from her lungs and the pores of her skin. I asked her if that made any sense. She appeared shocked and informed me that she and her mother owned a flower shop for thirty years. I told her the left lung appeared more stressed than the right lung. Because the left lung was more affected, I knew she struggled more with a female. This client immediately agreed.

I then walked Jane through an energy healing for her lungs. Many of your clients will have no idea how to accomplish their "energy homework," so you will need to walk them through the steps. As your client practices, watch their energy field to assess their ability to understand and accomplish the assignment. Ask your healing specialty guides how often and for how long the client should do their homework. It may come like a prescription for medication.

Jane's body and energy told me a story about the thirty-year struggle with her demanding mother. Her mother was in spirit, so I became the medium as well. Healing does not stop between two people just because one of them is in spirit. The medical intuitive then becomes the communication bridge for the living and the deceased client. A profound healing took place between Jane and her mother.

An example of a common physical location that causes physical or emotional illness, or tensions, could be a train track crossing that has a reputation for many deadly wrecks with automobiles. Many people who have been killed at that crossing remain there. Many continue to carry the emotion of shock just before the train hits them. Many deceased used the train as a means to commit suicide, which causes that extremely heavy burden of emotions to remain there as well.

Many people drive across those tracks every day and think about the train slamming into all those cars. Many people worry they might be in the next trainwreck. All that continual worry and fear is dense, and each day it builds up a little more all around that certain train crossing. People are literally driving through dense thought forms, which then begin to affect them. These people's negative emotions will add to these thought forms, and in return, the thought forms gravitate toward the person, adding to their struggles even more. Living people also affect the land, water, and the earth itself. As a result the land becomes toxic, and it circles around to create illness of the living people. The natural environment is thought to be the trigger for many allergies. People think their allergies are caused by pollen from trees, shrubs, and grass when, in fact, what lies beneath these allergies is an emotional cause.

The clearest example I can think of comes from one of my mentoring clients. She seemed to be allergic to the world around her. I commanded: "Tell me or show me now the exact point of origin causing all the allergies negatively affecting Lori." I instantly perceived her as a small child with the number six hovering over her head.

"I see you at the age of six with an older couple who seem like grandparents," I said. "They were talking about their allergies. Right then and there you decided that you wanted to have allergies too so you could be just like your grandparents."

Her emotions had sent out an empowered request to the Universe to receive allergies, and so she created allergies. If we have that much power at the age of six to create an illness, we adults have even more power and wisdom to create our health. Believe it first, then power up! (To heal allergies, refer to the Soul Retrieval Steps in chapter 7.

The entire Earth is our environmental home. Hugh Newman, author of *Earth Grids* and speaker on the History Channel, is known for his exploration of the ancient sights and the energy matrix that is associated with the Earth. The Earth itself is a living entity, and it too is about 70 percent water. Emotions within the human body and the body of the Earth affect the water. The Earth on its own has its high-energy places and its lower-energy places. It has its ley lines, energy grids, vortices, and patterns. We humans also have our own influences on the Earth's energy field. The Earth affects us and we affect it.[13]

Healing Technique:
Releasing Spirit People from Your Environment

The actions and powerful emotions of humans can affect any location on the surface of the Earth. They affect intersections with repeated automobile wrecks, train crossings where people have died, or houses where traumatic events have taken place, such as abuse or murder. The healings you facilitate will often involve the Earth, as it is a living being.

Here are simple guidelines to create a conversation with a deceased human that will lead to a powerful healing and release for them. They need your help.

1. Ask your Divine and Sacred guides if there are deceased people in your environment, especially if you do not see or perceive them. If you receive a "yes," then go to the next step.

2. Ask the deceased person: "Who are you? Why are you here in (my house, land, workspace, etc.)?" Pause after each individual question to receive the answers that pop into your mind.

3. Then ask: "Do you realize you are dead? Do you realize staying here in this location is not the best place for you?" Pause for the answers.

4. Inform the deceased person that you are calling in specialists to assist them into a new and special life.

5. Call in your Divine and Sacred guides who specialize in transitioning the deceased and take the deceased person to the highest place for their transformation into Light and Love.

6. If the deceased person resists, be firm and consistent. Tell

13 Hugh Newman, *Earth Grids: The Secret Patterns of Gaia's Sacred Sites* (Glastonbury: Wooden Books, 2008).

them: "This is not the greatest life for you. There is nothing here for you anymore." If the deceased person resists, then command that the specialty guides wrap them in warm blanket of loving white light. Tell the deceased person to feel the love coming from the guides.

7. When anything is released or removed, in this case a deceased human, it must be filled and replaced with something powerfully positive. Call in your Divine and Sacred healing specialists and command: "Fill every single space and place where that spirit person used to be with Light, Compassion, and Love."

I want to remind you that just like there are specialists in the physical world for everything, there are specialists in the nonphysical world for everything too. Even the Bible says, "As above, so below." Who knew it applied to spirit specialists too?

Healing Technique:
Clearing Negative Thought Forms from Your Environment

The beginning of this chapter describes how human violence affects the earth. The negative emotions people feel in certain locations, such as fear or hate, will build up a density that will collect over time in these locations. You need to cleanse and heal these thick collections from these environments. If a thought form is not healed and released from that particular area on Earth, its energy will continue to affect other humans. Healing these negative thoughts forms is like giving your environment a good, long shower. Here are the healing steps to release these negative thought forms from your environment:

1. Call out to Divine and Sacred guides who specialize in removing and cleansing all types of negativity.

2. Command: "Now completely and permanently remove all accumulations of negativity on all levels and in all places associated with me, (your full name)."

3. Then command: "Now cleanse all spaces and places where the negative used to be with precious, pure, clean energy. Permanently place it within, throughout, and around on all levels and in all dimensions."

Healing Technique:
Clearing Physical Toxins from Your Environment

Raymon Grace is well known for using these steps to clean up and heal schools for children, and to clear toxins from water and land. Invite in your most powerful Divine and Sacred healers, then command the following in these exact words:

- Command: "Now completely and permanently scramble all the exact points of origin causing the toxic, contaminated *(name the land, water, or area)* at *(name the exact address or location)*."

- Then command: "Now completely and permanently neutralize all the exact points of origin causing the toxic, contaminated *(name the land, water, or area)* at *(name the exact address or location)*."

- Then command: "Now completely and permanently transform all that has been scrambled and neutralized into *(clean, wholesome, vitally alive, etc.)* *(name the land, water, or area)* at *(name the exact address or location)*."

Essential Points

- The environment is the cause of many emotional struggles such as anxiety, nightmares, depression, and many other symptoms.
- Your environment becomes anywhere you are located at the time.
- Spirit people are focused on a certain environment because of the powerful negative emotions that surround it.

- Every time a living person has a heavy negative thought and its subsequent emotion, the energy of it accumulates in that same location over time.

- Communicate with negative spirits that are attached to an environment in a matter-of-fact manner. Do not add to the trauma or the drama with your own emotions.

Chapter 14

Ancestors Causing Illness or Life Struggles

I want to clearly state here that, in this second edition of *Advanced Medical Intuition*, I have added ancestors as its own separate category, making a total of eight causes of illness, challenges, or life struggles. I mentioned ancestors in my other books, but I neglected to give them their own category of causing illness and challenges. The more I hear from people about their ancestors, the more I recognized the need to identify ancestors as its own category of causes.

Someone once sent me a Facebook post written by a person named Chris Swart. I think you will find it as thought provoking as I did. He called it "Ancestral Mathematics." In other words, for you to be born today with twelve previous generations, you needed a total of 4,094 ancestors over the past four hundred years.

- 2 Parents
- 4 Grandparents
- 8 Great-Grandparents
- 16 Second Great-Grandparents
- 32 Third Great-Grandparents
- 64 Fourth Great-Grandparents
- 128 Fifth Great-Grandparents
- 256 Sixth Great-Grandparents
- 512 Seventh Great-Grandparents
- 1,024 Eighth Great-Grandparents
- 2,048 Ninth Great-Grandparents

Think for a moment: How many struggles, battles, or diffi-culties; how much sadness or happiness; how many love stories or expressions of hope for the future did your ancestors have to undergo for you to exist in the present moment?

Ancestors and People from Our Past Lives: Are They the Same?

I hear over and over again that students automatically place their ancestors and past-life family members into the same group. Most people, in my experience, seem to readily assume that our past-life family members are the same people who are now our ancestors. In truth, I have only come across that interconnection a few times over decades of being a past-life regressionist and a medical-intuitive medium. People are extremely surprised when I declare, after working with thousands and thousands of people over many years, that I have rarely seen the same souls participate in both a person's past lives and in their ancestry. It happens so rarely that I was the one who was amazingly surprised the few times it occurred.

We living humans are affected by the lineage of our ancestry but also the individuals in our past lives. But this does not mean they are the same people or the same souls. Before our birth, we apparently come to an agreement that we are born into a certain lineage. This lineage gives us the genetics, heritage, facial structure, and the body form that our soul will reside in. This lineage, of course, is also part of our current-life experience and often a powerful portion of our learning experiences. So, our ancestry forms the physical body for the experiences in this current life.

The individuals who share one or more past lives with us usually have nothing to do with the genetics of our current physical body. They do, however, seem to have a great deal to do with our experiences in this current life. You and your past-life colleagues seem to be a general plan to come into each other's lives for a split second, or a week, or a year, or possibly from birth to death and then beyond again. You have opportunities to learn and advance with them, and they have opportunities to learn and advance because of you. The past-life individuals help create current-life traumas and relationships, and both current and future emotions.

The people in our ancestry lineage, however, help to compose our physical body in this current life. Your ancestry certainly impacts your body and existence, but you may be completely different from who you were in a multitude of past lives. Generally, physical body characteristics come down through our ancestors. This is your current family history for the current physical body you are inhabiting in your current life now. This is not the same as your past lives.

Again, emotions cling to us throughout our past lives and carry into our current life. Our emotions and the thoughts that caused them, influence the genetics we received from the ancestors. Emotions from our current life trigger our genetics as well. Our thoughts and emotions either turn on our genes or turn them off.

In his book, *The Biology of Belief*, scientist Dr. Bruce Lipton states: "Positive thoughts have a profound effect on behavior and genes . . . And negative thoughts have an equally powerful effect. When we recognize how these positive and negative beliefs control our biology, we can use this knowledge to create lives filled with health and happiness."[14]

Dr. Lipton also states:

"My life-changing moment occurred while I was reviewing my research on the mechanisms by which cells control their physiology and behavior. Suddenly I realized that a cell's life is fundamentally controlled by the physical and energetic environment with only a small contribution by its genes. Genes are simply molecular blueprints used in the construction of cells, tissues, and organs. The environment serves as a 'contractor' who reads and engages those genetic blueprints and is ultimately responsible for the character of a cell's life. It is a

---

14 Bruce Lipton, *The Biology of Belief: Unleashing the Power of Consciousness, Matter & Miracles* (Carlsbad, CA: Hay House, 2016), xxviii.

single cell's 'awareness' of the environment that primarily sets into motion the mechanisms of life . . .

"If a protein did not have a complementary signal to couple with, it would not function. This means, as I concluded in that 'aha!' moment, that every protein in our bodies is a physical/electromagnetic complement to something in the environment. Because we are machines made out of protein, by definition we are made in the image of the environment, that environment being the Universe, or to many, God."[15]

I love it when science comes together and their findings work together with the world of energy medicine. Again and again, science continues to discover the power of our thoughts and emotions, and how they create an environment within us and throughout our genetics. Those same positive or negative emotions follow down through generations by sharing emotional family stories with the next generation. My mentoring student received intuitive information regarding her client's health, and found the cause of his illness stemmed from his ancestors. Jade Osera, from Australia, shared her experience:

"The Ancestral healing does deserve its own category. I have heard many times over the years people calling in their ancestors, and it makes me wince for all the reasons you clearly state. It really needed to be addressed. I have adapted your medical-intuitive steps already to take clients back to the ancestor who created the inherited condition.

"I worked last year with a man who had a heart condition (he had already had two heart attacks and he was only in his early fifties, but he was otherwise very fit and healthy). This condition was already known to him and known to have come down his father line. The client then discovered the cause himself. The point of origin was a woman four generations back. Our guides assisted the healing on her and two subsequent people (in the ancestral line) who inherited it also. When we

---

15 Bruce Lipton, 207.

had finished healing the point of origin that began four generations ago, we both saw that the pattern was cleared from his energy field. He said he instantly felt better, and many months on (even after having COVID-19) he has not had any heart trouble since.

"At the end of this ancestral healing, this man and I were guided to check the energy of his (current-life) children to make sure the pattern was completely clear in them too. Perhaps for his peace of mind? Which it was. I then finished the session with a future progression forwarding my client to a scene where he could see himself healthy, walking a beach as an older man and embodying the feeling of contentment. He knew his children were grown and he had been there (as this was his fear, to not see his girls grow up). I suggested he allow that feeling to fill his body. It felt like a merging with that timeline occurred.

"This is powerful, life-changing work. I guess we are, at all times, healing the past and the future by healing the now."

There is one more detail that may clarify a common false idea. Most people consider all their ancestors as positive guides for them, and they call out to them and invite them into their lives and decisions. Please do not do that. Just because they are dead does not mean they are positive or developed, and it does not mean they have reached the status level of guides or angels. When we leave our bodies, we pretty much take with us the level of awareness and thoughtfulness we had achieved at that moment of death. Calling out to your ancestors for help does not define any status or development as a guide, let alone the status of being divine and sacred.

The Traumatic History of Your Ancestors

Most of our ancestors suffered such cruelty and hardships of which we can barely conceive now. Life was brutal, and people's thoughts were raw and inflamed with emotions, especially a horrible fear of the world around them and of the unknown. Curses and vows were rampant. Those volatile events and emotions naturally travel down the ancestry lineage on a physical level of the genetics, but those emotions also follow down the lineage through family stories.

Powerful and dramatic negative emotions hold tight within the essence of our soul and follow the soul into the next life and the life after that. There are two primary reasons for this: 1) Emotions cling to our souls and follow these souls on their journey. These emotions tend to stay with us because traumatic negativity is extremely thick, dense, and sticky. 2) We human souls carry the trauma, and sometimes even memory of it, into the next life because we are trying to learn from it and advance into a healing and a total release.

Instead of learning, healing, and releasing, we humans often get caught up in these old patterns because the heavy burden is so familiar to us. One primary thing I have noticed about past lives is that we keep repeating the same old patterns because those energies of trauma linger within the soul. It seems the grand plan is to give us as many opportunities as we need to learn, heal the burden, and then release it forever.

Our ancestral lineage is fundamentally about the choice of our body and its traits, our brain, and intellectual abilities. The dense energy of negative emotions follows along the genetic lines of the body that you and your sacred guides chose for you in this current life. Remember that science is finding that emotions either turn on genetic keys or turn them off.

Not only do genetics affect us, but the beliefs (thought energy) of the lineage do as well. Here again is the power of our thought energy. Many families have stories that happened in their ancestors' lives. These stories can be about suffering under prejudice, traveling across the world to save themselves, the family's story of being cursed, or thousands of other situations.

Families tell their stories over and over again. Those stories become intense beliefs. Beliefs have emotions interwoven within their history. You would think that as each generation moves on to the next, the family stories of hardships, curses, and beliefs would subside, but in fact, they build strength with each generation. What family beliefs hold you back or cause you illness or challenges? You can heal and release these negative stories for yourself and your entire ancestry. Here is a small portion of a session that addresses a client's suspicions that their ancestry was causing dark thoughts.

Case Study:
Ancestors' Struggles Affecting a Current Life

Client: I ruminate. I can get dark about things. I think it is how I was set up astrologically or with my ancestry.

TZ: There are steps to take, and we have the ability to heal our ancestry and our past.

Client: Ooh, wow!

TZ: Oh my goodness, that sounds like you really like that idea. So, let's begin with you calling in a Divine and Sacred guide who specializes in healing and releasing struggles through the ancestry. I will be quiet, put that call out to the Universe, and see who responds to your call.

Client: Okay. It is a Native American, and he is huge! Nearly up to the ceiling and powerful. I feel him in my heart. My grandfather collected a large book of correspondences. They were pioneers and seemed to have no problems writing letters about the terrible treatment they did to the native people. Real sadistic stuff. I feel so much grief about this.

TZ: Ask your huge guide what to do about this history in your ancestry. Go ahead and ask him.

Client: *(Long pause)* I see this guide beaming tidal waves of Light through time and through souls who needed that Light. Then the Light spread to the Earth plane. He was like pulling an old, corroded, rusty chain away from my ankles, and he was doing it through time. I had been held like a prisoner. I want to keep up this ancestral work.

TZ: Now, would you be willing to talk to your big guy *(the specialist she is working with)* and take care in forming the command? Command him: "Show me or tell me the exact point of origin that my ancestors' struggles began." Then just wait to see what you notice.

Client: I see the 1500s, and I see a blond, curly-haired man. He is a monster and slaughtering the poor people.

TZ: Ask your guide if you are accurate in what you just perceived?

Client: Yes. I have always been fascinated with this time frame. I hope that man was not me in the past?

TZ: Now, stop right there and notice how you keep getting information but then you do not continue to ask more short, precise questions.

Client: Yes, you are right! I do not ask the next questions.

TZ: Then ask your guide right now if you were the man that you were just shown.

Client: No, I was not, but I was born into that line. Your progression has been that you have been on the aggressor's side and the receiver's side. It is a dynamic that you carry. You will let it go . . . You will let it go . . . You will let it go . . . I am shown that I am put on a stone bed, and I am being worked on by Spirit. They are pulling stuff out of me. I am being healed. It was a whole ceremony. Four Native Americans with wooden staffs were pulling all this negative energy out and spinning like yarn around their staffs. It was coming out of me and the ages too. They sent it up into the Light and cleared me too. The guide who yells said, "You will not have that energy anymore! You will do your work!" I think he means that I am to use all my training to help others.

Healing Technique:
Releasing You from Your Ancestors' Struggles

1. Ask your Divine and Sacred guides to tell you or show you the exact point of origin causing your illness or challenge. You are in some manner informed that it is your ancestry.

2. Ask: "How many generations does *(name the illness or struggle)* go back to?" You will see a number, or you will need to count back through a line of people who represent the number of generations.

3. Command your guides to show you the exact moment it happened to the ancestor with whom the ancestral problems began.

4. Command: "Go back to that exact minute, and completely and permanently remove all negativity and all darkness from all people involved and throughout all generations from that moment on, and remove all negativity and all darkness from every person who has ever been affected by that original moment now." Watch what they show you.

5. Command: "Fill every moment and every person with compassion, benevolence, empathy, and unconditional love now."

Time is not linear and you are not limited. Remember, you are only as limited as your thoughts. You and your guides are entirely skilled to heal throughout many generations of your ancestry and past lives across time and space.

Essential Points

- We living humans are affected by the lineage of our ancestry but also the individuals in our past lives. This does not mean they are the same people or the same souls.

- Our ancestors affect our current physical-body characteristics.

- The people who share one or more past lives with us affect our current-life experiences.

- Emotions cling to us throughout our past lives and carry into our current life.

- Our thoughts and emotions from our current life trigger our genetics.

- Calling out to your ancestors for help does not define any status or development as a guide, let alone the status of being divine and sacred.

- The events and emotions of our ancestors travel down their lineage both genetically and through family stories.

- Powerful and dramatic negative emotions hold tight within the essence of our soul and follow our soul into our next lives.

- We keep repeating the same old patterns between lives because the energies of trauma linger within the soul.

Chapter 15

Past Lives Causing Illness or Life Struggles

"One afternoon, Mum and I talked . . . We decided cancer or any illness was a life lesson, an unexpected event that we had to master ourselves. Mum said she'd been shot, hung, burned at the stake, thrown off a cliff . . . lived many lives. Perhaps this one was mastering illness . . . the spiritual growth within. For illness tests our inner strength and beliefs . . . especially fear."

—Shona Wong, talking to Denise Wong
just before her passing

Our past lives are truly fascinating and nothing to be afraid of. Knowledge of our past lives sheds light on the struggles you and your clients experience. If this knowledge brings you to understand the point of origin of your client's current-life illness or struggles, you can conduct a more permanent healing. I want to share my experience with my own past life and the spontaneous healing that took place.

I was vacationing in Colorado for about a week. No one was sleeping through the night due to having so many strange dreams. Because of all the struggles we were having, I did a cleansing of the room, the building, and the grounds where we were staying by using a dowsing technique I learned from Raymon Grace. The next evening, the spirit of a very traditional-looking, Old West cowboy came to me in the room.

"I am Roy Garrett. The work you did (I wasn't sure, but I think he meant the energy cleansing) made it possible for me to come in and connect with you."

As he spoke to me, he stood tall and lean. His hair was long, a little below his shoulders. He wore a dark shirt, jeans with leather chaps, and a cowboy hat. He wore traditional cowboy boots and a coat that hung down to the top of his boots. One minute the coat would be visible but the next minute it would disappear, almost like it was flickering.

He said, "I love this land. We used to live here. You were an Indian woman and you were my partner." When he said this, I had a feeling he had purchased me. I did not think to confirm that feeling with him. I told him I thought I had been a male Indian and not a female. Images appeared in my mind's eye. The images told me I was correct, but I was a male in the life before the one with Roy Garrett.

I witnessed scenes of my life as a male Native American. In deep remorse, I left my tribe on horseback and traveled a narrow trail high up in the mountains. The past-life me looked straight ahead, down the length of my horse's neck and focused between my horse's ears. I never looked back at the people I chose to leave. (I have seen that moment a hundred times before in my current life.) I left because the white man was coming, but my community stayed because the chief told them to. I knew they were doomed to die. I lived the rest of my life alone, living in a cave and dying in that same cave as a very old man. At the time of my death, I left my old, worn body and lifted up through the rocks as if they were gentle clouds.

The puzzle pieces dropped into place. I reincarnated into that life as a Native American woman sold to a white male. I had to live with Roy but discovered he was a good and kind man. That life gave me the opportunity to make peace within myself about "white people" and the two vastly different cultures of white and Native American.

As Roy stood there in spirit form, I asked, "What am I to do with this information now in this life?"

"Just love the land," Roy said. That will bring healing to the land and also to both of us."

I continued to feel his presence during my stay in Colorado. The point of origin of my own healing came through a gentle man who was gentle in his past life and remains just as gentle as a person in spirit. The point of origin is sometimes simple and gentle, but it is often painful and surprising.

Time is eternal. Time and the human soul are intertwined in a timeless eternity. Try to wrap your mind around living within an eternal continuum. A majority of the population think human life is a one-time experience, while others believe they have lived past lives but those memories are far away and unreachable. Still another faction of the population can access past-life memories with hope of learning about their history and advancing beyond it.

We can consciously experience our past lives, our future lives, and our current lives. We are only limited, as usual, by the boundaries of our thinking mind. We humans are capable of a consciousness that retains important information throughout time. Not only can we decide to go back in time, but we can also go forward into our future potential and its possibilities. Déjà vu seems to happen when we humans journey forward into those future possibilities. Then, when we arrive there at a later time, we vaguely remember those future moments and call it "déjà vu."

Past-Life Trauma Creating Energy Signatures

In a violent or otherwise extremely shocking event, our emotions are at a peak. The emotional intensity in a past life will frequently transfer into a current life. Because the existence of life is in a continuum and not chopped into segments of this life and that life, you and your client are able to journey back into past lives. Usually, a highly emotional event—whether positive, negative, or traumatic—produces a thought form that is a dense globule of energy. That globule is actually "unfinished business" that remains dense, heavy, and even sticky. That is why past-life trauma may still affect our current lives. We travel through the continuum of time and space, lugging around an unconscious weight. This energy signature may remain with us until we reach a level of awareness when we are capable of learning something important from the old event.

Heartache and trauma is not the only energy that moves with us. Profound healing also flows freely across time and space. The medical intuitive's primary goal is to uncover the precise moment the negative energy signature was created. Once they discover that moment in time, together the medical intuitive and the client will begin the healing process for that particular past-life moment. The client will soon understand the painful past-life events as opportunities to learn and advance in wakeful consciousness. We always have that choice.

When I sit with a client—be it on the phone, Skype, or in my office—we eventually get to the moment when I intuitively call out to the cosmos, asking for the point of origin of my client's illness or struggles. I know we are heading into a past life when I feel a pull to my left, which would be to the client's right. That is my signal from the guides that we are heading into a past life. You may have the same signal or a completely different one.

Case Study:
Negativity Follows from One Life to Another

This excerpt is a clear example of negative energy signatures following this client through time and space. In this case, the client was brutally criticized in a past life and that energy followed her into her current life. As a result, this woman is barraged by her own brutal self-criticism and judgment of others.

Practice Experience:

Imagine you are the medical intuitive speaking the words in this transcript. Read it aloud or, if possible, with a study buddy, one taking part as the medical intuitive and one as the client. Practice this session as if you are actually giving these steps to someone who needs your guidance.

TZ: I just asked to be shown the exact point of origin of your struggles. I am getting that in past lives, you were under extreme criticism. You yourself were not doing the criticizing, but you were under extreme criticism in many past lives.

Client: Do you mean many lives, or more than one at least?

TZ: Many past lives under extreme criticism. That is what came up right away. You carry that energy signature, so now in this life you are going to criticize others. I keep getting the word "retaliation." It is because you were under tremendous duress of judgment and criticism coming from family. As a result, in this life, you have minimal family now.

Client: I don't want to be around family.

TZ: It is purposeful to not have family this time around.

Client: Oh, it makes sense to me.

TZ: Does it?

Client: Oh God, yes.

TZ: You were crushed under violent criticism. Crushed.

Client: That's why today, if I get the slightest criticism, I take it on like it's a major, major deal.

TZ: Oh, yes. It looks like a steel bar, or a rod, of anger. It has become solid. I see it in your head.

Client: So, it's strong. And when I pop out that anger, I am also criticizing.

TZ: You're criticizing. And it involves women.

Client: Really?

TZ: Well, they are showing me that you are cowering down, and some big old chunky woman, who was your mother, is letting you have it constantly, constantly. You are still carrying that energy signature, and so criticism just flies out of you as if you don't know where it is even coming from.

Client: I don't have any control over it. When it comes flying out I think, "What the hell? This isn't that important. Why are you this upset?" Then I feel guilty because I'm criticizing.

TZ: Now the female part of this is really standing out. Is it usually about females?

Client: Mothers. And just today some woman was driving a van, fumbling around with something. The light had changed and I was trying to get here to this appointment. I honked my horn and said, "Some f'ing mother!" I said, "Damn women van drivers! I'm going to be late 'cause of her!" Yep. I'm going to examine that from now on.

TZ: I am getting that it is time for you to be aware this is all in your subconscious.

Client: Yes, it is.

TZ: They are saying it is time for you to knock it off.

Client: I agree. Oh, I need to stop that criticism. I'm just bellering at the TV, walking through the house grumbling about the neighbors and everything. And I certainly did not become a mother, did I?

TZ: No, and yet here you are in a female body.

Client: Yeah, I'm probably mad about that too.

(Here, information from this client's future life comes forward.)

TZ: I actually see you as a little boy in your next life that is coming up. So, you came in as female this time, and I think I have said this to you before, and you have not had any lives as female, or not very many.

Client: Not very many. All right, here is what I think *(about women)*. For God's sake, you were given a brain, use it. You don't need to do that kind of girly stuff. Wow! This is amazing to understand this. I think I am cleaning out. I am not taking this with me again *(to her next life)*. It's out of my luggage.

TZ: It seemed to be more about anger as a result of criticism. Oh, I have to say this too. You are losing a lot of your power as you do this.

Client: The anger?

TZ: No, the criticism. You are losing a great deal of energy from your solar plexus.

Client: I have been told that recently from someone else.

(Many people will tell you they have heard the same information from other intuitives. I happily respond, "If you are going to real intuitives, we will tell you similar information, because that information actually vibrates within your energy field.")

TZ: You are losing your own power with all that criticism. It is as if you are cowering.

Client: Well, that makes sense.

TZ: I see a little sister of yours in the scene, and the mother didn't do anything about your abusive sister.

Client: Was the little sister a girly girl?

TZ: Yes, she was a very girly girl.

Client: There it is! That's it! That's it! How best can I clear that out?

TZ: Well, we went to the point of origin. The point of origin I am getting is from this life, which is your most recent life. The one we have been talking about. Your little girly-girl sister was taught by your mother to be demeaning to you. She was brought up in the same environment as you but in a different way. Your mother would start the criticism and be demeaning, and your little sister would chime in and she would stand there with a big smile on her face while you cowered like this *(a fetal position)* on the floor. The little girl did not know any better or any different.

Client: You know, I have a tendency that if somebody is cowering or even sick, sometimes I think I want to get away from them. I don't want to even look at that kind of thing! Yes, there might have been some of that going on with that little girl too.

TZ: Well, your little sister saw her mom do it, so that must be what we do.

Client: Yeah.

TZ: Now, I am also getting that your current mother and your current mother's twin sister were very critical in your current life. Is that true?

Client: They were both extremely critical of themselves. They both were.

TZ: Your mom's twin, your current aunt, was your girly little sister in your past life.

Client: You're kidding! My aunt in this life is also frilly, frilly, frilly! When I walk into her house even now, I say, "Oh, your house is so pretty, Aunt Susie!" Inside I'm thinking I could never live like this!

TZ: So, it makes sense to me, and to you, that I see your aunt was your sister in that past life?

Client: Yes. That does make complete sense to me.

Past lives can be a potent factor affecting one's current life. When people say phrases like the following, those words often originate from vague memories from a past life:

"I don't know why I keep doing that."

"I keep thinking these thoughts and I cannot stop them."

"I feel like I know that person and I don't know why."

"I have never met that man, but I cannot be around him. He scares me."

"The second we met, it felt as if I had known you forever."

The following case offers an example of a violent past life that still affects this woman's current life. During the years of her current life, she occasionally picked up signals that reminded her of something painful. It was information about this past life that allowed the puzzle pieces to fall into place.

Case Study:
Past-Life Torture Manifesting in the Current Life

This case study describes how the energy signature of torture is carried into the client's current life. This study incorporates a certain healing technique for healing a painful past life. Notice these steps as they happen in this transcription.

Practice Experience:

Imagine that you are the medical intuitive speaking the words in this transcript. Read it out loud and, if possible, read it with a study buddy, one taking part as the medical intuitive and one being the client. Practice this session as if you are actually giving these steps to someone who needs your guidance.

Client: I have a condition in my vagina which is a white patch of cells. I had it a number of years ago, and I had it treated homeopathically and it went away. It's supposedly incurable and it came back again. I've been working on healing the uterus stuff because I think it is related to my past life. I had a C-section in this life, and I had terrible periods when I was a kid. I had a past-life reading of being a concubine in China and being treated very poorly. I was too young to have a child, yet I gave birth to a female child. I think I died as a result of problems after childbirth. There has always been something that freaked me out about women dying in childbirth. My first husband *(in her current life)* was Asian. I had a very strong preference for having a son and I did have a son. All that stuff has been bubbling up. I've been practicing what you said about going back and healing. I felt such compassion for this poor young woman who was really just not valued. She was just nothing.

TZ: I just realized that as I described your tailbone and the two other places in your lower spine *(earlier in the session)*, I already asked you to bring in that red sparkly energy. This whole area *(of her lower abdomen)* is very low energy and not flowing in those three places in your spine. This extremely low energy allows illness to happen in that area of the body.

As you talk about this past life, I am just sitting here listening to you and checking out your energy. *(A gruesome scene was developing within my mind's eye.)* Tell me, how you are healing it. *(Notice how it changes as they speak. Tell them what you perceived.)*

(As your client talks, just sit, notice, watch, and feel the client's energy.)

Client: I try to touch in with her *(the concubine)*, and I tried to go back to that life and tell her it's okay.

TZ: What did you notice happen as you did that?

Client: I felt like she had more peace when she died. I felt like she wasn't alone when she was dying. I also had another weird experience. Somebody lent me a book last year. She said she felt like she was supposed to lend it to me. It was about a woman who had a past-life memory of her being a witch. It gets to the part where she's being abused and tortured before she died, and it was so powerful to me. I related to it so much, and I realized that torture and abuse was in my past life for having practiced healing.

TZ: And to get more specific, are you aware of sexual torture? Because that is what I am getting. It wasn't just that they drowned you, or burned you at the stake; it was a sexual torture.

(It is important to say the hard things with great sensitivity and compassion.)

Client: Yes. When I read this part of the book, I couldn't put it down. It was like, oh my God, I really related to that! She was tortured for a couple of days. This is her own past-life memory of what happened. I can't tell you . . . I don't know how . . . I guess I need to hear that somehow. I think part of my physical issues are related to that.

TZ: Yes. There are also some issues with men in general. You are carrying the energy signature of the sexual torture from men. This is a strong word, but it is about feeling helpless or victimized by the men and carrying that into your current life.

Client: Yes, oh my God, I just have to share something.

TZ: Please, please yes.

Client: Just as you said that, I was remembering a situation when I was seventeen years old. My boyfriend had dumped me and I was feeling awful. A friend of mine, who was a lot older, fixed me up with his brother on a date. I went out on a date with this fellow and we were drinking. We were making out, and I realized that he was intent to have sex with me. I didn't want to, but I couldn't get out of it. I knew I was either going to be raped or I was going to go along with it. I said to myself, I'm not going to be a victim. I just went along and prayed that I didn't get pregnant, or get herpes, or whatever. After that I said to myself, "I'm not a victim!" I did that, and I am never going to be in that situation again, and do you know, I never went out in a car with a guy again. If I didn't know him very well, I would be very careful and very deliberate. Even in my mind I said, "I am not going to be a victim." I'm going to go along with this because if I fight him I'm going to lose, and I will always have the stigma of having been raped.

TZ: Yes. Look how all of that, all the puzzle pieces, are falling into place here.

Client: Yes, wow! So, how do I heal this?

(The following description of this past-life trauma may be too graphic for some readers. I ask that you try to stay with it so you can understand the healing that comes from delving into the horrible.)

TZ: Let's go back. Just follow your history back to that moment. In other words, just follow that sense of the victim, or that sense of the torture, and see what unfolds in your awareness. I will be quiet until you speak about it. It feels like a specific place.

Client: I'm getting a very specific . . . I think I was burned. I think something very hot, burning hot, was shoved up deep inside of me.

TZ: Yes, I agree.

Client: I think I feel like it was a religious thing. I don't know if it was the Inquisition, or just crazy religious people, or this authority thing happening. I couldn't defend myself against it. It was like a kangaroo court, and then I was tortured just for being a healer.

TZ: Yes.

Client: For understanding things that other people didn't understand. It's interesting, because I've been an astrologer for over twenty years and there are people who have known me forever who don't know things like this about me.

TZ: You know, we tend to keep things like this covered up. We tend to have some hiddenness about it, so it is okay. When I mentioned about the sexual nature of your torture, I sat here and I thought, "I don't really see intercourse," and I was not seeing rape but things being jammed up inside of you. I didn't see the burning hot thing. Do you realize that the diagnosis you have right now is a white patch of tissue inside of your vagina?

Client: Yeah. Dead tissue in the vagina, like the skin is dying.

TZ: Yes, I keep seeing white. Do you know if it is white?

Client: Yes.

(Never demand that the client must go to the traumatic past-life event. Strongly encourage they do so. The healing will be just as profound as the trauma ever was.)

TZ: That is what I am seeing. Think about what the tissue would do in that area when it was burned. *(Pause.)* Okay, now I want the current you to go back to that event, if you would, and if it feels right to you. Stand there before the torture began. It is important to go before it happens. It could be a moment before, or five minutes before, it doesn't matter. Go and be with the past-life you . . . back then, before it all started, and just see what you notice and just tell me.

(Long pause.)

Client: I feel terrified. I'm really scared, because I don't know if I can get out of it, or how long it will last until I die.

TZ: Now, I want you to get her attention, the past-life you who is back there. Make sure that she *(her past-life self)* notices you. Take your time and see how you two do that. Just be there with her. Let yourself feel like you're dreaming it up, because it might feel that way. *(Long pause.)* Does she realize you're there?

Client: *(Crying)* I think so.

TZ: Okay, check that out and see what makes you think so.

Client: She said there's something there.

TZ: Okay, excellent, excellent. Now I want the two of you to talk it over. It can be telepathic, just thoughts bouncing back and forth, or you both being verbal to each other. I want you two to talk it over, and then I want you two to take your power back from that situation, and take it back from the people involved.

I want you to take your power back. I want you both to put that command out there that you are taking your power back, then just wait to see how that happens. Take your time. I am going to be quiet until you speak.

(Very long pause.)

(Never direct the healing. The client will always know the perfect way to heal.)

Client: Okay.

TZ: Now, what did you two notice?

Client: I sense we were drawn together, and I put a pink bubble around the two of us. I told her I couldn't stop this from happening but that she was going to be okay. She would be in the bubble and she didn't have to be the victim. She would be in a future life and it would be very, very different circumstances.

TZ: Ohhhh boy, there is something very perfect about that, because I have goose bumps from head to toe. There is something deeply, deeply right about that. Okay, and then what did you two notice? If anything.

Client: I felt a real connection to her. I was glad there was one of my fragmented personalities, or former personalities. She's a part of me, but I don't have to have the pain.

TZ: Now the next step is very, very important. The two of you together, give back all the crap, all the pain, all the terror, all of it. I want the two of you to take all of that stuff out of you and give it back. Give it back to that moment, give it back to the people involved, and make sure you take it out of both of you and give it back to them. Take your time and see how that unfolds and let yourselves both feel it.

Client: Okay.

TZ: My guides are asking me to tell the two of you to look them in the eyes with all your power, all your strength. Look at every single one of the wrongdoers. Look them right in the eye.

Client: Okay.

(A few minutes go by before she opens her eyes and looks at me.)

TZ: Now, just tell me what you noticed. What did it look like? What happened? Then I have something I need to share with you that was a very different experience for me. It is connected with what you just did. Tell me first, what did it look like? What happened?

Client: I felt like I was physically giving all the energy, the dark energy, to these people. When you said to look them in the eye, I didn't see humans! I saw these monster figures I was looking at.

TZ: Did you? That makes sense.

Client: I felt stronger. I felt a release in my lower chakra, and I—I feel more in my own power about it, and I understand it can't hurt me again.

TZ: And what did they do with it when you gave them back all their crap and looked them in the eye? What did you notice about them, if anything?

Client: Maybe they got a little smaller, shrinking back.

TZ: Excellent, excellent. Okay, now are the two of you still together? Are you still right there together?

Client: Yes.

(The soul retrieval begins here. Direct the client to bring their fragmented piece of soul back and merge it into their current life. Do not tell them how to achieve this.)

TZ: All right. There is another step. Would you two talk it over and ask her if she is willing now to completely release that moment and come forward with you?

(Pause.)

Client: Yes, I am able to take her away from there.

(Tell the person it will always feel like imagination. Never tell them how to do the steps.)

TZ: Just see how you two do that and describe it.

Client: I told her I couldn't stop the torture that was going to happen to her physical body but that her soul could leave and come with me so it wouldn't be recorded on her soul.

TZ: Oh, that's beautiful! And so she did that?

Client: Yes.

(Asking the person to share details when a step is complete will solidify the reality of the healing.)

TZ: Where is she now in proximity to you? Does she have a location?

Client: I feel like she's in my heart center.

TZ: Okay, excellent. So, inside of you?

Client: Yes.

TZ: Okay, very good. See, I did not ask you to merge together. You just did it very naturally.

Client: Yes.

TZ: All right, just sit there for a moment if you would, and I want you to notice whatever you notice. I also want you to feel the aliveness and this beautiful sparkling red coming up through your vaginal area, filling your whole groin, your whole hip area, and all your female organs. Let it fill you with cellular vitality. I'll be quiet. *(A few minutes pass before she opens her eyes.)* Is it all right if I tell you a couple of things?

Client: Yes, please.

(Always give homework. That sends a message that they have the power to create and sustain their own healing.)

TZ: Well . . . besides the sparkly red, there is also this beautiful pink too, a very rich kind of rosy pink. Sparkly red is cellular health and vitality. This rosy pink is self-love that you are bringing up through your body. What they *(my healing specialists)* want me to emphasize to you is to make sure that you deliberately send it into your tailbone and into your spinal column. You are getting some homework about this. Let me see what they're saying . . . They don't want you to work at this. I could tell you to do this eight times per day and you could just work at it like crazy. They are telling you not to work at this but to let it rise up through you and to let your physical body feel a healing warmth.

Everything is too cool down in your pelvic area. But it makes sense because of all the burning torture. They want you to let it be a gentle warmth now, with self-love rising up into you and through you. Along with the candy-apple sparkly red, you are also bringing in that rosy pink of love and the gentleness of warmth. So, they want your physical body to show you how it can now feel the healing warmth in that whole area of your body. Does that kind of make sense?

Client: Yes, it does make sense.

TZ: Now they are telling me, just one time a day. You could go to sleep at night or you could deliberately run your energy in this way the first thing in the morning. But they are saying, if you would, just do this one time a day. I'm getting for thirty days. You will really feel a difference.

Client: Okay.

TZ: So, this is your prescription. You're getting a thirty-day prescription. Now, I want to tell you what I saw as you were taking your power back. I want you to be really honest with me and tell me what happens when I describe this to you. Okay, when you were looking them right in the eyes, I actually saw one man in particular, in some sort of armor, who was your primary abuser.

Client: Okay.

TZ: The work you just did for yourself also assisted him *(the abuser/torturer)* in his work as a soul. As you were doing this for yourself, I saw that it had a domino effect for him as well. I actually saw him lift up, and rise up and out of there.

Client: Wow!

TZ: Now, stay there with that for a moment, and see what emotions come up, and see where you go and try not to censor it.

Client: Wow, this is interesting! I think some of my classmates at the spiritual center are also connected in various ways, in various lives. One of my classmates gave me a reading last year and said we knew each other and that we were friends. We were playing with things we weren't supposed to and we got caught. They took her away and we couldn't do anything to stop it. I started crying *(during the reading)*, and I know it was her. There's one male classmate who I have felt very uncomfortable with, and who always is trying to ingratiate himself with me. When he was doing a healing on me once *(at the spiritual center)* I was uncomfortable because he was touching me. I could see him as a monk. He abused the children with his power as a religious figure. I'm really uncomfortable with him in the class too, and I try to avoid him. He's always trying to ingratiate himself with me because he sees me as something special and I don't know why . . .

TZ: Yes, you do know why.

Client: Yes, yes I do. I feel like he was a religious figure who abused his power. *(In her current class)* He said to me that he's sexually attracted to me. One time he said to me that we needed to do some healing. He wanted to go outside and put our hands all over each other. I looked at him, and I said, "Are you asking me to do a healing?" I knew exactly what he was asking. When we were talking about the knight *(her abuser/torturer)*, I don't know if he was the knight, but I think he was there.

TZ: And do you realize you're not being a victim to him now?

Client: Yes!

TZ: That's really important for you to realize this right now.

Client: Yes, yes!

(Validate the ways they have been healing and advancing through their current life experiences.)

TZ: Now, I don't feel he is the knight who lifted up and out, but he certainly was there, because that is what you are getting.

Client: It's interesting, because my boyfriend in college was what we would now call a stalker. He was very possessive. It was a very sexually intense relationship, and part of that excited me and part of that scared me. He was very, very possessive. I can see he was related to one of those past lives. It's like he wanted to own me in this life.

TZ: You know, all those experiences *(in her current life)* are ways you are healing. You know that these were opportunities for healing? You know what else I have to say? I just turned and looked out my window, and a great big hawk just dove past the window and landed on a tree branch. Are you aware of that symbol for yourself?

Client: Yes, hawk has been showing up a lot the past year . . . hawk and eagle.

TZ: It's a very powerful symbol for you.

Healing Technique:
Past Lives

Here are some important points to remember when helping a client to heal a past life. Review them, then if it feels right to you, go back and read through the case again with these points in mind.

1. Remind the person that this work will always feel like a daydream, but reassure them it is real.

2. Clearly state to each client, "Do not try to make anything happen. Wait and let it unfold like a movie."

3. The client will forget to include their past-life self in every step throughout the healing process. Remind them repeatedly that they must do each step together with their past-life self. This process will achieve the greatest reconciliation and the most profound healing results.

4. The client will tend to hurry because they know you are waiting. Direct the client to always take their time.

5. Clearly tell the client they will need to let you know when the step is complete. This prevents you from interrupting the healing at crucial points.

6. During the silence, send Source energy to the client to support the sacred space of healing.

7. Observe the client's energy field while they take the healing steps. You can then report meaningful, positive changes during their process. This will validate their own abilities and the reality of the healing process they just participated in.

Past Lives Causing Current-Life Physical Challenges

For thirty years, I facilitated and specialized in regressions of both past lives and life between lives. Time and time again, my clients, when in a deep state of hypnosis, would describe phenomenal and complicated past-life scenarios that defy description. In many cases, an individual would uncover a profound explanation for the physical challenges they were born with. One person would describe a past life where they had been wounded in a battle that took place two hundred years ago, and that same wound would be duplicated in their current physical body in some manner. This duplication could be as minor as a birthmark in the exact place a spear had run through them, or as severe as a birth defection like a malformed spinal cord or absence of legs, or some other serious disorder.

Timothy was twenty-five years old when his mother brought him in for Reiki sessions. Timothy was unable to speak and could only create vocal sounds. His body was twisted and he used a walker to move around. He absorbed the Reiki energy and became quiet and peaceful during the sessions with the three of us. During the fourth or fifth session, I suddenly looked up at his mother with surprise and declared, "Timothy is talking to me. I can hear him!" His mother was thrilled.

Using me as his spokesperson, he told her: "I do not want you to get rid of Cindy (one of his homecare nursing assistants). I like her. I am not in as much pain as you always think I am." But then he said, "My life is harder than I thought it would be." His mother became tearful. Timothy went on to say that, in another life, he had worked himself to death. As a result, his current life was about being cared for. He repeated, "This is harder than I thought it would be."

For many individuals, the next life seems to offer dramatic changes in lifestyle, and in Timothy's situation, he was born with severe physical limitations. This dramatic change stimulates a potential learning experience, which seemed to extend from one of Timothy's lives to another.

Sitting before me in my office, a client named Carl described physical pain that suddenly began two years ago at the age of twenty-four. For the last two years he saw many physicians in the surrounding area. No one could find the cause of the severe physical pain that tortured his entire body. Despite the many pain medications and different types of treatment, the pain continued. A physical cause could be never be found.

Listen for key words as a person tells their story. They unconsciously tell you what is vital. It is common for people to reach a certain age in their current life when there is an instant onset of physical symptoms or emotional symptoms. Many times, it is the arrival at a certain age that signals physical symptoms, disease, or an illness in their current life. A sudden onset for which medicine fails to find a cause is often a key signal for a past-life trauma. The traumatic past-life event, in this example, took place at the age of twenty-four. In this life, when Carl reached the age of twenty-four, the energy signature of a certain past-life trauma was triggered. Here is what happened during our medical-intuitive session together.

As Carl spoke, a dreadful movie-type vision appeared within my mind's eye. I first envisioned a grassy field. Far off, I saw two fully armored men in violent combat. No one else was visible as I moved closer to the two men. Although they were fully covered in shining armor, I instinctively knew Carl was losing the battle. His opponent skillfully swung his sword over and over again. He repeatedly sliced and stabbed the younger man until he fell to the ground, dead.

I described the scene to Carl. I gave a detailed description of his injuries because my guides told me to be detailed. When I finished describing this grizzly scene, Carl told me the wounds I described were the same painful places in his body that he suffered from. My guides instructed me to tell him that the pain was triggered in this life at the same age he died in the past life. I gave him the details of his injuries because I always follow the advice of my guides. Surprisingly, Carl was not shocked. He actually said it made sense to him, especially because no one else had come up with an explanation.

The healing steps began.

I asked Carl if he was willing to take some steps with me to heal this dramatic event. He readily agreed. I emphasized that he must allow his imagination to go wherever it wanted to. I instructed him that it would feel as if he was imagining it, but to go with the flow no matter what happened. He agreed.

Again, emphasizing imagination, I asked him to imagine traveling back to that field a few minutes before the fight actually began. I told him to let me know when he was there and what he was doing. After a long pause, he said he felt the weight of the armor and his sweat. I then directed Carl and his past-life self to do the following together:

- Command the Universe to show them how to take their power back from the precise moment, and from that man.

- Ask for the perfect, most effective, permanent healing to take place in that exact moment. (I emphasized that he should let it unfold like he was imagining a movie. I told him to take his time, and that I would be quiet until he was ready to speak.)

After a few minutes, Carl said he and his opponent both stood facing each other for a long time. Then, together, they agreed to walk away. With trust, they turned their backs to each other and walked away.

"Excellent," I responded. "That is perfect." This encourages the client and lets them know they are participating with the healing correctly. Remember that the client works out how to do the healing. The medical intuitive does not get the information for the client, nor do they do the healing for the client. Turn it over to the individual clients and the healing specialty guides.

Now, here is the very interesting part of this session. As Carl and I continued to discuss his experience, I began to hear sounds of metal banging against metal out in the hallway of my office. The sounds grew louder and closer to the door of my room. Carl said he could hear the sounds also. Carl's opponent, the large man in armor with an enormous sword hanging at his side, materialized in my room! I was shocked, but Carl did not seem startled at all. I told Carl that this man had something to say to him, and was he open to hear what this man from his past life had to say? When I received permission, I gave the man's message to Carl:

"I want him to know that whatever he did just now released me and healed me. I am now free to go. I thank him and honor him."

We intuitives are not imaginative enough to make up these stories. Nonphysical reality is much more than we can ever experience through our physical senses. It truly has structure and an organized intelligence that encompasses many more dimensions than we can incorporate with our limited human intelligence. Not only does heartache and trauma transmit across time and space, following us wherever we go, but—thank goodness—healing does as well. Healing shifts seamlessly from past lives into current lives and into the future.

I ask for the exact point of origin for the person's specific current illness or struggle. Our spirit guides will develop indicators with you that will efficiently indicate what is about to happen. My past-life indicator is that pull to my left, or the client's right. Without rushing the process, I allow the pull to happen. I watch, feel, and notice everything about the pull and where it takes me. I often perceive dates coming toward me, but then they float on by. Sometimes scenes rise before me and then fade away. I still wait until the pull settles to a stop. There, I might sense or see an exact date. I may hear sounds of wooden wagon wheels crunching dry soil. A battle or a scene of torture may appear as if a movie began in my mind. I might also perceive the happiest life that my client has ever lived. Any great emotion, at either end of the emotional spectrum, may disclose itself to you. Remember, you have called out to the cosmos for the precise moment that began your client's specific hardships.

I describe what I perceive to the client, but sometimes I do not describe the exact details and images of the event if it is excessively violent. In that case, I state what is happening in a general way. I then ask the client if that makes any sense to them, or I might ask if they were already aware of this past life or this event. Most of the time, your client will tell you they are already aware of trauma during that era or in that part of the world. Rarely will your client say they had no idea about that lifetime. Either way, I continue with what my guides have given me.

I will then ask my client to allow themselves to pull back to the original moment the problem began. Direct them to take their time and see where it takes them in that life. Remind them it will always feel like a dream or feel as if they are just making it up. Tell them you will be still until they speak. Allow for quiet time so your client may access the information. Ask them to simply wait and allow the awareness to unfold in front of them like a movie. I will then instruct the client to call in the perfect Divine healers to show them how to heal and alter that particular moment. I never tell them what action to take. Again, I ask that they do not try to make anything happen either. Direct the person to call out for a healing and then wait to see or feel what happens next.

You might receive other variations regarding the healing steps because you are dealing with an individual who is totally different from all your other clients. You are also being guided by Spirit, so you never truly know what will happen next. I will often ask the client to give me a moment while I ask my guides for directions to bring about a complete and permanent healing. There are distinct variations to any of these steps. Your guides may strongly direct you to have your client stand before their wrongdoers and look them directly in the eyes. Your guides might tell you to have your client go back a few minutes, a few hours, or a week before the traumatic event took place in the past life. The spirit guides will then direct the client, through you, to call out to the guides to heal the situation before it even begins to unfold. In other words, your client and the healing guides work together to alter that past life to prevent the trauma from happening in the first place. The guides might even direct the client to allow a healing after the traumatic event took place. There is no end to the variations your guides may give you, so do not lock yourself into any definite healing pattern or healing steps.

Describe and explain the healing steps your guides give you, but never tell your client what must happen. Your client and spirit guidance will come up with the most precious healing moments you could never have created alone. Again, always allow your client to take those steps and do not direct the client how to do these steps or what needs to take place. The most powerful healing for an individual becomes something way beyond what you, as a practitioner, could ever come up with. Simply get out of their way, watch, and support their energy field while things beyond our expertise take place.

Healing Technique:
Past-Life Trauma

1. You have identified an issue. Command to your Divine and Sacred medical-intuitive guides: "Show me or tell me now the exact point of origin causing *(client's full name) (name the issue)*."

2. A past-life situation unfolds like a movie. Inform the client of the details you just received about this past life. Ask the client if that makes sense to them.

3. Tell the client to stretch their current self back to that moment in time. Tell your client to make sure their past-life self really knows they are there for him or her in that moment.

4. Direct both your current client and their past-life self to call in a Divine and Sacred healer who specializes in healing and releasing past-life events or traumas.

5. Tell your current client and their past-life self to command together: "Completely and permanently remove all forms of negativity from this past-life moment, from our bodies, from our energy fields, from our spirits. Remove all forms of negativity across all timelines and all dimensions. Remove all negativity from both of us now!"

6. Tell the client and their past-life self to observe everything happening and everything releasing.

7. Once they remove all the negativity, your client's current

self and past self must command: "Divine and sacred healers, come to us now and fill every single space and place throughout all timelines, and all dimensions, with unconditional Love and Light of the Eternal Divine."

8. Direct your client to ask their past-life self if they need any other healing. If they receive a "Yes, there is something else," then they must ask what it is and repeat the entire process for the other issue.

9. If your client receives a "No, the healing is complete," then direct your client to completely leave your past-life self behind. Tell the client to release that moment and pull themselves back to their current body.

Note: Do not ever bring the past-life self back to the client's current life. The past-life self cannot possibly be as advanced as the client currently is now. We do not want to bring a less-evolved part of us back to this current life.

Repetition of Past-Life Patterns

Sometimes intense emotions from a past life might manifest as negative behavioral patterns that repeat from one life to another. I have seen some of these repetitive patterns in people whose lives are centered around anger, suicide, abusive relationships, an obsession with a particular individual, or an addiction to street drugs or alcohol.

I frequently hear people say that karma is to blame. These same people think of karma as a cycle of punishment repeating over and over again for wrong deeds, wrong love, or wrong religion. In my experience with thousands of individuals experiencing past-life regressions, not one of them described karmic punishment. What I do hear, day after day and year after year, is the cycle of learning, achieving, and transformation. Each life is another opportunity to experience, make choices, and think more deliberately. It offers an adventure in discovering how we humans are really creators.

You may find a common thread that repeats throughout multiple lives. For example, I often hear from an individual in spirit who committed suicide that they have done so in many of their past lives. They will tell me to inform their loved one they deeply regret their actions but felt as if they had no other options. Many of your living clients will tell you they keep repeating the same mistakes as they made in past lives such as remaining in poverty, marrying an abusive person, or getting caught up in jealousy, just to name a few. It seems that a pattern becomes more ingrained as subsequent lives are lived. When requesting the exact point of origin of the pattern, the Universe will take you back to a very specific past life where the original pattern began.

Case Study:
Healing Repetitive Patterns Found in Multiple Lives

This session is about healing multiple past lives within a session. The case demonstrates how an issue can transfer from one life to the next, creating patterns of behaviors and emotions. Become consciously aware of the pattern and its exact point of origin to bring about a clear healing experience.

Practice Experience:

Imagine that you are the medical intuitive speaking the words in this transcript. Read it out loud and, if possible, read it with a study buddy, one taking part as the medical intuitive and one being the client. Practice this session as if you are actually giving these steps to someone who needs your guidance.

Client: Nothing is too out-there for me. I can take it!

TZ: Well, even as I was dialing the phone, I saw a large eye in your energy field. The eye is very open, so it is symbolic of being open. And look how you started the conversation by saying how open you are. When I say this, just accept whatever jumps into your awareness.

You looked at me, then turned and looked back over your left shoulder. Now, that is another symbol from my guides that tells me the past is still bothering you. There are memories coming up, or unfinished business in your personal history. Now, as I say that, what or who jumps into your mind?

Client: What jumped into my mind was patterns.

TZ: Patterns?

Client: Yeah, patterns that are interfering with my life now. Behavior patterns from my childhood, I guess.

TZ: When a pattern in our life repeats, repeats, and repeats, it simply means we have not learned the deeper message about ourselves. We tend to think patterns are about everybody else, but patterns are really about ourselves. They repeat because we have not learned the deepest sense of knowing about ourselves. Now, as I say that, really check out the patterns you are talking about and just see what comes up.

Client: I saw a past life where he *(this client experienced herself as a male in this past life)* cut himself . . . I did a suicide attempt, so I wasn't expecting to see that one!

TZ: You accepted what popped into your awareness out of nowhere. It is always intuitively the clearest information. So, you saw yourself in a past life cutting your wrists. Is that what you meant?

Client: Yes. It didn't look like me because I was a male, but he cut his wrists in a past life. This life I did it too. But the past few years I picked myself up and I've done okay. But it could be that there's unresolved stuff around it.

TZ: Yes, it means there is something else you need to notice. It is not ever a punishment, or anything like that.

Client: It doesn't feel good though. I'm not happy that you know about it, but I have to look at that.

TZ: Give me a second. Let me ask what we should do here. *(Brief pause.)* First of all, did cutting your wrists lead to your death back then? Check that out. Don't try to make anything happen. Just feel like you are being pulled back there in the past life and just wait.

Client: I think he did commit suicide. I don't know if he ended up dying by cutting his wrists. I think he tried more than one thing.

TZ: Well, I am getting that too. They are telling me to ask you to notice any threads that tie you to that past life, and also your current life when you did something similar.

(When a past life negatively affects a person's current life, you might perceive a string-like substance, a cord, a path, or some other informative symbol that shows a connection between lives.)

Client: He could not conceive of going forward in his life. I did feel like that, and it was like being disabled. I don't know . . . disabled by death or disabled by life. Does that help?

(Let the client know you are about to give them difficult information. In this example, the word "victimized" could be a loaded term causing a huge response.)

TZ: It is not about helping me at all. My guides are telling me to use a power-packed word. "Victimized," or feeling no hope as a victim would feel. Victimized and moving into a place of powerlessness. Oh wow. Now my guides are cheering you on! You have actually broken that pattern this time.

Client: Oh good, because I felt like I had!

TZ: This is huge, huge, huge! You broke a multi-life pattern! I am getting that you have killed yourself multiple times. I am getting as many as five lives where you have killed yourself in some similar way. I want you to just sit there and see if it feels right to you. Always tell me if what I say doesn't feel right.

Client: I just had to change my mind. I wasn't on antidepressants.

I wasn't doing any of that stuff. I just literally changed my mind. I just decided I am not going to live in depression. I am not going to live this way. I'm going to live another way!

TZ: You broke the pattern in that moment.

Client: That was a number of years ago, and I haven't had issues with depression or anything since then. I feel like, at that point, I was able to just change my mind.

TZ: Well, one of the main concepts I teach is to get more in charge of one's life, and you actually did it. So, I am asking my guides right now . . . If she broke the pattern, or altered the pattern, why are we attending to this right now? Why are we talking about it? *(Pause.)* They are saying it is time to stand even stronger in your empowerment. You still feel like a victim in more subtle ways.

Client: I can't relate to it! It's either not the current case or it's really below my awareness. Before, I was the queen of victimization leading up to my suicide. I felt victimized on every level. So, I've been working hard to move away from that. I mean, like, to clear it, not to suppress it, but to clear it! You know it's possible, there is still a thread of it there. I can't connect to it, but you know it's possible. It's there.

(Your client may express disbelief. Give them time to process the information. Trust the information you receive even when your client rejects it.)

TZ: Okay, my guides are giving me this information. When we struggle to heal something in our current life, it means we haven't directed the healing to the original event that caused it. The original event actually popped up in your awareness. You were that man, cutting your wrists in a past life. See, you already knew where we needed to go.

(The session now moves toward healing the struggle at the point of origin.)

TZ: Okay, would you be willing to send the current, more powerful you back into this past life and stand with your past-life male self? Make sure he knows you are there with him. I will be quiet now, and just let me know what you notice back there. Go to him just before he cuts himself. Just let it unfold.

(Remember, the greatest healing takes place on an energetic level and at the point of origin, or the instant the issue began.)

Client: He is aware of me. He is aware of me.

TZ: How do you know that?

Client: Because I saw him before. I saw him just a few days ago. Do we start getting ready for sessions before the sessions start?

TZ: Yes, many clients tell me they have had a spiritual experience just before their session.

Client: He is aware of me now.

TZ: Excellent. I am asking you to go back just before the cutting. Ask him what you need to know just before he does that. Just take whatever pops into your awareness.

Client: He says he had doubt, self-doubt. So, there was something in him that made him do it anyway.

TZ: Right, right. Ask him to be clearer about doubting. Just take whatever jumps into your mind.

Client: He says he doubted the existence of love. Everybody talks about love and everybody tries to get love. They feel love and give love, you know, but if you don't know exactly what it is and you don't think it actually even exists, then that would be challenging.

(Throughout the session, intuitively request your specialty guides to create the most profound permanent healing for the client. Follow the steps they give you.)

TZ: Very interesting. All right, ask him if he is willing to work with you now.

Client: Yes, he is willing to work.

TZ: I want the two of you *(the client and her past-life self)* to talk it over. I am getting that this is a matter of struggling to receive in life, struggling to receive the goodness from life. Ask him if that makes sense to him.

Client: Yeah, he said he was very conscientious, and he always did what he thought he should be doing and what he was trained to do. He was told to do the right things. He really wasn't enjoying doing that. It's not that he didn't enjoy being kind to people, or helping people, but it was kind of prescriptive. It wasn't from his heart, I guess.

TZ: Here is what I am getting. He is still talking about doing, doing, doing to help others. I am going to ask the two of you to allow yourselves to receive. Not doing more, but actually just receiving right now. The two of you need to do this together right now and see what unfolds. It is not about doing more, or doing it right. Just receiving. See what comes into your awareness.

Client: He sees the life he could have lived if he had been open to receiving. How it came through is that he had the goose that laid the golden egg. He saw how quickly he could have had it all. You know.

TZ: Yes. They keep showing me that you two, together, need to allow yourselves to receive the most profound compassionate healing right now. I will be quiet and just see how that happens.

(As the medical intuitive, I did not tell the client what to receive but to generally allow receiving to happen as they stand together. Spirit will guide the client and you.)

Client: *(After a long pause.)* Well . . . I could feel my crown get all prickly, like activating. But I have difficulty connecting with feelings, and perhaps he has the same difficulty; I don't know. I think we did receive, but we couldn't feel what we were receiving. It's how it seems to me.

TZ: Okay. I am directed to tell you that the two of you are struggling to do everything on your own. I keep seeing multiple angelic-type beings coming in to give you the healing if you would allow yourselves to receive it. Ask for a healing to feel the sensations of receiving. Slow down and let it unfold.

Client: *(Very long pause.)* Well, I guess I feel calmer. I feel peaceful. I don't know where he is.

TZ: Well, let him tell you. Just let him tell you.

Client: He said he cried a lot of tears. He just said something else. He said he is ready to move forward now.

TZ: Wow! How did you two receive that healing? Can you describe it?

Client: For me? Because I didn't see what was happening to him because that was his.

TZ: Well, but his is also yours.

Client: It kind of seemed private, I guess.

TZ: Interesting. Okay, go ahead then.

Client: I was basically covered in a lot of slime. That's what it looked like to me, and they were cleaning the slime off me.

TZ: Who are they, and how did the cleaning happen?

(Discussing the details out loud will solidify the event for your client.)

Client: Well, it was the angelic beings, so I asked for their help. They were using their hands from a head-down motion. It was a sweeping down motion with their hands, clearing away gooey slime.

TZ: Now I want you to check your sensations. Is the slime removed and gone?

Client: My cough feels better. I'm breathing better. I feel confident, and I feel strong, like an empowered strong. I forgot to mention that whenever they were doing this with him, he enjoyed it and he was happy. He liked it.

TZ: Okay. I am getting a couple other steps for the two of you to take, if it seems okay. I want both of you now to go forward together in his current life and allow his life back then to continue to move forward so the two of you experience how the rest of his life unfolds.

Client: He does get married! The reason he wanted to die was because his relationship had died and he felt responsible for her death. He does meet somebody else. He does marry and he had two children. He felt that he contributed, that the world was a better place. He was happy. Not all the time, he said, but he was happy . . .

TZ: What about his goose?

Client: His life had value and he enjoyed it.

(If a word jumps into your mind that the client mentioned earlier, that is a signal from Spirit to bring that back into focus.)

TZ: See how the goose with the golden egg manifested. Ask him to check that out.

Client: He said he could have had it all. He had his honor. That's a word that comes up. That was important to him. He was valued. He was valued for his wisdom and his contributions. He was good at what he did, whatever that was. So he felt, at all levels, he had a very valuable, honorable life, which were qualities that were important to him. It wasn't really about gold.

TZ: No, it was symbolic about abundance in all kinds of ways.

Client: Yeah, prosperity. He is saying that when he was in alignment, for lack of a better word, with his existence and with spirit, there was a trust. He always felt supported and taken care of. I think that is what he is trying to say. He never felt alone, and he never walked alone.

TZ: Excellent. All right, I have asked my guides what we are to do next. The two of you together can now come forward *(through other past lives)* together with all your empowerment and all this new ability to receive, healing every moment along the way with your healing spiritual guides, healing everything all the way as you sit with me right now. I will be very quiet and just see how you two do that and what happens.

Client: I already see one woman *(from another of the client's past lives)*. She didn't kill herself, but she didn't feel empowered. She received the healing. She was able to see what her life would have been had she been able to receive. It was in that lifetime that she took a lot of stuff, and she thought she was receiving. She basically stole money from people. You know, she thought that was receiving. Now she was able to receive more abundance. Now she doesn't have all the bad feelings about herself. I felt better for her. See if that's now completed.

(Guide the client to allow their experience to unfold like a movie in their mind.)

TZ: Let me ask. *(Pauses to ask my guides.)* You know, this fascinates me. I heard there is still one dark spot, or one more event, before you are finished. Just let it unfold. Don't try to find it. Just pause and see where it takes you.

Client: Well, I see the girl, maybe twelve or something, and she was really labeled as being deeply mentally ill. She was in an institution. She seemed to be a manifestation of a tortured soul. And I guess people thought she was crazy and locked her up. So, that's what I see.

TZ: Okay. My guides are becoming very loud with their directions. They want you to call on her behalf, and I am doing that as well, for specialty guides to cleanse her of negativity, cleanse her of negative attachments—cleanse her, cleanse her, cleanse her. "Call them in on her behalf" is what I keep getting. And I will do that to support you.

Client: *(Long pause.)* She is now able to speak. She says she just wants to go home.

TZ: Let me add this, if I may. I saw that black spot become the shape of a diamond. Lots of greens and orange were filling her. I am covered with goose bumps.

Client: Me too.

TZ: Oh good, good. That always means you and I are on a deep level of truth here.

Client: I see that she went from being tortured and completely unaware, to wish to go home, but I don't know what home is.

(It is not necessary to know everything that is taking place. We only need to be aware that healing and transformation is happening.)

TZ: We don't need to know. Together, let's call in spirit guide specialists that will know what she means and let them attend to it.

Client: Oh, okay. Well, to me it seems they supported her. She did say to me that all anger and all victims are leaving me now. I got peace, not anger that I picked up on. Wow, this has been a pretty busy time!

TZ: This is phenomenal. This is amazing. I am also watching your energy field, and you are getting brighter and brighter. And I see a thickness leaving you and in comes brightness. A lemony spring green is coming into your current physical body. Coming in now is a pinkish purple rising up your spine. I am perceiving these changes as they happen. You are changing. They are telling me you also had an energy signature that kept coming through these different lives and into your current life. This energy was of struggle, the inability to receive, and victimhood.

Now they want you to also call in more cleansing. You have been traveling through all these past lives *(during this session),* and you have not fully merged into your current physical body and current life. Call in specialists to assist you to completely return to your present life and body.

Client: *(Long silence.)* Okay, I think it's done. I'm in.

TZ: I am getting that this has been such a multifaceted session that they want you to realize a complete assimilation will take thirty days. It is going to settle in over the next month or so.

Client: Pretty incredible! It felt pretty complete like I'm really going toward like a transformation.

TZ: I probably do not need to say this to you, but this is very real. This will bring a different awareness and understanding into your current life. These are very, very powerful changes here.

Client: Far more than I expected. I didn't know what to expect, but this is amazing!

TZ: Well, Spirit can only be as amazing as you allow it. The first thing out of your mouth was that you are willing to go anywhere! I rarely hear that.

There are many different lessons throughout this medical-intuitive session, but there is one that is important to remember. This client, at first, rejected the possibility that she had not already healed her suicidal ideation and attempts. I agreed that she had done a great deal of healing on her own, but then I pointed out that a past-life memory had popped into her awareness. I explained this was because a past-life experience was truly the point of origin of her struggles. For a profound and permanent healing to take place, that past-life moment needed to be healed and released.

Past-Life or Current-Life Vows and Curses

Remember, science has discovered the importance of focused thoughts. "Intent" is another word for focused thought. I have attended workshops where the instructor simply said, "Now set your intent." At that time, I had no idea what that meant, how to do it, or what implications intent even encompassed.

Vows are real. If our thoughts and our spoken words can move pinballs in a research experiment, then our focused thoughts are able to create an intense energetic configuration, commonly known as a vow. A vow is a certain dedicated commitment or a binding promise. A vow has a distinct electrical vibration that attaches and intertwines throughout our eternal essence, our soul. That distinct frequency has the power to follow us from one life to another. Here are some examples of vows people have made throughout history:

- Poverty
- Chastity
- Silence
- Servitude
- A certain religion
- Battling for a certain belief
- Battling, or protecting, a certain person
- Dying for a cause
- Marital commitment for eternity
- Family commitment for eternity

Some of these vows could open up so many negative possibilities that I do not even know where to begin. For example, if you tend to develop spiritually faster than your current spouse, that person could actually interfere in your soul's contract or your evolutionary progress. That spouse may become a negative factor in your current life, and you may later divorce that individual. The vow had already been invoked, so it will seem that the two of you continue in a negative manner throughout your current life. At death, the divorced spouse to whom you made an eternal vow could then become a spirit attachment to you. That person could remain attached as if going along for the ride and not spiritually develop themselves. You, on the other hand, would be unable to achieve the higher level of conscious awareness you had hope for because your attachment weighs on you and interferes with your development. Now, this is simply a thought-provoking example for you and does not necessarily resemble a traditional marriage vow of "till death do us part." This traditional marriage vow has an end time, which is at the time of death.

Evelyn quietly sat down. Her physical posture was very good, but despite that, I intuitively saw a thick rope around her neck, pulling her head back and over to her left. I described this strange image to her and her eyes widened. She then described how she had gone to so many energy workers and chiropractors recently to help pull her head back into the correct position, but nothing had helped. Evelyn went on to say that she always found herself with her head and neck leaning to her left. She was not, however, aware of any sensation of a rope pulling at her. As I do with everyone I see, I asked her not to tell me anything else about her condition until I intuitively checked in with her more thoroughly. As she agreed, I sent my laser beam intent back to her physical body. The rope, of course, was still tied around her neck. My guides verbally directed me to follow the length of the rope, which faded off into the distance behind Evelyn's back. The rope pulled me over the client's shoulders and back behind her physical body. This told me it was a current-life issue. In my mind's eye, I deliberately directed my intent to extend along that rope until I perceived the end of it. I found a man firmly but gently holding the other end and pulling back on it as if he were pulling Evelyn back to him. I described my perceptions and described the man who I saw. She calmly stated that I had described her husband. I intuitively asked her husband what this was about for him. He said he was afraid that her expanding spiritual beliefs would pull them apart. He was trying to pull her back from a life path that felt very right to Evelyn.

Since I was not sure how to begin to heal this dilemma, I asked for the highest, most loving guidance for this couple. Instantly, thoughts leaped into my mind. I asked Evelyn to intuitively tell her husband whatever she needed to say about their life together. I also asked her to talk to him about the rope and that it needed to be removed. I told her to take her time and I would be still until she spoke. After a few minutes of silence, Evelyn described the discussion they had. My specialists then asked that I direct her to take a quiet moment to feel her own empowerment. My guides could have instructed us to do any number of things next. However, the message they gave me was that it was vitally important for Evelyn to take the rope off by herself without any help, and then to give the rope back to her husband. Notice that I did not tell her how to take action with these steps. This healing encouraged Evelyn to demonstrate her own sense of confidence and learn self-reliance.

Vows create powerful energetic cords, linking future lives to our past lives. The energy of a vow or curse tends to build throughout lives rather than dwindle, because more people talk about it and believe it as time goes on. If our words create a pledge that potentially lasts forever, then our words can also be a powerful tool capable of revoking that same vow. Before we revoke a vow, we must know as clearly as possible the exact words that were declared in the original vow. We can discover this during a medical-intuitive session or a past-life regression. You will know when you perceive the vow correctly, because people will have a powerful sense that it is correct. One must then feel a powerful commitment when they revoke a vow. The revocation needs to vibrate with as much emotional certainty and empowerment that is equal to the original vow. Knowing and believing that we can revoke a command with a different command will free us from the chains that may have bound us for centuries.

Case Study:
Past-Life Vows Blocking Current-Life Progress

This client could not excel in her current life. The ongoing theme in her mind was "I must keep doing good for others but I must never get paid for it." An ancient vow is disclosed in the case study.

Practice Experience:

Imagine that you are the medical intuitive speaking the words in this transcript. Read it out loud and, if possible, read it with a study buddy, one taking part as the medical intuitive and one being the client. Practice this session as if you are actually giving these steps to someone who needs your guidance.

TZ: I keep seeing you in a castle as a female. You're not the slave. You're the daughter of the aristocrat, or the daughter of the royalty in the castle. Does that make any sense?

Client: I get to wear the good clothes.

TZ: Yes, you have very nice clothing on. Do you ever sense life in a castle?

Client: I once had someone do a past-life thing and it might have been there.

TZ: This is about what you sense and not what someone else discovered for you.

Client: Yeah, I joke with my husband that I was born in the wrong historical era. I should have been in the era where you went out and played croquet or sat around.

TZ: Do you know why you're saying that?

Client: 'Cause there was nothing expected of you, probably, as women. You weren't the working class and you were not expected to work. You were just there. I wouldn't want to do that in our era. You know when you watch those period shows like *Downton Abbey*, I think I would feel that I'm not okay with that. You're the savior of the world and all that. So, if I was in a different era, the castle era, I would be more comfortable not being paid. It would be more acceptable.

TZ: How about you go back to the castle time and notice that this is not about me doing it for you. This is about you just letting yourself travel back and see where you find yourself. Just see what you notice and where you go. Just let it pull you. You don't have to do anything, just let it draw you there.

Client: See, that's easy because they have those beautiful gardens, you know?

TZ: Well, in your experiences there was a beautiful garden. Is that where you find yourself?

Client: Yeah, the gardens and the lawns and the libraries . . . all the things I love to do.

TZ: Check yourself out. What are you seeing about yourself and feeling while you're there? Really check that out.

Client: I was thinking of *Downton Abbey*. I don't know why. Who I liked best was the daughter who ended up going to be the nurse during the war because it wasn't enough to sit there. It's not enough.

TZ: I want you to check that out. Did you actually end up doing something? I was picking up that you found out something about the real life of the community (*outside of the castle*).

Client: There's something more out there and you have to make a contribution.

TZ: So, what did you do? Check that out, if you would.

Client: It would make a difference to go outside.

TZ: How did you actually do that? Or did you do it?

Client: Just go out to the people.

TZ: Did you see yourself doing that?

Client: Yeah.

TZ: What did you find out about your father? Check that out if you would, and just see what you notice about that. I keep getting that you discovered something.

Client: I think he would like it. Because in order to be able to express those feelings, he must allow me to express myself and talk about those kinds of issues, not internal. You know what I mean. And so yeah. I must educate the people. They *(the community around the castle)* will see there is not any difference between me and another human being.

TZ: So, educating the community?

Client: Yeah, it's similar to what you said, because I am a teacher *(in this current life)*.

TZ: You see how that all fits in? Notice what happens inside you when I say this. I hear you back in that past life, making a vow of some sort that is still affecting your current life now. See if that feels correct or not correct.

Client: Okay. Well, it would be a vow to change the world, probably to make a difference. I mean, that's what I would think. And is it true with past lives that, until you resolve what you do, you keep reliving them?

TZ: Yes.

Client: I heard that once.

TZ: A vow that we take actually tends to build with each different life. Whatever the vow is tends to get stronger and stronger. I'm looking over there because I see it over there. *(I am pulled to my left.)* How would I say it? It's like you are carrying an energy signature of guilt to have prosperity.

Client: That's it! I remember!

TZ: I'm getting goose bumps.

Client: I have total goose bumps.

TZ: Okay, when goose bumps happen we have touched in with some big important stuff.

Client: Cause I had a friend in college. I'll never forget, he said: "You know your problem is that you have middle-class guilt. You know you're sorry for all the good you have, and you want to make a difference in other people. You want to help people because you feel guilty for what you have." And I always remembered that.

TZ: It's a vow you made.

Client: I always remembered that because it resonated. Yes, I think that's it! And so I'm not happy in my skin because I'm not doing either.

TZ: See, that is why all the stuff you're doing in your current life is not healing you. Because we have to go to the point of origin to heal something. And look how lively you are about this.

Client: Well, because it's so clear, and it also fits everything I feel and what I think, because I'm constantly pulled to that. The other day my husband said, "You have the worst you. You live like the worst." This is not a mean thing he is saying. It's an observation that I live the worst of both worlds because instead of realizing and making a difference, I feel guilty or bad for what I have. It's what you just said!

TZ: Yes.

Client: So I don't get the good on either side.

TZ: Now for some people, the point of origin is in their current life. But for you, I'm pulled back to the castle. There you made a vow, and probably many vows. One thing you discovered was that your father wasn't the kindly person to others that he was to you. When you got out of the castle walls and saw what was going on, you were devastated and then you made the vow.

Client: That makes perfect sense to me.

TZ: For you and me to both burst forth in goose bumps, that always tells me we just tapped into a deep, deep truth for you.

Client: I would say so. I mean, it plugged into a bunch of things in my life.

TZ: Does it?

Client: I would say that I never feel I have the right kind of gratitude for what I have. And it's because of this guilt that you said. The word "guilt" was the trigger. It wasn't the vow. It was the guilt.

TZ: Yes.

(Healing the vow begins to take place.)

Client: And so I can't enjoy what I have. So, do I have to go back to the other life where it has to be resolved?

TZ: Yes. When I ask you this, take whatever pops into your head. How far back does this go, and what year do you get when you lived in that situation?

Client: I don't know history well. 1700s popped in, but I have no idea.

TZ: Take that. Make sure that your past-life self knows you are there with her. What are you noticing?

Client: That she came. She came.

TZ: Excellent. All right. I want you two to talk it over and ask for a complete healing for the both of you right there and just wait and see what happens.

(Notice this client resists having a healing experience.)

Client: She said I am healed. But I'm not.

TZ: Just stay there. What are you noticing?

Client: Well, she's happier because someone is paying attention. Someone's there.

TZ: Okay. Now . . . I want you to talk with her and ask her if she's willing to come forward now with you. Tell her it is all healed now. Then ask her to lift up and out of that past moment and come forward with you. At the same time she will mature and merge together all that happiness and healing with you right now.

Client: I've just done so many things that haven't worked.

TZ: Have you brought her back from this particular moment?

Client: No. I don't think I remembered that moment. It's kind of like it feels hopeless and fake.

TZ: Well, you don't feel like you're in charge of you. My hope is that you realize you are in complete charge of you. If you're not in charge of you, who is?

Client: Is that the reason I have no confidence?

TZ: I'm wondering if it's because she is so darn happy. You said she's happy.

Client: Yeah.

TZ: Just check that out and see what creates more of a struggle. Have you gone back (*into your past lives*) and got pieces of yourself before, have they been happy pieces?

Client: I can't remember, but I don't think so.

TZ: Then this is very different and you don't need to continue.

Client: Well, I do want to be free of it. You know I'm tired.

TZ: Do you know what is in that sentence?

Client: I get a lot of good feedback from people, but I don't see it.

TZ: You don't soak it in either.

Client: I get the negative stuff I grew up with. I'm used to that. I can see negative real easy. I can take that in.

TZ: Did you hear what you just said? You are used to the negative. You are aware of the negative, and you know what I said just a minute before that? Have you ever brought back (*from your past lives*) the happiness?

Client: You're probably right. And you told me.

TZ: I got goose bumps.

Client: I'm so afraid of achieving anything, but if I do it for free then I feel okay, but if I get paid for it, then I get all uncomfortable. That's what I chose to do, because it was easier.

TZ: People always think they get this stuff stuck in their head because they have watched a movie or a TV show, or they read a book. But it is the other way around. They're drawn to the TV show, or the movie, or the book because they have lived it in a past life. People get it turned around.

Client: I know when I went to England I was very taken by the castles. The whole idea of opulence . . . I had difficulty there because I knew what was going on.

TZ: Do you realize what you just told me? That you had an opulent life in England and you also had a life repeated in England. Now, what do you think about this? Are you less hopeful because it's a vow, or are you more hopeful? Check out your awareness.

Client: To me, it sounds like the vow was to make a difference for those who haven't been as blessed, or haven't been as fortunate. And what that is would vary with probably each generation or each place you relive.

TZ: Or was it a vow to serve without profiting?

Client: Oh, that's interesting.

TZ: This vow was very powerful. It covered all the bases at the time. For a vow to continue this long, and for me to pick it up so readily, means a profound emotional energetic signature is linked to it, giving it power.

Client: I feel more hopeful because anytime you know something, it also makes me feel less guilty because it's almost like there is a power you can't fight against but you can't win. I was living the life of the vow.

TZ: Yes, and you continue to do that. Doesn't mean you need to keep continuing in that way. I want to at least drop this idea with you. You can powerfully revoke a vow just like we can revoke a curse.

Client: What if it doesn't work?

TZ: If you resist it and think it won't work, then it won't work.

Client: You have to believe?

TZ: A belief is just a thought we think a lot. That's all it is. But your belief that it will not work is very, very powerful. There would be no revocation of it because you wouldn't believe it anyway. They *(spirit guides)* are telling me you will not even try to revoke it today because you're not ready and do not want it.

Client: Well, I believe in you. I probably don't believe in me.

TZ: Then it wouldn't work anyway because it is your vow. It's not mine.

Client: Yeah, I know. I don't think I am ready.

TZ: When you took that vow in the 1700s, it wasn't some quiet thing you did in your castle bedroom. You stood on a balcony or something way high up, and you declared it to the Universe. It was a like a bellowing declaration that vibrated out into the Universe. Doesn't mean you can't revoke it.

The client was not able to actually take the steps to revoke the vow. For most people, change is frightening. Do not force positive changes if a person resists. You may need to settle for increasing your client's awareness rather than accomplishing a complete healing.

Healing Technique:
Revoking Vows

1. Ask for the exact point of origin when the vow was made and took effect.

2. Ask for clarity regarding important keywords used in the vow.

3. Each time you state the following command, also imagine the physical formation of the vow, such as an energetic cord, completely disintegrate and float upward. Direct the client to imagine the sensation of freedom and liberation each time the client commands the following:

   "I now completely and permanently revoke anything and everything on all levels relating to the vow of (state the key words). I am now completely and permanently released and free from any negativity related to this past moment."

4. Repeat this revocation on a daily basis until there is a deep sense of release.

5. Direct the client to notice even the subtle shifts or changes in their life.

Curses are also real. I often hear that a curse will not work unless the person receiving the curse believes in curses. I would describe the power of a curse in a different way. The recipient of the curse does not necessarily need to be aware of it. That person, however, needs to vibrate in a similar frequency to the curse's vibration. If the person is full of shame, guilt, self-hatred, or generally thinks life is horrible, then the person's energetic frequency will correspond to, or even match, the focus of the curse placed on them. This energetic match will subsequently link the energy of the curse with the individual's energy field.

A stunningly beautiful, well-dressed aristocratic woman sat down with me for a session. As I tapped into her energy field, I was shocked to see that her face was overlaid with a deformed, grotesque blackened skull. Wormlike forms and insects came out of the skull's eyes and mouth. I told her that an ugly black skull covered her actual face, but I did not describe the bizarre details to her. Without hesitation, Monique stated that she had been cursed ten years ago. I asked that she not tell me any more details until I received more intuitive information about her situation. I immediately saw an older woman yelling a curse with an alarming degree of hatred. My client said, "Yes, that is my ex-mother-in-law. She has put a curse on me."

I have noticed one interesting issue regarding curses, either coming from a past life or coming down through generations. The power, strength, and intensity of a curse tends to escalate rather than diminish over time. How could that be? Its potency increases because people tend to repeat all the stories about a curse. With each past life and with each generation, the story is renewed and reexperienced. Discussing the curse continues to feed energy into it. The harm the curse causes becomes even more real. In other words, more and more people speak of it and usually embellish the stories. As a result, the curse becomes more alive and more potent.

Many curses originate from the hysteria of being tortured. An example that I can think of began in the 1700s with one of my clients. In one of her past lives, this woman was a midwife and failed to save a woman who was giving birth. The woman and the newborn died during the birthing process. The woman was the wife of the nobleman who governed that area of the country. As the midwife was about to be burned at the stake for their deaths, the midwife screamed out, "Death to all your babies!"

While some women delivered healthy babies, a few women had miscarriages or stillbirths. In fear, the people in that area focused much more on the deaths than on the living infants. That focus of thought energy gave life to the curse. The tales of those times continued to thrive, and an expectation of newborn deaths rose. That fear traveled from one generation to another, making the original curse from a horrific, torturous moment in a midwife's life into a reality.

Healing Technique #1 for Curses

The steps apply if the client was the perpetrator or the victim.

1. Ask your spirit guide specialists to give the exact point of origin of a person's illness or struggle. In this case, you will perceive a situation when a curse was formed and launched into reality.

2. Inform your client about the intuitive information your guides gave you. Ask the client to notice if it feels accurate to them.

3. Ask the client to imagine going back in time before the cursing event happened. Ask them to notice and describe the moment before the trauma began. In the example of the midwife, the person may go back to the moment of assisting with a positive birthing.

4. Ask your client to call out to the most divine, compassionate healing guides. Strongly request a complete and permanent healing to take place immediately for all people involved, and for love and kindness to prevail.

Healing Technique #2 for Curses

Use the Raymon Grace Dowsing Steps, which can be used to clear and heal many different situations or illnesses. You do not need a pendulum. The power of focused thought is required. Say them in the order that is stated below, and all in one sitting so the process is completed.

1. Command: "Permanently scramble all negative thought forms on all levels regarding (person's full name)."

2. Command: "Permanently neutralize all negative thought forms on all levels regarding (person's full name)."

3. Command: "Completely transform all that has been scrambled and neutralized into Divine Love."

Self-Inflicted Curses

Not all curses originate from another individual. We humans are actually capable of cursing ourselves. Self-inflicted cursing probably happens more often than someone else cursing us. Once again, the words we use in our inner mind and the words we use aloud are critical to our well-being and the well-being of others. Our words shape our existence. With that in mind, take a moment to really assess how critical or judgmental you are of yourself. Do you mumble self-hatred comments to yourself or call yourself names? People also repeat mindless statements such as: "I am poor and I always will be," or "Nothing good ever happens to me and it never will." Can you sense the power in these statements and how they may be considered as self-inflicted curses?

Healing Technique:
Self-Inflicted Curses

1. Point out the negative self-talk that your client is doing. Ask that person to share their negative self-talk with you. Carefully listen to the exact negative words that the clients use against themselves.

2. Describe it as a form of self-cursing. Teach the client about the power of their thoughts.

3. Assist the client to form a command that revokes the negative self-cursing talk. Allow the client to help develop the command and find the one that feels the most powerful to them.

4. An example of a command is: "I completely and permanently revoke and reject all negative comments about myself. I now fill every thought with positive Love and Light of the Divine."

Healing Affirmation:
Self-Cursing or Self-Hatred

Note: Names can be changed to fit one's personal spiritual beliefs.

"Only God's compassionate Love and Light and the purest sacred Consciousness completely fill **every cell in my body** now."

"Only God's compassionate Love and Light and the purest sacred Consciousness completely fill **my mind** now."

"Only God's compassionate Love and Light and the purest sacred Consciousness completely fill **my emotions** now."

"Only God's compassionate Love and Light and the purest sacred Consciousness completely fill **my energy field** now."

"Only God's compassionate Love and Light and the purest sacred Consciousness completely fill **my higher self** now."

"Only God's compassionate Love and Light and the purest sacred Consciousness completely fill **my spirit** now."

"Only God's compassionate Love and Light and the purest sacred Consciousness completely fill **my eternal soul** now."

Essential Points

- The emotional intensity in a past life will frequently transfer into a current life.
- A sudden onset for which medicine fails to find a cause is often a key signal for a past-life trauma.
- Healing shifts seamlessly from past lives into current lives and into the future.
- Describe and explain to your client the healing steps given

to you by your guides, but allow the client to do the healing themselves.

- Intense emotions from a past life can manifest as negative behavioral patterns that repeat from one life to another.
- Vows create powerful energetic cords, linking future lives to our past lives.
- The recipient of a curse needs to vibrate in a similar frequency to the curse's vibration.
- Self-inflicted cursing happens more often than someone else cursing us.

Chapter 16

Current-Life Trauma Causing Illness or Life Struggles

"The bad news is time flies. The good news is you're the pilot."

—Michael Altshuler

You will find a deep satisfaction when you discover and heal a client's current-life trauma. The client will feel an intense and heartfelt appreciation once the trauma is healed and released. They will experience an even deeper level of gratitude when the fragment of their soul merges back into their body.

Taking Back Power after Abuse

It is very important that you listen closely to your client and remember key words they use repeatedly or give emphasis to as they describe their upbringing, their life, or the traumatic moment. Some of these words and phrases might be "abandon," "desert," "assault," "made fun of," "sorrow," "guilt," "shame," or "hatred." I then use those same words to focus and to personalize the healing process for each person. In this next case, the key word was "vomit."

This gentle woman, whom I will call Abby, had a family full of abusers. She named them and gave me details of how they repeatedly harmed her throughout her childhood. I listened intently to the descriptive words that she emotionally used. Abby used the phrases, "I could just vomit!" and "I can't even look at them to this day!" "Vomit" and "can't look at them" stand out as key words that should be involved in her healing steps.

She began to act as if she was going to vomit, so I invited her to actually vomit into the wastebasket or allow herself to imagine vomiting up all the harm, the abuse, and the ridicule. She did so in her imagination and stated that she vomited all over their heads. This is the most aggressive that any of my clients have ever become with their wrongdoers. All others have experienced more loving and gentle ways in their healing process.

I asked Abby to sit and notice how she felt after vomiting all over their heads. She immediately felt so much better. I asked her to take a quiet moment to actually experience the sensations of "feeling so much better." Abby expressed that she felt stronger and more confident. These are now her positive key words to work with. I asked Abby to take another moment to feel her new strength and confidence. After a minute or so she opened her eyes and told me she had done so. I then asked Abby to line up her family members in front of her, which she did. Next, I asked her to look directly into their eyes and hold that look for as long as it took until the family member changed in some way. With a small smile on her face, Abby described in detail how all her abusive family members either shrank in size or turned away from her.

Because we humans are energy beings first and foremost, healing at this energetic level is profound. This simple experience is real, authentic, and power-packed with healing.

Healing Technique:
From Abuse to Empowerment

1. Ask the client to describe what they are missing inside of themselves due to the abuse.

2. Listen for key words that the client uses. The key words will be full of emotion, both negative and positive. Use the key words to transform the negativity into a positive experience.

3. Instruct the individual to take a moment and let the positive words create physical and emotional feelings inside of them. Tell them to just think the positive words and imagine the

positive feelings within. Pause and wait until they speak. Have them repeat the experience until the client can identify that the positive feelings are quite strong. Do not move forward until that strength happens and is recognized.

4. Direct the person to imagine the wrongdoer standing before them. Ask the client to look directly into the wrongdoer's eyes and hold that gaze until the perpetrator changes in some manner. Do not tell the client how the individual needs to change. Tell them to take their time and not to rush. The old proverb, "Our eyes are a window into the soul," is a valid truth and an extraordinary tool for self-empowerment.

5. Ask the client to describe what happened. Teach them that this experience is very real and it actually did happen.

6. Ask them to sit and feel the difference within and describe it to you. This will confirm and validate the reality of the experience.

Soul Fragmentation

When an individual becomes a victim in a painful or disturbing event, a portion of the soul may actually break away and remain imprisoned in a precise moment of the event. The remainder of the soul continues to move forward in life, leaving the fragment behind. Fragments may continue to disconnect throughout life if dramatically disturbing incidents occur again. Our language suggests that humans are unconsciously aware that fractures of the soul can happen. We hear it when someone says, "My heart was instantly broken when that happened," "It's like I lost a piece of myself when I heard that horrible news," or "I have never been the same from that moment on." Your client will describe the event in detail and will feel very emotional about it. It seems so raw that you will assume it happened last week when it actually happened twenty years ago. That happens because the fragment remains in the trauma, reliving it over and over again. It is the alive, energetic fragment of one's soul that keeps the memory just as alive.

Medical intuitives find themselves facilitating soul retrievals because it is a vital and successful healing method. A soul retrieval is a process of finding the soul's fragments, bringing those lost pieces forward, and placing them back into the energy field of the damaged person. Soul retrievals have been exceptionally valuable in my medical-intuitive practice. This healing technique ultimately heightens one's health and vitality in phenomenal ways.

Soul retrievals have been common in Native American cultures for hundreds of years. The shaman performs the soul retrieval on behalf of the ill or troubled person. The shaman himself journeys back to a traumatic moment in the person's life and brings the soul fragment forward for the client, placing the fragment into the individual's energy field.

With strong leadership from my specialty guides, I have altered a few steps from the traditional Native American technique. I do not travel back to the traumatic moment on behalf of my client. I direct the individual to journey back into their own past for themselves. I then verbally offer steps for the individual to bring back the fragment of themselves they left behind. With the medical intuitive's guidance, the individual takes action for themselves, on their own behalf. I received these changes in the middle of a session one day. As that session came to a close, I knew a tremendous difference had taken place for the client. Allowing and assisting the client to journey on their own and reclaim their suffering fragment has exponentially increased the healing benefits for many, many people.

There are four basic points that create the fundamental steps for this healing process. To understand the most basic structure of the soul retrieval, I have listed them here. I also give a thorough step-by-step explanation at the end of this section.

Healing Technique:
Retrieving Soul Fragmentation

1. Direct the client to go back to their younger self.

2. Together, the client and their younger self must take all the horrible suffering out of themselves and give it back to the wrongdoer.

3. Next they take back all that had been taken from them, and place it all back into their current self and their younger self.

4. Direct the client to ask their younger self to move forward and merge into the current moment in their current life.

Case Study:
Soul Retrieval Through Mediumship

This session demonstrates finding the age of the soul fragment and the subsequent soul retrieval. This brave client took back her power from an abusive father and brothers. This case is about brutalization, empowerment, and healing a relationship with a deceased family member through mediumship.

Practice Experience:

Imagine you are the medical intuitive speaking the words in this transcript. Read it aloud or, if possible, with a study buddy, one taking part as the medical intuitive and one as the client. Practice this session as if you are actually giving these steps to someone who needs your guidance.

TZ: I feel like you have really been working on your energy and your energy field because there is a lot of orange and yellow. The orange vibration is in the shape of a flower that is opening up and bursting forth like petals. Then in a split second, I saw a curvature in your spine. Then in a split second, that image was gone. Now I am noticing the center of this flower. You are changing very, very quickly. I hardly get something stated to you, and by that time you look different. There are positive changes and I really want you to hang on to that. Now, in the middle of this flower there is a dullness. This dullness keeps shifting around all over your body, which I find very interesting too. So let me check this out in a deeper way. (Pause.) There is your spine and I also see your nervous system. Your whole nervous system is coming into my awareness. Let me just say a few more things before you speak. You turned from me and looked back over your left shoulder. That sign from Spirit tells me that some of your physical struggles are also based in your past. I can head back in that direction if you want me to, but first I want to pause and let you respond. It feels like you want to respond to something I have said. So, where does your mind go about all this?

Client: Well, it all seems extremely accurate. I've been working very hard for a long, long time.

TZ: It's paying off or I wouldn't see this big, bursting flower.

Client: It is nice to hear that though, because sometimes you forget that and there are positive things going on too. I found someone who's been able to massage my shoulders, which have been extremely forward, and over the past three months she's been able to dissolve the adhesions. My shoulders are in a normal position now.

TZ: When our shoulders move into that direction, it is about shouldering a great deal of responsibility and, I have to say, sorrow. It started way back in your past. It started in your early childhood. In fact, I am pulled to when you were five years old, maybe six. I also get around twelve years old. Tell me the first thing that leaped into your thoughts.

Client: Well . . . I have had extreme anxiety my entire life. I was raised in a family, an extremely abusive family. There was a lot of abuse. That was hard for me. That affected me.

TZ: Your shoulders moving forward is about getting weighed down from this. It is protection of your heart. When our shoulders move forward and crunch inward, it is about protection. Your soul feels dear to me. You were a poodle among a bunch of pit bulls.

Client: Yes, yes!

TZ: That's the picture that's coming to my mind.

Client: That's what it was like.

TZ: Well, that also takes me back to your nervous system. Your nervous system is very sensitive.

Client: True. True. That's part of it, and then the emotional trauma of the abuse.

TZ: You are still hypervigilant.

Client: Yeah, yeah, I've been like that my whole life.

TZ: Your left jaw and the left side of your neck is inflamed, and so is the base of your neck. You have been chewing on the past over and over again. Clenching our jaw is about chewing on old issues that never go away. The left side of our body is about a female, a mom figure or a grandma figure. I'm drawn to your left side a lot. See if that makes any sense to you.

Client: There's issues there, (with females) but my dad was the big abuser. That's what I've been struggling with. I was sexually abused for the first three years of my life, and I never even had a chance at happiness. You don't trust anybody. You have no growth or development. There's no base for the first few years of your life. I always feel that's the root of all my problems, because my siblings weren't abused and none of them have my health issues or the challenges that I have.

(Inform the client that you are about to mention some difficult issues. This gives the client a moment to prepare.)

TZ: Well, here are a couple of things I want to bring up and they are very sensitive things.
    (Pause.) Are you aware of any physical or sexual abuse with your mouth?

Client: The abuse happened before I could talk, so I think that's a lot of the problem.

TZ: Yes, you are very insightful about this. Again, I want to emphasize how beautiful your energy looks. Down in the core (*of the symbol of the flower*) it is still dim, like we are looking at a big, dark hole.

Client: And that's what I want to clear up!

TZ: Well, here is where I want to go with that. I hear that you have done a lot of work around your father issues. I keep seeing struggles on the left. The left is about our mothers, or the female side. Tell me about your thoughts, about your mother being your protector or not protecting you.

Client: She didn't protect me!

TZ: Well, that is the direction I am going. You are very aware of the pain and work that you have done with your father, but there is more to do about your mother.

Client: Okay. Yeah, I can go with that.

TZ: Now, is your mother in the living?

Client: No, my parents are both dead.

TZ: Do you want me to check in with her? Because I can do that if she comes forth.

Client: Sure.

TZ: I need to ask her for permission. Give me her full name.

Client: Nora, and her maiden name was Stephens and her other name was Taylor.

TZ: Let me see about Nora. I have to ask her for permission. She is trying to hide. She is coming forth, but she is ducking over to the side and behind things. See if that makes sense in how you knew her. She does not want to be noticed, but she's coming forth on your behalf.

(Now you have two clients that need help and healing.)

Client: Well, I think she did the best she could.

TZ: She seems shy and cautious. Let me see . . . She says she was brutalized.

Client: Yes, she was. She was brutalized by my father. She had a horrible life. I mean, once she married him, she had a terrible life.

TZ: She has not moved on in the spirit realm. She still feels like a victim and brutalized. She is not a lost soul or anything like that, but she lost so much of her value in this life. Now she is saying she didn't protect any of you.

Client: Well, my dad was abusive to everybody but in different ways. My brother had learning disabilities and my dad berated him, called him stupid. My sister would fight with my father. He would call her a lot of names. He called her a whore. Everybody had their own different types of abuse.

TZ: Your mother is carrying some of the responsibility. She feels like she is still hiding, trying to get away. She is very aware that she was not a protector for you. She is very aware of that. Are you aware of her presence around you in your life? In spirit is what I mean.

Client: Not really.

TZ: Let me see what she is showing me here. She is showing that she comes to your home and she stands out in the hallway. Is there a hallway in your home?

Client: Yes.

(Do not assume that your client in the physical wants to connect with their deceased people.)

TZ: She shows me that she stands on the other side of the hall from your bedroom. She doesn't want to scare you. She does not feel worthy to connect with you. She is still carrying this life around even though she has left the physical body. What would you want to do with your mother? She is present here and she is making herself known. Is there anything that was unfinished for you with her?

Client: I would hope that she could heal from this lifetime.

TZ: She is working on it. She hopes for an understanding between the two of you, not even forgiveness. She feels that asking you to forgive her is not possible. What do you think?

Client: I don't think that's too much.

TZ: Your tears tell me this is very important.

Client: I don't think that's too much to forgive her. She really did the best she could do. She didn't protect us, but she didn't put herself before us either. It wasn't like she benefited, but she didn't really have anywhere else to go. I know she had no support. She couldn't even drive. What do you do with four kids? It would have been really hard to divorce him. She just kind of did the best she could.

TZ: Okay, while you are saying these words, I am just watching the two of you. I see the two of you, her in spirit and you in the physical, sitting at a kitchen table and you are writing a letter to her saying everything you want to say to her. It might be two pages or it might be twenty pages. She, in spirit, will sit with you at the kitchen table while you write this letter to her.

Client: Okay, I'll do that.

TZ: Yeah, and make sure you don't censor it in any way. Say the hard stuff in the letter. She is showing me that she will sit right there with you as you write it. I am covered with goose bumps, and that tells me we are touching on something very, very important.

Client: *(Crying)* It feels like it.

TZ: She is emphasizing that no matter what you say to her in that letter, she will stay right there with you at that table. She will not leave you. She will sit right there as you write that letter no matter what.

Client: Okay, that sounds good. *(Her crying continues.)*

TZ: She says she will be with you now when she couldn't be with you then. She is going to be right there with you no matter what you say to her, no matter how horrible it was. You need to write the horrible things.

Client: Well . . . it all seems extremely accurate.

TZ: Keep writing the letter until it feels complete, no matter how long it takes. You will know when you have said everything. Please remember, it will always feel like you are pretending and imagining her sitting with you. Okay? This feels enormous to me! She is coming out from behind that wall where she has been hiding. She will be out in the open and sit there at that table with you. *(Pause.)* Now it is coming to my attention that there is one particular memory that keeps coming up regarding your father's abuse? Just one particular moment or instant.

Client: I have one memory of lying on a bed, maybe even wanting for him to come.

TZ: How old do you feel you were?

Client: I want to say three. I don't know. I feel like I'm probably still holding guilt and low self-esteem. I mean, that's like one of my huge issues.

TZ: Well, your flower *(in her energy field)* shows all this work that you've done. The oranges and the yellow-orange tell me you have been building your confidence throughout all your work. The dark center of the flower is settling in your solar plexus, which is right above your belly button. That tells me you felt powerless with your father. Where does that take you?

Client: There are just a couple of things that come to my mind. One time walking to church, he held my hand and I had this most disgusting feeling touching him. I learned some of the songs when I was in the first grade. You had to quack like a duck and you kind of wiggled your bottom. The way he looked at me was just disgusting. When I was a teenager my sister was actually in college. One day he decided that everyone needed a new toothbrush, so he threw out everybody's toothbrush. He didn't get any new ones, so my parents got into a major fight. I thought he was going to hurt her when he came after her. To protect herself, she ran toward the kitchen window, and she screamed out the kitchen window so the neighbor would hear. These are the three things that come to mind.

(Notice the powerful healing steps taking place.)

TZ: Would you be willing, as the more mature adult, to imagine going back and standing there with your little one? Are you willing to go back and hold her hand?

Client: Yes.

TZ: Okay, I want you to imagine you are right there with her. What are you noticing? What's happening? There is no way to do it wrong. What did she *(her younger self)* notice? It will feel like you just dreamed it up.

Client: I feel a lot calmer, so I kind of feel like the tension is gone.

TZ: Yes. Did she notice you? Did you talk? Or did you just see each other?

Client: I kind of had my hand on her shoulder and then I got in front of her.

(Repeatedly asking for permission sends a message to the client that they have a choice, and they are in charge and in control.)

TZ: Excellent. Okay, is it all right if I ask you two to do something else?

Client: Sure.

(Doing energetic healing work is new to most people. Tell them they cannot do it wrong; it will always feel like imagination, but it is very real.)

TZ: Just let it unfold in front of you. You don't have to make anything happen. Let your thoughts go wherever they go, or if you're visual, just let it unfold. I want the two of you together to talk it over. I want you both together, to take all his *(the father)* energy out of the both of you and hand it back to him. Take all his abuse, all his guck, everything, and I want you two to give it back to him. See what he does with it. Everything, everything! It is his crap so give it back to him. And I'll be quiet until you speak.

Client: *(Long, long pause.)* Okay.

TZ: What did you notice? What happened?

Client: Well, I felt more connected with the eight-, seven-, six-year-old, whatever I was, and she looked happier when we were finished.

TZ: And what did it look like when you were giving it all back to him? Did it have a certain appearance, or what happened there?

Client: I really couldn't see it.

TZ: Okay. You are more of a feeling person. What did it feel like when you gave it all back to him?

Client: Kind of fun.

TZ: Okay. Now is it okay to do one more thing?

Client: Sure.

TZ: All right. I want the two of you together to take your power back from him. It might look like an energy, or a color, or a form, or something else. I want the two of you, hand in hand, to take your power, your own self-esteem, and take it out of him. No cutting or anything, just take it away from him and give it back to the two of you.

(Shorter pause.)

Client: Okay.

TZ: Ooh, that was faster. What did you sense about that?

Client: Well, it went right into our hearts! That's kind of the gist of it. I kept doing it just to make sure I got it all.

(Emphasize that the younger self must be included and participate with each step.)

TZ: And what about your little one?

Client: It was kind of like we enjoyed doing it.

TZ: Now I want you to notice what has happened with him *(her father)* about all this. And just take whatever jumps into your mind.

Client: It did not send him into a seizure, but it kind of made his body frail.

TZ: Yes. Just let your father have his own process.

Client: Okay.

(Sometimes a person has more than one memory that stands out. Repeat the healing steps again for each painful event.)

TZ: Excellent. Ask the little one if she is willing to mature with you, and go to your next memory and do that same thing: take his horribleness out of you two, and you two take back your power. Go to that next memory.

Client: I can't remember. What am I supposed to give him first?

(Do not say too much, too fast. Your client may not be able to comprehend the information.)

TZ: Just give him back all his guck, all his nastiness, his brutality. Just take it out of you and your little one, and give it back to him. Let him have his own process. Get all his energy out of both of you.

Client: *(Another long pause.)* Okay.

(Inform the person of the energy changes you are perceiving.)

TZ: I actually felt his energy pulling out of your chest on the right side of your heart. You were pulling him out of you. I actually felt an ache release from your body. Now make sure that you and your little one take all your empowerment back from him and put it inside of you once again.

Client: *(Quiet pause.)* Okay.

TZ: I want you to really listen to this recording. Your voice, just then, was the strongest it's been since I've been talking to you.

Client: Oh, wow!

TZ: You were very firm and confident when you said "okay."

Client: That'll be interesting to hear the difference.

TZ: Yes. Now, the next step is that you talk to your little one and allow her to mature and merge together with you. My guides are showing me it is a process over the next five to seven days. You will notice all kinds of things.

(Long pause.)

Client: Okay.

(The goal for healing is not forgetting the event. True healing, on an energetic level, transforms the pain into neutral information about one's life. The events no longer have any emotional impact. Remind the client of this.)

TZ: You left so much of yourself back there in the past. Looking back over your left shoulder signals to me that a great deal of your physical problems are connected with your past abuse. Your little one will continue to mature and merge with you. It is important that she comes forward into your present moment. When that is complete, you will look back into the past and it will simply be information with no emotional grief. You will notice it as neutral information about your history. Information is very, very neutral and really has no emotion. We are not affected physically by it anymore. You will not forget your history, but the impact will be released.

Client: Okay. You want me to notice that?

TZ: Yes. You now have two homework assignments. You are asked to sit with your mother at the table and to write her that letter. The other homework is to allow the younger you to mature and to merge with you over seven to eight days.

Client: Excellent. That was excellent! Thank you so much.

I am forever amazed that people implement their healing steps in the most compassionate and benevolent manner. Even people who have suffered the most hideous and violent attacks and have lost all sense of self-empowerment do not seek vengeance. It does not seem to occur to them. Instead, every person I have worked with over the years takes healing action steps with their wrongdoer in beautiful, respectful, and empathic ways. The client is not reacting in retaliation, but instead they are responding with dignity. Spirit is certainly supervising each step.

Healing Technique: Soul Retrieval

Use this when a painful memory in the client's current life has come to the forefront.

    1. Tell the client you want them to let their imagination unfold like a movie in their minds.

2. Ask them to imagine going back and standing with their younger self in the exact moment of the painful trauma.

3. Ask how they know their younger self is aware of them being together.

4. Direct both the young self and the current self to pull everything out of both their bodies that is not theirs. Completely pull out the traumatic event, the pain, the memories, all the ugliness, and give it back to their wrongdoers.

5. Tell the client to take their time and make sure they get absolutely all of it out of them and give it all back. You will be still until they speak so you do not interrupt their process.

6. Watch the client's energy field as they attend to your request. If there is any residual darkness, tell the client to go back and get it all out of both of them. Remind your client to do every step in partnership with their younger self.

7. Now direct both to call out for healing guides to create a perfect cleansing filter. Wait until the client informs you that the filter is present.

8. Next, firmly tell the client and their younger self to take back absolutely everything that has been taken from them. Bring it through the cleansing filter and place it back inside of both of them. To encourage the client, use the same emotional words that the client has used in describing the traumatic event. Some examples to say aloud might be:

Both you and the younger you, take back everything that was taken from you.

Both you and the younger you, take back your confidence.

Both you and the younger you, take back your ability to love.

Both you and the younger you, take back your personal empowerment.

Both you and the younger you, take back all of your energy.

Both you and the younger you, take back all of your health.

Both you and the younger you, take back all of your strength.

Both you and the younger you, take back all of your intelligence.

Both you and the younger you, take back all of your body.

Both you and the younger you, take back all of your beauty.

9. Let your client know you will be still until they speak, and to take their time making sure they get it all.

10. Ask them, their current self and younger self, to talk it over with each other to see if there is anything else that needs to be done for a complete and permanent healing. Pause and allow both of them to check that out. Follow through with anything that seems incomplete for them.

11. Direct the current self to ask the younger self if they are ready to leave that moment forever. If yes, tell both of them to release that event and to move forward, merging together physically and coming back into the client's present moment sitting in the session with you. Tell them to take their time and you will be still until the client speaks.

12. Watch the client's energy field and, at the end of the session, inform them of the positive energetic changes. Reinforce that healing on this energetic level is real.

In some cases, your guides may inform you that the merging and assimilation may take a certain number of days. Give that information to the client. You might be told to give the client some homework they are to do over a certain number of days following the soul retrieval. You might become aware of amazing physical changes with the client. They may have a sparkle in their eyes when, before the session began, their eyes were lifeless. The shape of their face, or their complexion, may be different. Finish the session by informing them of all the physical and energetic changes you have witnessed.

Current-Life Patterns that Keep Repeating

Your future does not need to look like your past. In fact, your past can only continue to affect you if you send energy into the past and maintain that energy. We keep our past alive in different ways:

- We believe the ugly criticism someone said to us.
- We swallow those false beliefs and make them part of who we are.
- We focus most of our thoughts on our memories.
- We give much less thought to our current life or our future life.
- We have unfinished business regarding events in our life.
- We hold on to extreme emotions about people or events in the past.

Notice any patterns that keep repeating in your life and the lives of your clients. A pattern is caused by some of the things mentioned above. While a life pattern is often caused by these things, a pattern continues to repeat because we are unconsciously attempting to heal the agony and learn specific attributes embedded within the pattern.

Remember this: Repeating patterns are a profound signal telling us what our true life's purpose is. There is always a consistent issue that threads through the pattern, tying it all together. Look for the consistent thread and you will discover the purpose of this person's life. The purpose of each lifetime is to learn, and to achieve the next level of awareness. Each level of awareness fine-tunes our consciousness, allowing us to expand in our personal evolution.

The healing of a pattern can only happen when we go to its point of origin—the instant it began—and positively alter the source of the pattern at the energetic level. Attempting to cure an illness or disease in the physical realm alone is only placing a bandage over the cause. The longer the bandage remains, the more the true cause festers, becoming more toxic as time continues.

Throughout the first part of my session with my client Amanda, I frequently heard the words "hopeless," "different," and "alone." When I brought this to her attention I also asked her if I could check in with her intuitively to find the source of her stress and ill health. She immediately agreed. I asked Spirit for the point of origin of Amanda's pattern, and that request took me to an intense event in her childhood. I immediately found myself drawn back over her shoulder. When the pulling sensation stopped, a large number twelve floated in front of me. I said to Amanda, "What happened to you when you were twelve years old? You had a traumatic situation happen, didn't you?"

Tears silently dripped down her cheeks. She looked at me and said, "My stepfather was a violent drunk. For the first time ever, I had three girls stay over at my house. I had never done that because he was drunk all the time, but that night he was supposed to be out of town. The girls and I were upstairs in my bedroom, and I was so happy that I might have friends now. A few minutes later I heard my stepfather yelling and pounding on things. I sneaked partway down the stairs, and by then he was beating up my mother. I went back upstairs and the girls were hiding in my closet. They were terrified and I was horribly ashamed and humiliated. They never came back or talked to me again."

That incident cascaded into a life pattern of feeling rejected, alone, and different from other people. The pattern kept repeating over and over. At first glance, one might miss the pattern because Amanda's negative experiences happened in different settings and with different types of relationships. Amanda kept using the same words to describe her life situation. Those words were the thread that tied them all together.

A similar shocking event took place for thirty-five-year-old Debbie. She had an unshakable depression that ruined every relationship anyone attempted to have with her. She could agree with me that there was a pattern in her life, but she was completely perplexed about the cause of this pattern. I was pulled to the number seven that hovered in the shadows far away behind her. I was not ready for her reaction when I told her that something dreadful happened when she was seven years old. Debbie gasped and physically threw herself against the back of the chair and sobbed until she could not breathe.

People will always know exactly what happened to them at the age you intuitively receive. I always allow my clients to feel the depths of their emotions without trying to calm them down or rush them in any way. Sometimes emotions burst open like lancing a huge boil that has built up a great deal of pressure over time. Debbie's mother had hung herself in an upstairs bedroom while Debbie and her father were downstairs and unaware. Debbie had placed this horrific moment back into the depths of her memory and her subconscious. The effects, however, tainted her ability to create loving and lasting relationships. There was the point of origin of her struggles and dismal health.

Case Study:
Emotions beneath Life Issues

This is a brief excerpt that demonstrates a physical issue of which the client is already aware. Underneath lies an emotional conflict, which in this case was never speaking their personal truth to others.

Practice Experience:

Imagine you are the medical intuitive speaking the words in this transcript. Read it aloud or, if possible, with a study buddy, one taking part as the medical intuitive and one as the client. Practice this session as if you are actually giving these steps to someone who needs your guidance.

Client: I'm worried about my neck.

TZ: I see you turning very stiffly.

Client: It's not good. I can't bend down too long, because when I do, it shuts off the nerve.

TZ: Well, when I look straight on at the back of your neck, your neck actually has a strange, odd curve in it. You have a couple curves, in fact, that seem to be causing kinks, and it looks squished in your cervical spine. I am being pulled up to cervical 2 and then also cervical 5 to 6. The energy doesn't flow at C5 to 6. There is a bit of a constriction. Oh, okay. C5 to 6, especially, is connected with your struggle to speak your truth. That has a lot to do with the emotion and your thoughts and beliefs that you should not speak your truth. That is right straight through to the thyroid. It has a lot to do with you holding back from who you are really meant to be. This is a pattern that has been repeating for a long time to the point that it has manifested in these physical struggles.

Client: That's neat. Did you see anything at my C1?

(Do not depend on what the client thinks is the cause of illness. Use your own intuitive abilities and the clear direction from your guides.)

TZ: Well, I keep getting pulled up to the top of your spine. It's up there.

Client: Because my C1 is fused with my occipital, so that is the reason you saw the C2. It is a congenital defect. I didn't find this out until I was fifty. I woke up after helping a friend move and I couldn't move. That's why you saw the C2.

TZ: There is stress there in C2, and it is hot and irritated. It also has a dark line through it.

Client: That's why, if I have any pain, it is most likely where it is compressed because I don't have a C1.

TZ: Remember that I said it is kind of squished. I am seeing stresses 5–6 and up there C2.

Client: I'd be curious about how much can be done about it when it is about not speaking. You are giving me hope. If there are things like speaking one's truth that I could do, it would be great. I will definitely consider speaking out! Absolutely!

Throughout this book I have given readers a multitude of healing techniques and the steps to accomplish that healing. That being said, you must also be ready for an individual to branch off unexpectedly, doing their own thing without a single bit of guidance from you. Let them go on their spontaneous way! Allow them to take a detour from the normal steps and go along with their unique flow. Something else is guiding them. The following case is my best example of uniqueness.

My adult client, Bridget, spontaneously went back to her abusive childhood on her own, without any directions from me. I quickly realized that I was the one who had to adjust. I was not in the driver's seat with this woman! She informed me she was aware that her five-year-old self was inside of her adult body.

Suddenly, the words just flew out of my mouth: "Take your little five-year-old self out of your older body!" I had never specifically given that directive before to anyone. So, we both had already received unique guidance.

I asked her to take her abused little one out of her body. I really did not speak again for most of the session. Bridget independently reported to me whatever was happening. Her extremely abusive older sister suddenly stood before her. My client described removing large wooden blocks out of her own body and her five-year-old body.

She spontaneously said, "I am now putting new toys back into their bodies."

I did not say, "Wait a minute. I did not tell you to take that step yet!" Instead, I listened, watched, and witnessed Bridget's own private process of healing.

Then she declared, "A little potted plant suddenly appeared, and I am placing it into my five-year-old's lower abdomen." Bridget then gave me directions to wait quietly because she needed to hug all her abusers. She informed me that her nasty mother, father, and older sister came for the hugs. I continued to do as I was told. I waited until she completed the hugs.

I did step in a little at this point and asked her to take back all they had taken from her and all she had unintentionally given away to them. I waited.

To my surprise, Bridget said, "I see fertilizer in my inner vision. The little potted plant is being fed the fertilizer!" I could have never imagined directing a client to fertilize a potted plant for their healing, but Bridget knew it was exactly what she needed.

We medical intuitives walk a fine line of giving direction without telling our clients how to specifically do each step. We also walk a fine line regarding nudging them forward in the process, while at the same time allowing them to spontaneously take a different road that has nothing to do with our own plans. In other words, when your client is in their own spontaneous flow of healing, go with their flow and not your own plans. Each person ultimately knows their own correct way to heal, to learn, and to expand.

Essential Points

- Use key words your clients emphasize to personalize their healing process.

- During a painful event, a fragment of a human's soul can break away and remain imprisoned in a precise moment of the event.

- A soul retrieval is the process of bringing the soul's fragments back into the energy field of the damaged person.

- Allow and assist the client to journey back to their younger self on their own and reclaim their suffering soul fragment.

- Your past can only continue to affect you if you send energy into the past and maintain that energy.

- Repeating patterns are a profound signal telling us what our true life's purpose is.

- A pattern can only be healed when we go to its point of origin and positively alter the source of the pattern at the energetic level.

Chapter 17

Structuring Your Medical Intuitive & Healing Session

In order to achieve an advanced level of training as a medical intuitive, people have read my three books about the subject, taken my in-person courses, or met with me in many private mentoring sessions.

You may now have the same question that so many others have had over my many years of teaching medical intuition and the healing methods. When an individual asks this question, I know in my heart that they will take their intuitive skills and healing abilities out into the world to create incredible, breathtaking, positive changes in the lives of many people. The question is: "How do I put all the pieces together in a medical-intuitive session, and what does it look like?"

My heart is singing even as I write those words. I want to begin the answer to that question here:

You first need to recognize and acknowledge that people will come to you with many needs, struggles, and illnesses. You cannot heal all their problems in one session. It is impossible.

For example, I was meeting with a dedicated mentoring student. In this session, Nita described a particular client.

Nita said, "I just could not do enough for her no matter how hard I tried." She went on to describe the multiple diagnoses her client suffered with, including many childhood traumas and a great deal of stress in her relationships. Nita described each issue and told me in detail which healing steps she took with this client.

I finally said, "This is impossible to get this all done in a one-hour session!"

Nita said, "Oh no, this session lasted a little over three hours!"

People will come to you for medical intuition with an entire lifetime of trauma, current-life stress, and a wide range of illnesses. You cannot heal their entire lifetime in one session. Here are a few reasons why:

1. People cannot understand, assimilate, or remember that much information in one session.

2. Energy is instant. People cannot tolerate the fast multiple energetic changes that the medical intuitive and their guides send through the client during the healings.

3. You cannot function at your best over so many concentrated, emotional hours.

I want to describe a structure that has proven to be the most successful not only for clients but for your own long-term well-being.

The Structure of Your One-Hour Session

Before the session even begins, insist the client not tell you anything about themselves at first. They will be shocked and may want to argue, but assure them that within ten minutes, they can share everything with you.

Help them understand that you want to work with your guides first, so they give you the clearest information about the client's energy field and their physical body. Then explain that you will want to hear the client's feedback afterward. This will calm the client so you can begin the session.

Here I offer two ways to describe the structure of a one-hour session for you:

Details of the One-Hour Session:

1. *5–8 minutes:* Immediately inform the client of all intuitive pops of information your guides give you.

2. *15–20 minutes:* Allow the client to respond now. Intuitively

look into the areas your client thinks is important and wants more information about.

Important Goal During This Segment: Determine one primary concern that both your client and your guides agree upon.

3. *10 minutes:* Direct your guides to show you the exact point of origin that caused this issue. Inform your client of the cause and discuss the details.

4. *25 minutes:* Call in your healing specialist. Ask them to show you the most powerful healing method to use. Engage the client to assist with the healing steps as they happen.

5. *5 minutes:* Ask your guides for the most powerful homework so the client may empower their own healing. Have the client practice the homework. Watch their energy field to ascertain they understand how to do it well.

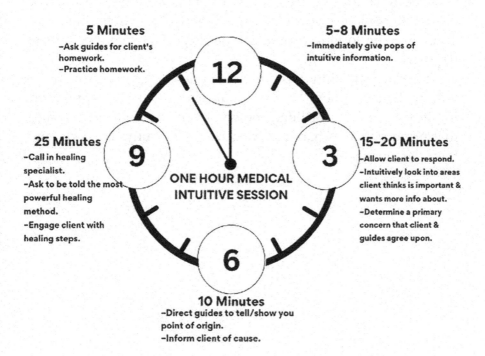

5 Minutes
–Ask guides for client's homework.
–Practice homework.

5–8 Minutes
–Immediately give pops of intuitive information.

25 Minutes
–Call in healing specialist.
–Ask to be told the most powerful healing method.
–Engage client with healing steps.

ONE HOUR MEDICAL INTUITIVE SESSION

15–20 Minutes
–Allow client to respond.
–Intuitively look into areas client thinks is important & wants more info about.
–Determine a primary concern that client & guides agree upon.

10 Minutes
–Direct guides to tell/show you point of origin.
–Inform client of cause.

Bringing Closure to Each One-Hour Session

1. You must point out to most clients the primary issue you gave them information about.

2. Point out that a deep healing took place, and that this healing needs to assimilate within their body and energy field.

3. Inform the client of any other issues you received information about but didn't have enough time to provide a healing.

4. Never push a client to schedule more sessions. Simply point out what still needs to be worked on, according to your guides. Then ask the client to go home and let you know when it feels right to make another appointment. The client will not feel any pressure if you address scheduling more sessions in this relaxed manner.

You might have already noticed that the medical intuitive must be in control of the time and structure of the session. The client will not know how to use the time with you in the best way. Even more important, people will not expect a healing process to happen.

It is rare when intuitives include honest-to-goodness healings within their sessions. My books and my courses magnify the intuitive's skills to facilitate powerful and permanent healings that bring positive changes for each person's physical body and their personal lives.

Chapter 18

Conclusion

*"The real spiritual progress of the aspirant is measured
by the extent to which he achieves inner tranquility."*

—Swami Sivananda

By now, you know that medical intuitives truly travel throughout
many dimensions. We will close this interdimensional experience
we have had together, with my own near-death experience. I share
my personal story with you for two reasons:

1. It feels deeply important to share my details with you
   because a near-death episode is a very special interdimensional experience.

2. You will read how three medical-intuitive friends of mine,
   in different locations around the world, received almost
   exactly the same information during my near death.

My Own Near-Death Experience

I was back in my hospital room after the second surgery on my
infected hip. I was septic. The infection had spread throughout
my body. I was looking up at the ceiling, and then the ceiling was
gone. I was moving forward through a white mist or cloud-like
substance. Then, quietly and gently, I heard sounds that I will never
forget. Thousands upon thousands of beings were humming, or
vocally creating tones that intermingled in a blessed harmony. The
sounds rose up and down as if following the waves of an ocean.

I moved slowly past all kinds of things. I saw the faces of

many, many people, none of whom I knew. We looked deeply but gently into each other's eyes as I passed. I drifted past babies and older people and people of all ages. I stopped for some reason and looked into the eyes of an elderly man. I remained with him for a short period of time as if I was examining him more closely. His eyes suddenly began to glow a menacing bright red. He was trying to be scary or even evil, but I just laughed and laughed, and then I moved on. I moved past vague formations and still more people and faces.

My drifting slowly came to a stop. I could not go any farther, so I remained standing, or floating, there. Brilliant colors surrounded me. The lights were so bright it was like I had placed my face an inch in front of a multicolored neon sign. It seemed like my eyes were burning out of my head, but there was no pain at all. The colors continued hovering all around me.

I began laughing with all my heart and could not stop laughing. Laughing so joyously just made me laugh some more. I felt so completely consumed with joy and elation that I had never felt before. I could hear myself laughing. The sounds echoed all around me. My laughter bounced off the wall of colors, while some echoed within the colors. My own laughter kept bouncing back to me from all directions.

As I watched the neon colors, I noticed the brightest light of all was white and it appeared ahead of me and a little to my right. The white light was blinding but without pain. The colors formed complicated geometric shapes. The shapes fit tightly together like puzzle pieces. Then the shapes changed and became one shape that duplicated itself. There were a multitude of shape changes. I remember one of a tree that duplicated, and each duplication fit with itself and repeated all around me. And then the form of a bird duplicated in the same way. I began laughing more loudly than before. I was truly ecstatic. I was elated, and then I was in my hospital bed again.

The following information comes from the observations and experiences of three medical intuitives. I will call them Chris, Lola, and Mark. According to Google, Chris and Lola live 8,419 miles away from me. The third medical intuitive, Mark, is also a scientist and lives an hour from me. Mark did not know that Chris and Lola were working on me at the same time he was.

All three, however, were doing medical intuition and supporting me energetically while my third emergency surgery was taking place.

Chris tuned into me during the surgery. This was her experience:

"When we started the healing, I saw a Light surgeon come from the Light and enter the body of the real surgeon. When he opened you, he pondered for a second on what bits to do. He got a shiver down his spine and then made the decision. It was awesome to watch.

"Next thing was the comment from you about your bum. I turned and you were out of your body. I saw it happening on my left-hand side. I said, 'What are you doing out?' You said, 'I don't know, but I can float.' You started floating on the ceiling and then said, 'Let's go visit a place.' I thought, 'We can't.' We (both medical intuitives) had our (energetic) hands on you doing the healing. Then suddenly a double of ourselves came out. There was a double of Lola and me. I was left to heal and the second duplicate of us went with you.

"You were floating on top of the surgery room having a laugh. You said, 'I hope my bum isn't sore after this.' You wanted to visit an ancient Pleiadian disc. That's when we found ourselves on a disc meditating. It was a see-through disc with ancient symbols on it. We all sat on it and meditated. We had to tie a white cord on your leg and pull you back into the room and make you heavy so you sank back in. You were having too much fun and wanted to go to visit other places.

"We *(the two medical intuitives)* knew you were light and wanted to go places. You were floaty. You wanted to go through a star gate and other places. Thank God for the white cord. We will keep it on until you are better. You were tremendously happy. I started the healing at 10:30 p.m. and it was 2:35 a.m. when I was back in my bed."

Lola described the experience she had as she sent healing energy my way.

"You were laughing and had to be pulled back in the room and into your body with a white cord. It was like a comedy . . . us convincing you we had to go back, and you were sort of on laughing gas and also worried about your bum."

Mark reported this:

"The morning of your surgery, I woke super early and felt strongly that I needed to work on keeping your silver cord attached. It wasn't easy either. I had trouble getting that done.
    "In summary, it was my intention to monitor you throughout your last surgery and broadcast accordingly. The area I found that was most important to address, while the surgery was underway, pertained to keeping the silver cord attached. The cord can become loosened via operations, accidents, drugs, falls, etc. The cord becoming loose is part of the dying process. It is quite possible that had your silver cord actually loosened, you might not have returned to your physical body after the surgery.
    "It was well after the surgery that your partner told me about the two people in New Zealand who were concurrently working to do the same thing I was attempting to do, during the same surgery, via different techniques. It was also well after the surgery that you told me you had the very distinct sense, just prior to surgery, you were not going to make it through

that surgery. I had no knowledge of either of these events (the other two healers) as I was attempting the work at that time."

I began this book by sharing my intuitive observations of my mother's death transition. I will end this book by sharing the experiences other medical intuitives had as they assisted me, and healed me, through my own near-death experience. Between the beginning and the end of this book lie true stories and examples of the infinite possibilities with medical intuition. My hope, from one medical-intuitive healer to another, is for you to recognize the vast realms your intuitive skills and your healing abilities will take you.

The medical intuitive travels throughout many dimensions of existence. Our work includes healing for the living, but also healing the dying, and those who have already made their transition. The medical intuitive travels throughout levels of energy from light to dark and back to the light again. We move through time and space at will because there are no restrictions and no limitations. Those borders are only in the limited mind.

I am very intuitive, and so are you.

I am a person in the physical world who is enriched with the electrically alive energetic information of the nonphysical world, and so are you.

I am immersed in an experience of both the physical and the nonphysical at the exact same time, and so are you.

I am able to perceive another person's eternal story, which brings a natural healing in their current life, and so can you.

You will never know the profound effects of how much your precious healing moments have blessed the eternal lives of others.

Appendix

Direct and Empower Your Toroidal Field

My guides have altered the order of directing your toroidal field. Directing the toroidal field in the following way is one of the primary reasons I decided to release the second edition of this book. My guides ask that you fill yourself with the following energy. The first two focus on healing, cleansing, and then purifying while the last two bring in power and protection because the negative cannot stand its elevated high frequency.

- **Each individual color of the rainbow.** Each color has its own focus of healing. So, directing each color individually provides a more powerful healing response within your body.
- **The violet flame.** This holds a purifying, cleansing energy.
- **Brilliant diamond-like sparkles.**
- **Shimmering, glorious, golden energy.**

Here are the steps to direct and empower your toroidal field using the energy listed above:

- Imagine inhaling through the soles of your feet.
- Focus your thoughts and inhale each color of the rainbow one at a time. Fill yourself with each color one by one in this order: Red, Orange, Yellow, Green, Blue, Purple, White.
- Every time you inhale, fill yourself more and more with each shimmering, glistening color.
- Focus filling every cell of your body on sending each color

up your spinal cord, every cell, every organ, every muscle of your physical body.

- Notice the fullness of rainbow energy within you.

- In your mind, direct the violet flame to rush through each cell of who you are, purifying all along the way.

- Think, imagine, and sense that brilliant white sparkles are inside every single cell of your physical body.

- Direct shimmering, electrified, precious gold energy to shoot up from the soles of your feet.

- When you are completely full of rainbows, violet, white sparkles, and gold, then allow that fullness to shine like a lightbulb. Shine in all directions, and especially empower your entire backside. (*Note:* Do not deliberately send your energy outward. Focus on being so full of brilliant light that you naturally shine like a lightbulb.)

- Notice you are so full that your brilliant light rises upward and out the crown of your head, shooting up into your higher self and into the heavens. The heavens notice and respond positively to your new positive energy field.

- Allow your energy, and the energy of the heavens, to flow back down like a fountain through you and back into the earth.

- Every time you inhale, continue this natural flow as it comes back up through your body and spine. Allow your body to feel the sensations of this flow. As you think about the flow circulating, your body will feel the sensations of it. The energy will often give you warm vitality and the sense of taking a perfect, heavenly shower.

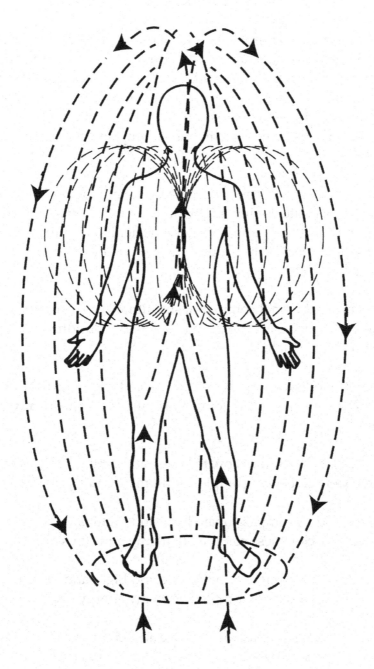

The Toroidal Field (*illustration by Jacqueline Rogers*)

Protection that Works with the Negative

"I, *(full name)*, completely and permanently revoke and repel *all* negative people and *all* dark-force energy from me and my clients in all ways and on all levels! I, *(full name)*, am indomitable, invincible, and unassailable to all negativity on all levels. Only the divine, compassionate, loving Light of Source fills my body, my mind, my higher self, my spirit, and my eternal soul."

"I, *(full name)*, invoke the greatest guardians of the divine, compassionate loving Light of Source, to constantly guard my physical body and my energetic field to create a completely safe, sacred space around me, my clients, and our healing work."

Note: For the final command, substitute "God" for any divine name that feels correct to you, such as "Buddha," "Christ," "Krishna," or "Allah."

"Only God's compassionate Love and Light and the purest sacred Consciousness completely fill **every cell in my body** now."

"Only God's compassionate Love and Light and the purest sacred Consciousness completely fill my **mind** now."

"Only God's compassionate Love and Light and the purest sacred Consciousness completely fill my **emotions** now."

"Only God's compassionate Love and Light and the purest sacred Consciousness completely fill my **energy field** now."

"Only God's compassionate Love and Light and the purest sacred Consciousness completely fill my **higher self** now."

"Only God's compassionate Love and Light and the purest sacred Consciousness completely fill my **spirit** now."

"Only God's compassionate Love and Light and the purest sacred Consciousness completely fill my **eternal soul** now."

Work Only with Divine and Sacred Guides

Step 1: Command

Use the following command to call out to a Divine and Sacred specialty guide:

"I invite in now, only the most Divine and Sacred guide who specializes in working with me, *(your full name)*, for the purpose of *(clearly define the specialty that you want or need).*

Step 2: Interview

Interview the guide so you are confident about who you are working with. Ask them these three questions. If they are truly Divine and Sacred, you will receive an instant "Yes."

- Are you truly Divine and Sacred?
- How did you achieve that status?
- What exactly is your specialty area?

Dismiss them if . . .

- They are silent and do not answer your question.
- They begin talking about something else to distract you.
- They clearly say, "No."

Step 3: Develop a Working Relationship

Communicate back and forth to develop a clear working relationship. Ask precise questions such as:

- What is my first step to working excellently with you?
- What is the first step you will take to work excellently with me?
- I just received this piece of information from you. Did I receive that correctly?

Note: The invitation is only an invitation. From this point forward, you must now clearly command each action you want or need the Divine and Sacred to take.

Disconnect Your Energy from the Client
After Every Session

Here are three specific steps to create good, clean closure with your client:

1. At the beginning of each session, ask that a sacred space be placed around you and your client for the most perfect work and healing to happen. Do not create the space yourself. Ask your specialty guide to create the perfect, sacred, and safe space for the work to happen. You may feel it, or you may see it. Intuitively invite each client to join you in that sacred space.

2. At the close of each session, or at least at the end of each day, invite in and direct a Divine and Sacred specialty guide to create the most powerful cleansing filter for you now. Notice the look and the feel of the filter in front of you. With deliberate consciousness, pull back your energetic laser beam from the client through the filter. You may feel the filter, or you may actually see it working. You can assist yourself by inhaling and imagining each inhalation pulls your energy back to you through that filter.

3. A possible command to use at the same time might be:

   I now bring me, and only me, back to myself, clean and

clear, through a perfect filter provided for me by my divine cleansing specialist.

Sometimes I see a thick substance clinging to the filter. I am so comforted and pleased to know that I am not bringing someone else's emotional density into my life.

Clarity Heals Your Clients

Here are some tips for maintaining vigilance regarding your clarity as an intuitive:

- Identify yourself as the healer standing strong and personally unaffected by the sorrows or negativity of your clients.
- Deliberately run your toroidal field. Identify with unconditional love and mental wisdom from the center of your heart and mind. Do not create a barrier around you. Your protection is the brilliant glow from the Light of Source within you and shining outward all around you.
- Do not do this work by yourself. Every day, invite specialty guides as your body guards to constantly protect you.
- Read and feel *The Invocation* by Betsy Bergstrom, or feel free to create your own invocation.
- Have no fear. Think and then manifest feelings of power, knowledge, and invincibility.
- Take a daily energetic cleansing shower provided to you by a spiritual guide who specializes in cleansing and healing.

Work with Your Guides

Here are the simple steps to ask your guides about a piece of intuitive information they gave you of which you don't know the meaning:

1. Create a very specific question and direct the question to your specialty guides.

2. Pause and wait for a moment.

3. Absolutely accept the first thought, image, knowledge, or sensation that pops into your awareness.

Finding the Point of Origin of an Illness

The following phrases can be very effective:

- "Give me the exact point of origin that started *(illness/ struggle)* for *(client's full name)*."

- "Show me the precise moment that started the *(illness/ struggle)* for *(client's full name)*."

- "Direct me right now to the instant that *(illness/struggle)* began for *(client's full name)*."

- "Give me the original cause when *(illness/struggle)* began for *(client's full name)*."

- "Show me the exact point of origin that is causing *(illness/ struggle)* for *(client's full name)*."

Healing Technique:
Negative Energy Caused by Substance Abuse

1. Describe the emptiness and its physical location in the person's body, such as how cold or dark it is.

2. Ask the client, "Where and when did you lose your empowerment?" Tell them to take the idea that instantly pops into their mind. Most of the time, they will share a current-life trauma. Sometimes they will become aware of a past-life trauma.

3. Guide the client to fill themselves up with the energy of the sun: breathe its warmth into their belly, push warmth along with a sparkling neon-yellow vibration into their abdomen. Do this with them so they feel they are not alone.

4. Ask the client to notice what they feel in the space that was previously empty. It will be warmer and fuller.

Healing Technique:
Psychic Surgery, Energetic Manipulations, Extractions

Remember, only provide a psychic surgery, energetic manipulation, or extraction if your specialty guides specifically direct you to do so, or you spontaneously sense it happening. Spirit will show you the exact steps you are to follow. Here are a few of the infinite possibilities Spirit may guide you to do:

1. Imagine your energetic hands gently penetrating your client's skin at the injured spot within the person's body.

2. Spirit will show you exactly what to do. For example, Spirit may tell you to . . .

   • Seal the leak by covering the bubbles leaking out of your client's body with your hands, like a Band-Aid or some type of wound dressing.

   • Energetically cut tough, gristle-like scar tissue out of a client's body.

   • Straighten a vertebra that has slipped out of place, or push the entire spinal cord into alignment.

   • Remove a cyst with your hand.

   • Smooth out a jagged or frayed tendon with your fingertips.

   • Remove an instrument from the energetic realm, such as an ancient sword, from the client's back.

   • Or, sometimes Spirit will heal the client for you.

3. When you remove anything from a physical or energetic human body, remember to fill the empty space with Love, Light, and perfect healing.

Healing Technique:
Allergies Caused by Thoughts and Emotions

1. Ask the client to remember the moment they first became aware of having allergies. Even if it was in infancy, ask them to imagine going back to whatever age they feel they were.

2. Direct them to imagine their adult self going back in time to join their younger self. Emphasize that they cannot do this wrong and to allow whatever comes into their imagination.

3. Tell them to let it unfold like a daydream or a movie. Inform the client you will be quiet until they speak. They will often feel they should rush, so make sure you ask for them to take their time. They will tell you when they feel they are with their younger self.

4. Instruct the client: "Make sure the younger you actually knows you are there with them." Then ask, "How can you tell they know you are there with them?"

5. Ask the adult and the younger self to notice everything around them and where they find themselves. (This helps the client settle into this new awareness.)

6. State: "Now talk it over with the younger you, and the two of you take all the negative emotions out of both of your bodies and give it back to wherever, or whomever, the negative emotions came from. Take out all the emotions from both of you and give everything back. Make sure you help the younger you to do this. Those negative emotions are not yours to keep. You do not need to carry them any longer. I will be quiet until you speak."

7. Repeat all the dialogue in the previous step but substitute the word "allergies" in place of the phrase "negative emotions." Then state, "I will be quiet until you speak. Take your time."

8. When your client states they have done that, ask: "What happened and what did the negative emotions and the

allergies look like when you released them?" Allow the client to describe their experience. Support them by telling them how real this is.

9. For the next step, direct the client by stating: "Now for a complete and permanent healing and release, take back everything that is positive for the younger you and the mature you. Take back all that is positive. Take back all that you gave away, and all that was taken from you, in that moment. Place it back inside both of you. Again, I will be quiet until you speak. Take your time."

10. After the client describes the experience, state: "I ask that the mature you and the younger you talk it over and see if there is anything else that needs to happen for a complete and permanent healing and release." (Take note of the power of the words "complete and permanent." Note that you are also encouraging the client to take any other steps necessary to release the allergies.)

Healing Technique:
Unresolved Issues

I asked my healing guides to show me the way to provide a complete and permanent healing for Eric. This is what Spirit directed me:

1. Tell your client to imagine sending his current self back to that specific moment and stand with his younger self.

2. Ask your client what they see and feel.

3. Tell your client to call in their own healing guides to join their younger self and current self in that exact painful moment.

4. Ask your client what they experience.

Healing Technique:
Secondary Gain from Illness

1. In a gentle manner, ask if they tend to be people pleasers and have a difficult time saying no to people.

2. Inform your client they do not need to become more important than everyone else, but just equally as important. You will need to repeat this important piece of information again and again.

3. Inform them they are in charge of their thoughts and emotions. They can refuse to think negatively about themselves. They will be surprised when you inform them they can say no without making any excuses or explaining in any way. You will see a light go on in their eyes. A spark of new ideas just happened.

4. Ask them how they might take the first baby step in this process.

Dowsing Steps

1. Completely scramble the point of origin of (person's specific struggle) on all levels and in all ways for (person's full name).

2. Completely neutralize the point of origin of (person's specific struggle) on all levels and in all ways for (person's full name).

3. Permanently and completely transform all scrambled and neutralized energy for (person's full name) into Divine Love and health.

The Raymon Grace Dowsing Steps for Miasms

1. Ask for the original cause of the miasm.

2. Command: "Permanently scramble all negative miasms on all levels regarding (person's full name)."

3. Command: "Permanently neutralize all negative miasms on all levels regarding (person's full name)."

4. Command: "Completely transform all that has been scrambled and neutralized into Divine Love."

Healing Technique:
Levels 1–2: Negative Thought Forms and Confused or Afraid People in Spirit

1. Tell the client you will ask the spirit person/thought form questions, but they are to receive the spirit's answers and tell you what thoughts leap into their minds. This engages the client with their own healing process.

2. Ask the person in spirit questions to create a sense of relationship with them. This engages the spirit person in their own recovery. As your living client receives the spirit's information, the living client will realize the cause of their own struggles and what led the spirit person to connect with them in the first place.

3. Call in Divine and Sacred guides who specialize in transformation of this spirit person.

4. After a brief pause, now direct the spirit person to count the specialists who have come for them. This engages the spirit but also begins their own sense of making positive choices and feeling empowered.

5. Direct the spirit person to feel the love emanating from these guides and to turn their care over to the guides.

6. Your living client must consciously and completely release the spirit that has been affecting them. Ask them to actively send the spirit person out of their body and energy field. (Many clients will selfishly refuse to send the spirit away. Do not accept this. Tell them they are interfering with the transformation the spirit person absolutely deserves.)

7. When something leaves, the medical intuitive as well as the client always need to request the most compassionate Light, Love, and healing to come in and fill every single space and

place where the spirit used to be. This is a powerful key for permanent healing.

8. Invite a specialty guide who excels in cleaning and clearing to create the ideal cleansing filter for you to return through to maintain perfect health for you.

9. Deliberately and consciously pull your energetic laser beam back from the client and the experience through the filter. You may feel the filter, or you may actually see it working. You can assist yourself by inhaling and imagining each inhalation pulls your energy back to you through that filter.

10. At the same time, command: "I now bring me—and only me—back to myself, clean and clear through a perfect filter provided for me by my Divine cleansing specialist."

Healing Technique:
Levels 3–4: Angry, Possessive, Vicious, Hateful, and Deliberate People in Spirit

1. Inform the client they have a negative spirit person interfering with them. You can describe the spirit to them. Clients can often identify who they are.

2. If the negative spirit controls the client to refuse consent to remove the entity, ignore it and continue giving instructions.

3. Ask the spirit person questions, and tell the client to listen to the spirit's responses and tell you what they are. This engages the client in their own healing process. Here are a few examples of questions to ask the spirit entity:

- How long have you been connected to the client?
- What drew you to this person?
- What goal do you have by staying connected?
- How many other people are you connected to right now?

- How is this connection not working for you any longer?
- Have you forgotten that you are a separate human being from this human?

4. Move on in conversation, emphasizing how separate and different the spirit entity is with statements or questions such as:

    - If they are different genders, emphasize that difference.
    - Do you know that you can never become your own self while attached to this human?
    - This is not a good life for you to remain with this human.
    - You cannot be happy or become who you are meant to be.
    - You will be forgotten by everyone if you remain attached to this human.

5. If the spirit person refuses to talk, state that they must be uncomfortable with what you are saying and that they do not want to answer. This will encourage responses to resume.

6. Tell the spirit person you have already called in specialty guides from the Compassionate Source just for them. Direct the spirit to count the guides that have come and to feel their love. Tell the spirit person the specialty guides do not care how terrible the entity thinks they are. The guides can only feel love for them, no matter what they have done.

7. Describe aloud how both the client and the spirit person are now separating away from each other. Repeatedly state how this is best for them both.

8. Throughout this session, internally ask guides to completely extract all levels of these negative entities from your client.

9. Ask the client to participate and allow the release to happen. Tell the client to declare, "I completely and permanently

release this spirit person and anyone who is associated with you now. Go with the specialists who are here for you."

10. Describe out loud to your client how you, as the medical intuitive, are perceiving the separation that is happening.

11. Ask your specialists to remove the being and take it to the best place for its highest transformation into Light, Compassion, and Love.

12. Call in your Purest Healing Specialists of the Light to cleanse every single space and place where negativity used to be. Request immediate special healing that is best for this client and this situation. Command that a complete and permanent healing and cleansing happen now.

13. Ask the client to accept the healing and to tell you when the healing is complete. Tell them you will be quiet until they speak.

14. Ask the client to describe their experience during the healing. This will help the client remember the details.

15. Invite a specialty guide who excels in cleaning and clearing to create the ideal cleansing filter for you to return through to maintain perfect health for you. Deliberately and consciously pull your energetic laser beam back from the client and the experience through the filter. You may feel, or actually see, the filter working. You can assist yourself by inhaling and imagining each inhalation pulls your energy back to you through that filter.

16. Command: "I now bring me, and only me, back to myself, clean and clear through a perfect filter provided for me by my Divine cleansing specialist."

Healing Technique Levels 5–6:
Nonhuman Entities and the Darkest Entities

You have just perceived a nonhuman being or the darkest entity. You have studied this. We have talked about it. You are ready now. Follow these steps:

1. Feel no fear. Ugly does not mean powerful. It only means ugly. When you sense these two levels, stop your assessment immediately. Electrify your energy field and body with rainbows and a violet flame throughout you and all around you, shining stars inside of every cell of who you are, and shimmering golden energy. Generate a fierce, powerful sense of yourself, and know you are defiant with that fierce attitude of invincibility. You are deliberately in charge because you are the true meaning of Light Worker, purposefully emanating tidal waves of Love, Compassion, and the Sacred Light of the Holy Source.

2. Immediately pull your laser beam back to yourself by your thoughts and by inhaling, through which you can create the sensation of pulling your laser beam back to your body.

3. Command: "Divine, Sacred healers who specialize in transmuting negative energy, completely and permanently transmute all negative energy coming at me into pure Divine, Sacred, golden healing energy."

4. Command: "I invoke Sacred Specialists from Source Light to instantly and completely encapsulate (or wrap) *all* the dark beings in a warm, loving blanket of Pure Sacred Protective Light."

5. Other commands to use:

   "I, *(full name)*, completely and permanently reject, repel, and revoke ALL negative entities and all dark-force energy from me and my clients in all ways and on ALL levels! Keep me out of this and keep me safe!"

"I, *(full name)*, am invincible and unassailable to all negativity on all levels. Only the divine, compassionate, loving
Light of Source fills my mind, my body, my soul, my higher
self, and my spirit."

"The Purest Healing and Cleansing Guides from Source, instantly create the perfect cleansing filter for me, and I pull
all my energy back to me."

6. Inform the client of negativity attached to them, but never
describe it. Do not scare them. Fear will constrict the client's
energy, and that constriction clamps down on the being too.
This is the opposite response you want to achieve.

7. Many people will say they do not want it removed. That is
the negative entity in control of the client. Strongly inform
them, "I am the specialist now in this process. You are not in
charge. I am in charge now, and the healing will continue for
everyone involved."

8. Ask the client to listen for the being's answers to your
questions. Do not let the dark being ask you questions. You
are in charge and the only one who asks questions. Here are
some examples of these questions:

   • How long have you been connected to this human?

   • What drew you, and why did you connect with this
     particular human? *(You are looking for vulnerable char-
     acteristics, actions, or an event that allowed the dark being to
     attach to the client.)*

   • What do you get from interfering with this human?

   • How many levels like you are connected to this human?
     *(There is often an entire network and hierarchy. Learn the
     full extent of dark forces. All need to be released by the end of
     the session.)*

   • Do you have a director or leader? *(You want to include all
     levels of dark forces that are involved for them to be released
     as well.)*

- How many humans total are you connected to right now? *(Often, many other humans are interlaced with a dark force. All affected humans in this particular network must be included in the release and healing.)*
- Have you forgotten where you originated?

9. Intuitively command: "I invoke Sacred Specialists from Source Light to immediately encapsulate and contain the dark beings with Pure Sacred Protective Light. Extract all negative/dark-force commanders, managers, and all beings within their network."

10. Ask the client how many specialists have come to remove the entities. (This engages the client in the healing process.)

11. Intuitively command: "I invoke Sacred Specialists from Source Light to immediately surround and contain the dark beings and the entire network, including any commanders, with Pure Sacred Protective Light immediately. Take every one of them to the best place for their complete and highest transformation into Love and Light." (Keep repeating this command as necessary for each level of the hierarchy.)

12. Repeatedly tell the client and the dark entities that they are separating and becoming individuals.

13. Direct the client to actively reject and push the negative entity out of their body, mind, soul, and spirit.

14. Intuitively call in healing guide specialists to completely remove all layers, all tendrils, and all sludge from the client now.

15. You and the client ask that Pure Light and compassionate Love immediately fill every single space and place where the negative used to be. (When something is removed, something positive must fill the empty space, or the negative will rush back in.)

16. Ask the client to allow the healing and inform you when the healing is complete. Be quiet until the client speaks.

Healing Technique:
Releasing Spirit People from Your Environment

The actions and powerful emotions of humans can affect any location on the surface of the Earth. They affect intersections with repeated automobile wrecks, train crossings where people have died, or houses where traumatic events have taken place, such as abuse or murder. The healings you facilitate will often involve the Earth, as it is a living being.

Here are simple guidelines to create a conversation with a deceased human that will lead to a powerful healing and release for them. They need your help.

1. Ask your Divine and Sacred guides if there are deceased people in your environment, especially if you do not see or perceive them. If you receive a "yes," then go to the next step.

2. Ask the deceased person: "Who are you? Why are you here in (my house, land, workspace, etc.)?" Pause after each individual question to receive the answers that pop into your mind.

3. Then ask: "Do you realize you are dead? Do you realize staying here in this location is not the best place for you?" Pause for the answers.

4. Inform the deceased person that you are calling in specialists to assist them into a new and special life.

5. Call in your Divine and Sacred guides who specialize in transitioning the deceased and take the deceased person to the highest place for their transformation into Light and Love.

6. If the deceased person resists, be firm and consistent. Tell them: "This is not the greatest life for you. There is nothing here for you anymore." If the deceased person resists, then command that the specialty guides wrap them in warm

blanket of loving white light. Tell the deceased person to feel the love coming from the guides.

7. When anything is released or removed, in this case a deceased human, it must be filled and replaced with something powerfully positive. Call in your Divine and Sacred healing specialists and command: "Fill every single space and place where that spirit person used to be with Light, Compassion, and Love."

Healing Technique:
Clearing Negative Thought Forms from Your Environment

The beginning of this chapter describes how human violence affects the earth. The negative emotions people feel in certain locations, such as fear or hate, will build up a density that will collect over time in these locations. You need to cleanse and heal these thick collections from these environments. If a thought form is not healed and released from that particular area on Earth, its energy will continue to affect other humans. Healing these negative thoughts forms is like giving your environment a good, long shower. Here are the healing steps to release these negative thought forms from your environment:

1. Call out to Divine and Sacred guides who specialize in removing and cleansing all types of negativity.

2. Command: "Now completely and permanently remove all accumulations of negativity on all levels and in all places associated with me, (your full name)."

3. Then command: "Now cleanse all spaces and places where the negative used to be with precious, pure, clean energy. Permanently place it within, throughout, and around on all levels and in all dimensions."

Healing Technique:
Clearing Physical Toxins from Your Environment

Raymon Grace is well known for using these steps to clean up and heal schools for children, and to clear toxins from water and land. Invite in your most powerful Divine and Sacred healers, then command the following in these exact words:

- Command: "Now completely and permanently scramble all the exact points of origin causing the toxic, contaminated *(name the land, water, or area)* at *(name the exact address or location)*."

- Then command: "Now completely and permanently neutralize all the exact points of origin causing the toxic, contaminated *(name the land, water, or area)* at *(name the exact address or location)*."

- Then command: "Now completely and permanently transform all that has been scrambled and neutralized into *(clean, wholesome, vitally alive, etc.)* *(name the land, water, or area)* at *(name the exact address or location)*."

Healing Technique:
Releasing You from Your Ancestors' Struggles

1. Ask your Divine and Sacred guides to tell you or show you the exact point of origin causing your illness or challenge. You are in some manner informed that it is your ancestry.

2. Ask: "How many generations does *(name the illness or struggle)* go back to?" You will see a number, or you will need to count back through a line of people who represent the number of generations.

3. Command your guides to show you the exact moment it happened to the ancestor with whom the ancestral problems began.

4. Command: "Go back to that exact minute, and completely

and permanently remove all negativity and all darkness from all people involved and throughout all generations from that moment on, and remove all negativity and all darkness from every person who has ever been affected by that original moment now." Watch what they show you.

5. Command: "Fill every moment and every person with compassion, benevolence, empathy, and unconditional love now."

Healing Technique:
Past Lives

Here are some important points to remember when helping a client to heal a past life. Review them, then if it feels right to you, go back and read through the case again with these points in mind.

1. Remind the person that this work will always feel like a daydream, but reassure them it is real.

2. Clearly state to each client, "Do not try to make any-thing happen. Wait and let it unfold like a movie."

3. The client will forget to include their past-life self in every step throughout the healing process. Remind them repeatedly that they must do each step together with their past-life self. This process will achieve the greatest reconciliation and the most profound healing results.

4. The client will tend to hurry because they know you are waiting. Direct the client to always take their time.

5. Clearly tell the client they will need to let you know when the step is complete. This prevents you from interrupting the healing at crucial points.

6. During the silence, send Source energy to the client to support the sacred space of healing.

7. Observe the client's energy field while they take the healing steps. You can then report meaningful, positive changes

during their process. This will validate their own abilities
and the reality of the healing process they just participated
in.

Healing Technique:
Past-Life Trauma

1. You have identified an issue. Command to your Divine and
   Sacred medical-intuitive guides: "Show me or tell me now
   the exact point of origin causing (client's full name) (name
   the issue)."

2. A past-life situation unfolds like a movie. Inform the client
   of the details you just received about this past life. Ask the
   client if that makes sense to them.

3. Tell the client to stretch their current self back to that
   moment in time. Tell your client to make sure their past-
   life self really knows they are there for him or her in that
   moment.

4. Direct both your current client and their past-life self to call
   in a Divine and Sacred healer who specializes in healing
   and releasing past-life events or traumas.

5. Tell your current client and their past-life self to command
   together: "Completely and permanently remove all forms
   of negativity from this past-life moment, from our bodies,
   from our energy fields, from our spirits. Remove all forms of
   negativity across all timelines and all dimensions. Remove
   all negativity from both of us now!"

6. Tell the client and their past-life self to observe everything
   happening and everything releasing.

7. Once they remove all the negativity, your client's current
   self and past self must command: "Divine and sacred
   healers, come to us now and fill every single space and
   place throughout all timelines, and all dimensions, with
   unconditional Love and Light of the Eternal Divine."

8. Direct your client to ask their past-life self if they need any other healing. If they receive a "Yes, there is something else," then they must ask what it is and repeat the entire process for the other issue.

9. If your client receives a "No, the healing is complete," then direct your client to completely leave your past-life self behind. Tell the client to release that moment and pull themselves back to their current body.

Note: Do not ever bring the past-life self back to the client's current life. The past-life self cannot possibly be as advanced as the client currently is now. We do not want to bring a less-evolved part of us back to this current life.

Healing Technique:
Revoking Vows

1. Ask for the exact point of origin when the vow was made and took effect.

2. Ask for clarity regarding important keywords used in the vow.

3. Each time you state the following command, also imagine the physical formation of the vow, such as an energetic cord, completely disintegrate and float upward. Direct the client to imagine the sensation of freedom and liberation each time the client commands the following:

    "I now completely and permanently revoke anything and everything on all levels relating to the vow of *(state the key words)*. I am now completely and permanently released and free from any negativity related to this past moment."

4. Repeat this revocation on a daily basis until there is a deep sense of release.

5. Direct the client to notice even the subtle shifts or changes in their life.

Healing Technique #1 for Curses

The steps apply if the client was the perpetrator or the victim.

1. Ask your spirit guide specialists to give the exact point of origin of a person's illness or struggle. In this case, you will perceive a situation when a curse was formed and launched into reality.

2. Inform your client about the intuitive information your guides gave you. Ask the client to notice if it feels accurate to them.

3. Ask the client to imagine going back in time before the cursing event happened. Ask them to notice and describe the moment before the trauma began. In the example of the midwife, the person may go back to the moment of assisting with a positive birthing.

4. Ask your client to call out to the most divine, compassionate healing guides. Strongly request a complete and permanent healing to take place immediately for all people involved, and for love and kindness to prevail.

Healing Technique #2 for Curses

Use the Raymon Grace Dowsing Steps, which can be used to clear and heal many different situations or illnesses. You do not need a pendulum. The power of focused thought is required. Say them in the order that is stated below, and all in one sitting so the process is completed.

1. Command: "Permanently scramble all negative thought forms on all levels regarding (person's full name)."

2. Command: "Permanently neutralize all negative thought forms on all levels regarding (person's full name)."

3. Command: "Completely transform all that has been scrambled and neutralized into Divine Love."

Healing Technique:
Self-Inflicted Curses

1. Point out the negative self-talk that your client is doing. Ask that person to share their negative self-talk with you. Carefully listen to the exact negative words that the clients use against themselves.

2. Describe it as a form of self-cursing. Teach the client about the power of their thoughts.

3. Assist the client to form a command that revokes the negative self-cursing talk. Allow the client to help develop the command and find the one that feels the most powerful to them.

4. An example of a command is: "I completely and permanently revoke and reject all negative comments about myself. I now fill every thought with positive Love and Light of the Divine."

Healing Affirmation:
Self-Cursing or Self-Hatred

Note: Names can be changed to fit one's personal spiritual beliefs.

"Only God's compassionate Love and Light and the purest sacred Consciousness completely fill **every cell in my body** now."

"Only God's compassionate Love and Light and the purest sacred Consciousness completely fill **my mind** now."

"Only God's compassionate Love and Light and the purest sacred Consciousness completely fill **my emotions** now."

"Only God's compassionate Love and Light and the purest sacred Consciousness completely fill **my energy field** now."

"Only God's compassionate Love and Light and the purest sacred Consciousness completely fill **my higher self** now."

"Only God's compassionate Love and Light and the purest sacred Consciousness completely fill **my spirit** now."

"Only God's compassionate Love and Light and the purest sacred Consciousness completely fill **my eternal soul** now."

Healing Technique:
From Abuse to Empowerment

1. Ask the client to describe what they are missing inside of themselves due to the abuse.

2. Listen for key words that the client uses. The key words will be full of emotion, both negative and positive. Use the key words to transform the negativity into a positive experience.

3. Instruct the individual to take a moment and let the positive words create physical and emotional feelings inside of them. Tell them to just think the positive words and imagine the positive feelings within. Pause and wait until they speak. Have them repeat the experience until the client can identify that the positive feelings are quite strong. Do not move forward until that strength happens and is recognized.

4. Direct the person to imagine the wrongdoer standing before them. Ask the client to look directly into the wrongdoer's eyes and hold that gaze until the perpetrator changes in some manner. Do not tell the client how the individual needs to change. Tell them to take their time and not to rush. The old proverb, "Our eyes are a window into the soul," is a valid truth and an extraordinary tool for self-empowerment.

5. Ask the client to describe what happened. Teach them that this experience is very real and it actually did happen.

6. Ask them to sit and feel the difference within and describe it to you. This will confirm and validate the reality of the experience.

Healing Technique:
Retrieving Soul Fragmentation

1. Direct the client to go back to their younger self.

2. Together, the client and their younger self must take all the horrible suffering out of themselves and give it back to the wrongdoer.

3. Next they take back all that had been taken from them, and place it all back into their current self and their younger self.

4. Direct the client to ask their younger self to move forward and merge into the current moment in their current life.

Healing Technique:
Soul Retrieval

Use this when a painful memory in the client's current life has come to the forefront.

1. Tell the client you want them to let their imagination unfold like a movie in their minds.

2. Ask them to imagine going back and standing with their younger self in the exact moment of the painful trauma.

3. Ask how they know their younger self is aware of them being together.

4. Direct both the young self and the current self to pull everything out of both their bodies that is not theirs. Completely pull out the traumatic event, the pain, the memories, all the ugliness, and give it back to their wrongdoers.

5. Tell the client to take their time and make sure they get absolutely all of it out of them and give it all back. You will be still until they speak so you do not interrupt their process.

6. Watch the client's energy field as they attend to your request. If there is any residual darkness, tell the client to go back and get it all out of both of them. Remind your client to do every step in partnership with their younger self.

7. Now direct both to call out for healing guides to create a perfect cleansing filter. Wait until the client informs you that the filter is present.

8. Next, firmly tell the client and their younger self to take back absolutely everything that has been taken from them. Bring it through the cleansing filter and place it back inside of both of them. To encourage the client, use the same emotional words that the client has used in describing the traumatic event. Some examples to say aloud might be:

Both you and the younger you, take back everything that was taken from you.

Both you and the younger you, take back your confidence.

Both you and the younger you, take back your ability to love.

Both you and the younger you, take back your personal empowerment.

Both you and the younger you, take back all of your energy.

Both you and the younger you, take back all of your health.

Both you and the younger you, take back all of your strength.

Both you and the younger you, take back all of your intelligence.

Both you and the younger you, take back all of your body.

Both you and the younger you, take back all of your beauty.

9. Let your client know you will be still until they speak, and to take their time making sure they get it all.

10. Ask them, their current self and younger self, to talk it over with each other to see if there is anything else that needs to be done for a complete and permanent healing. Pause and allow both of them to check that out. Follow through with anything that seems incomplete for them.

11. Direct the current self to ask the younger self if they are ready to leave that moment forever. If yes, tell both of them to release that event and to move forward, merging together physically and coming back into the client's present moment sitting in the session with you. Tell them to take their time and you will be still until the client speaks.

12. Watch the client's energy field and, at the end of the session, inform them of the positive energetic changes. Reinforce that healing on this energetic level is real.

Details of the One-Hour Session

1. 5–8 minutes: Immediately inform the client of all intuitive pops of information your guides give you.

2. 15–20 minutes: Allow the client to respond now. Intuitively look into the areas your client thinks is important and wants more information about.

   Important Goal During This Segment: Determine one primary concern that both your client and your guides agree upon.

3. *10 minutes:* Direct your guides to show you the exact point of origin that caused this issue. Inform your client of the cause and discuss the details.

4. *25 minutes:* Call in your healing specialist. Ask them to show you the most powerful healing method to use. Engage the client to assist with the healing steps as they happen.

5. *5 minutes:* Ask your guides for the most powerful homework so the client may empower their own healing. Have the client practice the homework. Watch their energy field to ascertain they understand how to do it well.

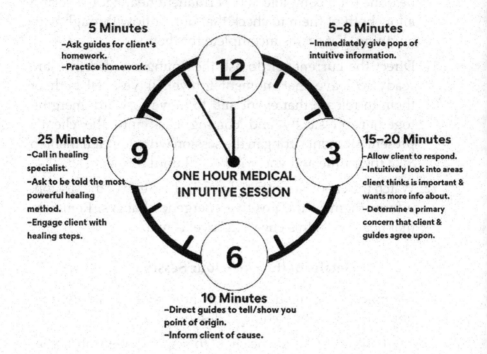

5 Minutes
–Ask guides for client's homework.
–Practice homework.

5–8 Minutes
–Immediately give pops of intuitive information.

25 Minutes
–Call in healing specialist.
–Ask to be told the most powerful healing method.
–Engage client with healing steps.

15–20 Minutes
–Allow client to respond.
–Intuitively look into areas client thinks is important & wants more info about.
–Determine a primary concern that client & guides agree upon.

ONE HOUR MEDICAL INTUITIVE SESSION

10 Minutes
–Direct guides to tell/show you point of origin.
–Inform client of cause.

References

Baldwin, William J. *Healing Lost Souls: Releasing Unwanted Spirits from Your Energy Body*. Newburyport, MA: Hampton Roads Publishing. 2003.

Baldwin, William J. *Spirit Releasement Therapy: A Technique Manual*. London: Headline Publishing. 1995.

Ellen, Gerry. "Understanding Synchronicity as a Tool for Conscious Living." *MeetMindful*. Accessed September 1, 2022. https://www.meetmindful.com/understanding-synchronicity/.

Lipton, Bruce H. *The Biology of Belief: Unleashing the Power of Consciousness, Matter & Miracles*. Carlsbad, CA: Hay House. 2016.

Loudon, Irvine. "A Brief History of Homeopathy." *JRSM: Journal of the Royal Society of Medicine* 9, no. 12 (2006): 607–610. Accessed December 13, 2022. https://www.ncbi.nlm.nih.gov/pmc/articles/PMC1676328/.

Morrell, Peter. "Hahnemann's Miasm Theory and Miasm Remedies." Last accessed December 13, 2022. http://www.homeoint.org/morrell/articles/pm_miasm.htm.

Moss, Robert. *Sidewalk Oracles*. Novato, CA: New World Library. 2015.

Newman, Hugh. *Earth Grids: The Secret Patterns of Gaia's Sacred Sites*. Glastonbury: Wooden Books. 2008.

Tansley, David V. *Chakras: Rays and Radionics*. C.W. Daniel Company. 1984.

Villoldo, Alberto. *A Shaman's Miraculous Tools for Healing.* Newburyport, MA: Hampton Roads Publishing. 2015.

Recommended Resources

The Art of Psychic Protection by Judy Hall

Chakras-Rays and Radionics by David V. Tansley, DC

Change Your Energy, Change Your Life (DVD) by Raymon Grace

The Unquiet Dead by Dr. Edith Fiore

The Biology of Belief by Bruce Lipton, PhD

E Squared by Pam Grout

E Cubed by Pam Grout

Ask Your Guides by Sonia Choquette

A Shaman's Miraculous Tools for Healing by Alberto Villoldo

Healing Lost Souls by William Baldwin, PhD

Spirit Releasement Therapy by William Baldwin, PhD

The Amazing Power of Deliberate Intent: Living the Art of Allowing by Esther Hicks and Jerry Hicks

Heal Your Body by Louise Hay

The Energy Healing Experiments: Science Reveals Our Natural Power to Heal by Gary Schwartz, PhD

The Freedom Path by Robert E. Detzler

Soul Re-Creation: Developing Your Cosmic Potential by Robert E. Detzler

The Secret Science Behind Miracles by Max Freedom Long

Ascension Help Blog by Cameron Day

The Quantum Doctor: A Physicist's Guide to Health and Healing by Amit Goswami, PhD

The Spiritual Universe by Fred Alan Wolf, PhD

Quantum Success by Sandra Anne Taylor

Matrix Energetics by Richard Bartlett, DC, ND

Quantum Healing: Exploring the Frontiers of Mind/Body Medicine by Deepak Chopra, MD

The Catalyst of Power: The Assemblage Point of Man by Jon Whale, PhD

Educational Radionic Workbook and General Information by Caroline Connor

About the Author

TINA M. ZION is a fourth-generation intuitive medium. She is globally considered an expert in medical intuition, healing methods, and mediumship and teaches these subjects internationally. She has worked in the mental health field as a registered nurse with a National Board Certification in mental health nursing from the American Nurses Credentialing Association. Tina is a gestalt-trained counselor, graduating  from the Indianapolis Gestalt Institute in 1997. She received her certification in clinical hypnotherapy from the American Council of Hypnotist Examiners, specializing in past-life regressions and was certified through the Michael Newton Institute.

Tina is the author of three award-winning, top-selling books: *Become a Medical Intuitive, Advanced Medical Intuition,* and *Be Your Own Medical Intuitive.* Her two Reiki books are *The Reiki Teacher's Manual* and *Reiki and Your Intuition.* She is a contributing author in Newton's latest book, *Memories of the Afterlife.*

Tina's private practice now focuses completely on teaching medical intuition, mediumship, and healing through teleconferences, workshops, and individual mentoring sessions.

Tina's website: www.tinazion.com

About the Artist

Corey Ford currently works with digital art and commissioned Fine Art pieces. Her art has been viewed on three seasons of the TV series *The Flash* as well as the TV series *Pawn Stars*. Her art is also on the book titled *12 Days of Terror* featured on CBS News Sunday Morning. Corey's digital art is selling on a worldwide basis with T-shirts, book covers, CD and DVD covers, computer games, and websites. Her favorite subjects to portray are dinosaurs, unicorns, Pegasus, horses, fairies, volcanoes, space (outer space), science fiction, Victorian era, Art Nouveau, American Indian, Egyptian (Old Kingdom), dragons, whales, sharks, Medieval Age, and underwater scenes.

Corey Ford's website: www.coreyfordgallery.com

About the Illustrator of Toroidal Field Drawing

Jacqueline Rogers is an illustrator of many books, mostly for children. You can see more of her work on her website, www.jacquelinerogers.com